Directors
an**A–Z**guide

Directors
an**A–Z**guide

Bob Tricker

THE ECONOMIST IN ASSOCIATION WITH
PROFILE BOOKS LTD

Published by Profile Books Ltd
3A Exmouth House, Pine Street, London EC1R 0JH

Designed by Sue Lamble
Typeset in EcoType by MacGuru Ltd
info@macguru.org.uk

Printed in the UK by CPI Bookmarque, Croydon, CR0 4TD

A CIP catalogue record for this book is available
from the British Library

ISBN 978 1 84668 167 7

Contents

Preface

This is the fifth time that this book (first published under the title *Pocket Director*) has been revised and updated. Indeed, this time it has largely been rewritten. In the 12 years since the first edition, some incredible changes have occurred which have brought the subject of corporate governance centre stage: Enron; the collapse of Arthur Andersen, one of the big five accounting firms; the Sarbanes-Oxley Act in the United States; a new companies act in the UK defining directors' responsibilities for the first time; the growing importance of state-owned enterprises on the world scene; and, most significantly, the clash between the American rule-based approach to corporate governance and the principles-based approach being pursued elsewhere in the world. And all that was before the global financial and economic crisis which began with the credit crunch in 2007 and which has highlighted yet again how essential high standards of corporate governance are.

The new entries reflect some of the significant developments since the last edition: hedge funds, private equity, sovereign wealth funds, state-owned enterprises, Chinese corporate governance, D&O insurance, the Societas Europaea European company, corporate social responsibility, sustainability, nomads and whistle blowing. A host of new organisations with their inevitable acronyms appear: ASP, APB, FASB, FRC, FSA, POB, SASAC. Recent years have also produced some fascinating new corporate governance cases to supplement the classics from previous editions: Conrad Black, Gazprom, HSBC, Marks & Spencer, Mittal, Network Rail, Northern Rock, Walt Disney, Yukos, even the University of Oxford.

There have also been profound changes in board-level thinking and practice, although many of important issues remain unresolved – for example, how to calculate director remuneration, should a chairman also be chief executive, should institutional investors take on corporate governance duties, can independent directors and outside auditors ever be really independent? What is undeniable in these fast-moving and complex times is the importance of how board directors do their jobs.

This book aims to help them understand and carry out their role, and once again, I hope that this new edition will not only inform and educate but also entertain.

Bob Tricker

Introduction

Many people become directors of family companies, subsidiary companies, holding companies and joint-venture companies, as well as public companies listed on a stock exchange. Other people find themselves appointed to the governing bodies of not-for-profit organisations such as educational and medical institutions, professional bodies, quangos and charitable societies. Governance is the role of these governing bodies, whatever they are called. This book is for everyone who serves on a board, council or committee. Governance is different from management. Managers run the enterprise; the directors make sure that it is being well run and run in the right direction.

Corporate entities are among the most important organisations in modern society. They satisfy societies' needs, provide employment and create wealth. Their actions affect the lives of everyone – whether they are employees, customers, beneficiaries, suppliers, investors, or members of society at large. These stakeholders in the modern corporate enterprise can make heavy demands on its directors. They expect visibility, accountability and performance. They can exert significant pressure, which is amplified by ever-increasing regulation and, in many societies, litigation.

This book examines what being a director involves, what makes a director effective, what brings board-level success and the way power is exercised over corporate entities. The introductory essay provides the basis for a broad understanding of directors' work. The A–Z section, which is the core of the book, gives practical insights into the world of directors today. It explores the basis of corporate governance, covers the factors necessary to be a successful director and shows how to build a better board. Cross-references in SMALL CAPITALS make it easier to find related topics. The appendices, with their codes of governance practice, board guidelines and director checklists, and details of over 100 internet sites, provide access to further valuable information. The quotations are intended to entertain as well as illuminate. This is a book for dipping into and exploring.

Effective directors and successful boards

Directors are involved in corporate governance not management, even though executive directors will have substantial management responsibilities as well. What is corporate governance? Corporate governance is as old as enterprise. Shakespeare knew about corporate governance, even though he didn't use the phrase. The merchant of Venice, watching his ship sail away over the horizon, worried that his wealth was now in the hands of the captain and his crew (Act 1, Scene 1). Corporate governance is involved every time the owners of a company or the members of a society leave the oversight of their assets and the success of the enterprise in the hands of other people. In the case of companies, the owners appoint a board of directors to look after their interests. In not-for-profit entities, including charities, clubs, professional bodies, hospitals and academic institutions, the members elect a governing body to direct their organisation. Although often known as a committee or a council, for the sake of simplicity in this book all governing bodies are called "boards".

Broadly, corporate governance concerns the way power is exercised over an organisation. As stated above, corporate governance is not management. Management is responsible to the board. Management runs the enterprise; the board makes sure that it is being run well and in the right direction. For years the major focus in business was on management: management schools, management consultants, management gurus. Today, the way companies are governed has become as important as the way they are managed.

Twenty-five years ago the phrase "corporate governance" was unfamiliar; today it is widely used. Every corporate entity, being distinct from its members, needs some form of constitution to define its boundaries and purpose, and to determine the relationship between members and governing body. In a company the constitution is provided by its memorandum and articles of association. In a society, such as a sports club, a trades union, or a community association, it may be a set of rules. In a partnership, the partnership agreement provides the governance underpinnings, and in a quango it is the founding legislation.

Poor corporate governance has ruined companies, resulted in directors being sent to jail, destroyed a global accounting firm and threatened economies and governments. Obviously, the relationship between the members and their governing body is central to effective governance. In the same way as the structure, the membership and the activities of the governing body are fundamental.

How companies have developed

The original concept of the company was immensely innovative, elegantly simple and proved superbly successful. In the middle of the 19th century, apart from companies created by the state or the crown, the only way to do business was as a sole trader or a partnership. If the business became insolvent, the owner could find himself in debtors' prison and his family in the work house; hardly an incentive for an investor to risk his funds in a venture run by someone else. Yet businesses growing out of the industrial revolution needed just such investment from outside shareholders. So the concept of the joint stock, limited liability company arose – incorporating a legal entity, separate from the owners, whose responsibility for the company's debts was then limited to their equity stake. Ownership was the basis of power. Shareholders elected their directors, who were accountable to them.

Initially, all companies were public companies, incorporated to raise funds from outside investors. Early in the 20th century, however, entrepreneurs and family firms realised that, by incorporating their businesses as companies, they limited their personal liability for the business debts. The private company had arrived.

By the 1930s, most public companies in the United States had many outside shareholders and a separation between owners and management had occurred. Self-perpetuating boards ruled companies and did not always act in the best interests of the shareholders. Investors needed protection and the US Securities and Exchange Commission was created.

In the 1970s, another governance idea surfaced. Large companies, it was suggested, owed a responsibility not only to their shareholders but also to other stakeholders, such as their employees, customers and suppliers, even to society at large. Such suggestions were, predictably, resisted by directors and proved inconclusive. The legal responsibility of boards to be the stewards of their shareholders' interests was maintained.

In Europe, meanwhile, in an attempt to harmonise company law throughout the member states of the European Economic Community, proposals were drafted which would have required all companies in the Community to adopt the German two-tier board model, instead of the unitary board used in American and Commonwealth jurisdictions. This proposal was strongly resisted by countries which favoured the unitary board approach and was not pursued.

The 1980s saw the opening of financial markets around the world. Hostile takeovers of companies reinforced the market for control in the Anglo-American economies. Many state enterprises were privatised. Unfortunately, the drive for corporate growth led to excesses and by the end of the decade there were some dramatic company collapses: Maxwell in the UK, Burnham Drexel in the United States, Nomura in Japan and many more. The need for better board-level behaviour was apparent. Codes of good corporate governance practice were published, Cadbury (1992) being the first. And the phrase corporate governance appeared for the first time.

The board

Boards seldom appear on an organisation chart. The idea of management as a hierarchy is commonplace: a chief executive with overall responsibility, heading an organisational pyramid with various managerial levels, delegating authority for management functions downwards and demanding accountability upwards. Management is depicted as such a pyramid in Figure 1.

The board, however, is not a hierarchy. Every director has equal responsibility and similar duties and powers. Company law recognises no boss of the board. The work of the board, the governing body of an entity, is depicted in Figure 1 as a circle, superimposed on the management. The management triangle is responsible for managing the enterprise; the duty of the board is to govern.

In Figure 1 the board has nine members. Six of them are non-executive directors, what in the United States would be called outside directors, that is, they are on the board but not in management, and shown as ○ in the figure. The other three directors, □

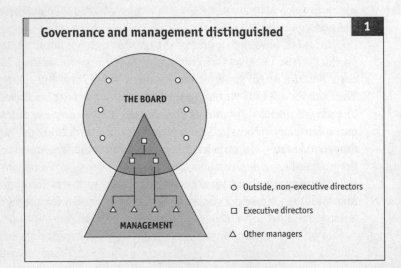

Governance and management distinguished   1

THE BOARD

MANAGEMENT

○ Outside, non-executive directors

□ Executive directors

△ Other managers

in the figure, are executive directors on both the board and in top management.

A board like this, with both non-executive and executive members, is known as a unitary board and is the structure adopted in most countries around the world. The boards of many family companies, small companies and subsidiary companies have a majority of executive directors, whereas the boards of many public companies and not-for-profit entities have a majority of non-executive directors. In a few countries, including Germany and the Netherlands, large companies adopt the two-tier supervisory board in which the top executives and the outside supervisory members serve on two different boards: executive and supervisory.

A further distinction needs to be drawn between non-executive directors who are independent of the company and those who have connections with it. As explained later, all the corporate governance codes around the world call for genuinely independent directors, that is, directors who have no link with the company, other than their directorship, which might influence the exercise of independent, objective judgment. Of course, a good case might be made to have a representative of a major shareholder, a retired executive from the company, or a family relation of another director on the board, but they cannot be considered independent.

Primary role: strategy formulation and policymaking

The board's task is to direct, which is why directors are so called. The primary role of the board is to determine the purpose of the enterprise, agree the strategies to achieve those goals, and lay down the values and policies that guide management as they run the business.

In formulating strategy the board works with top management, looking ahead in time and seeing the firm in its strategic environment. In some cases the board as a whole plays a major part in analysing the company's strategic context, exploring alternatives and determining the company's direction. Such boards often set aside specific times, perhaps a weekend retreat, to discuss their strategy. Other boards expect their top management to undertake the strategic review and come to the board with clear proposals. The non-executive directors can then question the executive on their underlying assumptions, the resources needed, the exposure to risks and the probability of success, referring the proposals back for further work if necessary.

Companies take different approaches to formulating strategy. For some the exercise is little more than an attempt to roll their annual budgeting exercise forward over a few more years. A more analytical approach is the well-known SWOT analysis, in which the strengths and weaknesses of the company are explored and set against its external opportunities and threats. But both these approaches suffer from a basic shortcoming: conceptually the strategist is inside the company looking out. The true strategist needs to see the company in its context, including competitors, markets and the economic, political and technological framework. A crucial issue, from this perspective, is working out what strategies competitors and potential competitors might be pursuing. As the hunter says: "To catch a tiger, you must think like a tiger."

The corporate strategy developed by the board should reflect the mission and values that the directors have laid down for the company. A comprehensive strategy is likely to contain a number of segments, including strategies for marketing, finance, human relations, operations, technology, risk and board development. Companies do not have perpetuity, they can die, but they do have an existence separate from that of their founders, shareholders and directors. An important challenge to boards, as they develop their strategies, is to balance short-term performance with sustained long-term success.

Other roles: supervising executive activities and accountability

Strategies, translated into policies, procedures and plans for management action, provide the basis for subsequent control. The board

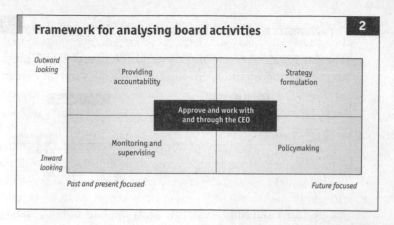

Framework for analysing board activities   2

| Outward looking | Providing accountability | Strategy formulation |
| Inward looking | Monitoring and supervising | Policymaking |

Approve and work with and through the CEO

Past and present focused   *Future focused*

needs to monitor and supervise the activities of executive management, looking inwards at the current managerial situation and recent performance. The board also has a responsibility to be accountable, reporting corporate activities and performance to the shareholders and other stakeholders with legitimate claims to accountability.

Boards vary in the extent to which the board as a whole engages in these functions or delegates work to the CEO and the management team. In some companies the directors are heavily involved; in others they delegate much to the CEO and the management team, while ensuring that the necessary control systems are in place to enable them to supervise. Figure 2 provides a simple framework summarising the work of directors.

Figure 2 also highlights an issue for a unitary board that has both executive and outside directors. The roles in the right-hand column – strategy formulation and policymaking – are performance roles, concerned with the board's contribution to corporate direction. Those on the left – executive supervision and accountability – are essentially concerned with ensuring conformance. But executive directors face the potential problem of being responsible as members of top management, while at the same time being responsible as board members for overseeing that management. Some call this the "two-hat problem", recognising

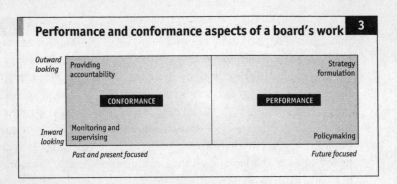

that executive directors inevitably wear the hats of both manager and director. When in the boardroom they should be wearing the director hat and not defending their managerial performance or seeking benefits for their area of managerial responsibility.

Figure 3 shows this important distinction. In a two-tier board the roles are separated, with the executive board responsible for performance and the supervisory board responsible for conformance.

Appointment to the board

The director's role

Because every company is different, directors' contributions vary. They bring different skills, knowledge and experience to their board. An appropriate balance of skills and experience is needed for an effective board. Ideally, directors will also have some basic core competencies: strategic vision, reasoning and planning capabilities, a decision-making ability, communication skills, political awareness and networking know-how. They need to have minds of their own, as well as being able to work as part of a team. There is a checklist of core competencies for directors in Appendix 4.

All directors need to know about the enterprise itself if they are to make sense of board information and contribute meaningfully to board discussions. This knowledge has three parts: knowledge of the company, knowledge of the business and knowledge of the financials.

Knowledge of the company includes a clear understanding of the basis of power (who the shareholders are and where the power lies to appoint the directors); the basis of law under which the company operates and what the governance rules and regulations are (for a listed company these include company law, the listing rules of the stock exchange, and the company's memorandum and articles of association); the board structure, membership and personalities; and the board processes, such as the use of board committees and the basis of board information. An awareness of the history of the company can also be crucial in interpreting the current situation and understanding the board culture and the perspectives of the other directors.

Knowledge of the business includes an understanding of the basic business processes, its purpose and aims, its strengths and weaknesses and how it measures success, the field of its operations (including markets, competitors and its current operating context), the strategies being pursued, the structure of the organisation, its culture, management and people, and the form of management control and control systems.

Knowledge of the financials includes an awareness of how the company is financed, a sound appreciation of its annual accounts and directors' reports, developing trends in key financial ratios, the criteria used in investment appraisals, the calibre of financial controls and who the auditors are. It is not necessary to be an accountant to be a good director: indeed, some might argue the reverse. But an ability to appreciate the financial aspects of the company is important.

It is said that "outside directors never know enough about the business to be useful and inside directors always know too much to be independent". Ideally, all directors, both executive and non-executive, form a team of independent, tough-minded individuals working together with trust and mutual understanding to achieve sustained success. For this to be the case the composition of the board in terms of skills and knowledge is crucial. So too is an awareness of what each of your fellow directors bring to the party – and what they don't. Self-awareness is also helpful, but perhaps more difficult to achieve.

Unless they have personal experience of board-level behaviour, many people expect board discussions to be rational and directors' decisions to be based on a rigorous review of alternatives, but board meetings typically involve a political process. Position and prestige of board members do not guarantee a successful board: the chairman of Enron's audit committee was a leading accounting professor.

In reality, corporate governance is more about human behaviour than structures or strictures, rules or regulations. Board interactions can involve intrigue, secrecy and conspiracy; just as they can involve honesty, fairness and trust. After the corporate collapses of 2002 and the financial sector crisis of 2008, many people felt that some directors were putting their own interests well before their duty to the company and its shareholders. In doing so, they had potentially undermined the trust and harmed the well-being of investors, employees and other stakeholders. The effectiveness and integrity of a board depends largely on the calibre of the directors and the style of board leadership.

Poorly performing directors may have insufficient time for board matters. They may lack interest, or worse be motivated by self-interest. Complacency, arrogance and domination are all board-level failings, as are being weak-willed and easily led. "Yes-men" who fail to speak out when they disagree are as dishonest as those who deliberately lie.

Integrity is at the heart of effective corporate governance. Directors are the stewards of the shareholders' interests. They have a fiduciary duty to the company to act openly and honestly for the good of all the members – minority holders of voting shares as well as a majority holder. The enterprise does not belong to the directors, personally, unless they are the sole shareholders. Private interests in corporate matters need to be disclosed. Making a secret personal profit from the company is illegal. So is trading in a listed company's shares on the basis of privileged insider information.

The director's legal duties and rights

Although company law varies from jurisdiction to jurisdiction, the essence of directors' duties does not. Essentially, directors have two duties: one of trust and one of care. The duty of trust, or fiduciary duty, requires directors to act with integrity, honesty and fairly for the benefit of all the shareholders. To achieve this, directors need to act within their powers in the company's constitution and promote the aims of the company to ensure its success. The universal principle is that directors should not treat a company as though it exists for their own personal benefit, unless of course they own all the shares, and even then they have to respect the legal rights of creditors and other stakeholders.

The duty of care calls for directors to exercise independent judgment with reasonable care, diligence and skill. What courts consider "reasonable" hinges on the knowledge, skill and experience that a director can be reasonably be expected to have: an accountant, lawyer or engineer would be expected to bring those skills to bear in their work as a director. The standard of professionalism now expected of directors is significantly higher than that expected a few years ago. Courts will not normally second guess board-level decisions even if they prove to be wrong, recognising that business decisions involve risk. This is frequently referred to as the "business judgment rule". Courts do act, however, if negligent or fraudulent behaviour is alleged. Increasingly, around the world, directors find themselves exposed to litigation from shareholders, employees and other vested interests. Cases do not have to be based on incontrovertible evidence: some litigants bring actions in the hope that settlement will be made out of court to avoid risk and reputational loss. Directors and officers (D&O) insurance can provide some protection against court fees and damages, but not against malfeasance or negligence.

Other crucial issues

Although in principle the shareholders appoint their directors, in practice nominations in public companies come from the board, often through the board's nomination committee. In private companies, for example family firms, subsidiary companies and joint ventures, of course, the shareholders are often directly involved. Before extending an invitation to join the board, the chairman should make sure that the prospective director has the skills, knowledge and experience expected, has sufficient time and dedication to serve on the board and its other committees, and that an independent director meets the independence criteria. It is important to note that the word "director" is used in various ways. Already explained is the difference between executive directors and non-executive or outside directors, of whom some may be independent and others may have connections with the company. Then there are representative or nominee directors, shadow directors, alternate directors, even employee directors. And in these days of "job inflation" there are more and more people who are given the title "director", perhaps as a reward or mark of prestige, who are not on the board at all.

A newly appointed director needs a proper induction programme to reduce the learning time taken before beginning to make a significant contribution. The quicker new directors master this knowledge, the faster and the better will be their contribution to board deliberations. There is an induction checklist for directors in Appendix 5. Appropriate director training and updating are also essential in today's changing governance climate. Many of the corporate governance codes now call for director induction, training and development.

Director remuneration, particularly the remuneration package of executive directors, remains a controversial topic. Investigative media challenge large benefits, which sometimes seem to be rewarding failure. Institutional investors criticise the scale of executive directors' rewards, claiming that they are out of line with the market and unrelated to performance. But what is the appropriate level needed to attract the best executives, to provide sufficient incentive and reward success, while keeping the best people in the company? The idea of a remuneration committee was designed to deal with this difficult matter. This is a subcommittee of the main board, consisting wholly or mainly of independent outside directors, concerned with making recommendations on director rewards. The underlying principle is that no one should be responsible for determining their own rewards. The establishment of remuneration committees has not done away with the complaints about executive remuneration or answered the question of who should fix the remuneration of the remuneration committee.

Governing the company: the corporate governance codes

The first code on corporate governance was the UK's Cadbury Report (1992) from a committee chaired by Sir Adrian Cadbury of the well-known chocolate company. Like almost all the subsequent reports around the world, this was a response to corporate collapses and perceived excesses by business leaders in the boardroom. The report defined corporate governance as the system by which companies are directed and controlled: notice the contrast between performance and conformance. The Cadbury code was quickly followed by others: the Hilmer Report (1993) in Australia, King (1995) in South Africa, Viénot (1995) in France and many more. The codes were not based on academic research but on current ideas of best practice. Nevertheless, their introduction brought a lot of changes to board behaviour around the world.

In most cases the codes were voluntary, relying on reporting and stock exchange listing rules for enforcement. In essence, they called for independent outside directors, argued for the separation of the roles of chief executive and chairman, and proposed board-level committees made up mainly of outside directors, including audit committees to provide a bridge between the external auditor and the board, remuneration committees to assess top management rewards, and nomination committees to suggest the names of new members for the board. The idea was that the outside directors on these committees would bring an independent perspective to the deliberations and avoid domination by overly powerful executive directors. For most commentators conformance and compliance was the central plank of the corporate governance platform. The pervading theme was for greater disclosure, transparency and accountability.

Subsequently, director induction, director training and development, the performance assessment of individual directors and boards, corporate risk assessment and, in some cases, corporate social responsibility were added to the codes of many countries. The country codes were followed by some international codes, such as the OECD Code (1998) and the Commonwealth Code (1999). Some institutional investors, such as CalPERS (California's state employees' pension fund), proposed codes for international companies looking for capital. Typically, they called for transparency and disclosure, the protection of minority shareholder interests and voting procedures, which enabled shareholders to influence corporate decisions. The argument advanced by these institutions was that if companies in other countries wanted to access their capital markets, they must meet their governance standards. However, this argument was turned on its head by the sub-prime credit problems that arose in 2007, after which financial institutions in America and the UK had to call on sovereign funds in China, Singapore and the oil states for funds. Many companies now publish their own corporate governance codes or policy statements, as a trawl of their websites will show.

However, governance problems were highlighted several years before when one of the largest companies in America, Enron, collapsed as a result of heavy and unreported indebtedness. Worldcom followed, bankrupted by an overpowering chairman/CEO. The financial transparency, indeed the viability, of other companies was questioned. Suddenly, from being the leaders of western economic success, entrepreneurial risk-taking and sound corporate governance, directors were depicted as greedy, short-sighted and more interested in their personal share options than creating sustainable wealth. Some blamed pressure from institutional investors, struggling to maintain the net worth of their funds as stockmarkets fell; others blamed board-level attitudes and greed.

Governance problems appeared in companies in other parts of the world: British Rail, Marconi and Tomkins in the UK, HIH Insurance in Australia and Vodafone Mannesmann in Germany, for example. Arthur Andersen, one of the big five global accounting firms – and auditors of Enron, Worldcom and other firms with dubious governance such as Waste Management – collapsed as clients changed auditors and partners changed firms. American accounting standards (GAAP) were now pilloried as being based on rules that could be manipulated, rather than on the principles of overall fairness required in international accounting standards.

New legal requirements for directors of all companies listed in the United States were rushed through in the Sarbanes-Oxley Act and quickly incorporated into stock exchange listing rules. Only independent directors could now serve on audit and remuneration committees, shareholders must approve plans for directors' stock options, subsidised loans to directors were forbidden. Auditors must rotate their audit partners, to prevent an overfamiliarity between the auditor and the client's finance staff. Auditors were forbidden to sell some non-audit services to audit clients, and audit staff must serve a cooling-off period before joining the staff of an audit client. As had happened before, corporate collapses led to changes in corporate governance thinking and practice.

Managing the board

Board style and leadership

The primary role of the board chairman is board leadership. This includes ensuring that the right mix of skills, knowledge and experience is available among the directors, establishing programmes of induction, director training and continuing updating, as well as creating the appropriate board culture, values and climate. Meetings are not just held: they have to be planned, managed and led. Directors need relevant and timely information. Some may need additional briefing. In badly led boards directors are allowed to play games (see GAMES DIRECTORS PLAY) and personalities and politics prevail. Successful boards have sound leadership.

The boards of different organisations will inevitably have different styles. At one extreme is the rubber stamp board, in which everything is already decided and the board meeting is a mere formality; indeed, sometimes it may produce minutes of meetings not held. Surprisingly, perhaps, there is a legitimate place for this style where, for example, the company is a mere legal convenience, a family firm where owners, directors and managers are the same people who meet continuously, or a subsidiary company where the holding company dominates its managerial decisions. Then there is the representative board, with directors representing different, sometimes conflicting interests. Many not-for-profit entities have such boards, with members appointed to represent the interests of various stakeholding groups. Meetings of such boards often more resemble a parliamentary debate than a governing body seeking consensus. Then there is the country club style of board. Typically old fashioned, full of ritual and reminiscence, more concerned with interpersonal friendly relations than tough-minded discussion, this style of board has little place in the modern world. Lastly, there are those boards with a professional style, balancing concerns for rigorous pursuit of success with trust and mutual respect for colleagues.

Performance evaluation of individual directors, boards and board committees used to be resisted if it was even raised in the boardroom. Many directors felt that the experience and ability that had brought their board appointment meant that evaluation of their personal performance was inappropriate. Moreover, they believed that a board's performance was the result of a team effort that could not be assessed other than in the company's results. A few directors still think this way. But most corporate governance codes now call for regular appraisal of the performance of directors, boards and board committees. In some cases this is little more than an informal assessment by the chairman, but increasingly a professional approach is adopted using an independent, objective and experienced assessment process. Various systems for rating companies have also been developed by credit-rating agencies, consultants and independent national bodies (see CORPORATE GOVERNANCE RATINGS).

Succession planning

An area of board management that is often overlooked is succession planning for directors. Frequently, companies seem to be caught out because they have not planned adequately for the replacement of the CEO or other executive directors, the chairman or independent outside directors. In many start-up and family firms succession proves to be particularly difficult. Planning for succession has to overcome the founder's apparent belief in immortality.

Succession planning can also be applied to the board as a whole. What should be its future size, balance between executive and independent directors, and functions of board committees? Companies regularly outgrow their boards. A strategy for board-level development should be a segment in all corporate strategies, which is consistent with the other strategic directions being pursued.

Philosophical and other issues

The academic, philosophical, legal and other corporate governance issues will no doubt run and run. Below is a summary of
what they are.

Agents or stewards?

Academics have two competing theories of corporate governance:
agency theory and stewardship theory. Actually there are three,
but the third, so-called stakeholder theory, is really more of a philosophy than a theory.

Agency theory addresses the agency dilemma: when the
owner of wealth (the principal) contracts with someone else (the
agent) to manage his affairs how does he make sure that the agent
acts solely in the principal's interests and not in his own? As Adam
Smith commented in the 18th century in his famous book *The
Wealth of Nations*:

*The directors of companies, being managers of other people's money,
cannot be expected to watch over it with the same vigilance with which
they watch over their own.*

This is the agency problem and the basis of agency theory. In
essence, the theory argues that directors, in trying to maximise their
personal benefit, take actions that are advantageous to themselves
but detrimental to the shareholders. In other words, directors
cannot be trusted to act in the shareholders' interests. Agency
theory lends itself to statistical analysis on data already in the public
domain so researchers do not need to go anywhere near the boardroom, and therefore their theoretical studies on the subject have
been somewhat inconclusive. This is because there is usually a lot
more going on than is reflected in the measured aspects of corporate governance and corporate performance. But it does seem that
there is a positive link between what is perceived as good corporate
governance and better performance. Certainly, many institutional
investors pay a premium for companies with acknowledged good

governance, not least because it reduces their exposure to risk.

Stewardship theory takes an opposite view. Ownership is the basis of power over the corporation. The directors are stewards of the shareholders' interests. They report to the shareholders on that stewardship, subject to a report from an independent auditor that the accounts show a true and fair view. Inherent in the concept of the company is the belief that directors can be trusted. Contrary to agency theory, stewardship theory argues that directors do not try to maximise their own personal interests: they can and do act responsibly with independence and integrity. Stewardship theorists believe this is what most directors actually do. Of course, some fail, but this does not invalidate the basic concept. Agency theory reflects the perspective of the financial economist, stewardship theory that of the lawyer. Neither offers a persuasive insight into boardroom decision-making.

Shareholders or stakeholders?

To whom are directors responsible? This is a fundamental question. In company law there is only one answer: the shareholders. Both agency and stewardship theorists accept that directors' primary responsibility is to the shareholders. They differ on whether directors fulfil that duty.

Exponents of stakeholder notions, however, question that perspective. They believe that directors owe a duty to the company's stakeholders – employees, suppliers, distributors, customers, suppliers of finance – indeed, any parties whose interests may be affected by the company's actions. For many that includes communities affected by local employment, environmental hazards, or the exploitation of water, minerals or forests, for example. Some add corporate responsibility at the level of the state, recognising a company's duty to generate wealth, provide employment and pay taxes. They argue that companies affect the lives of far more people than the shareholders and, consequently, should be accountable – some say responsible – to them.

Critics of stakeholder thinking complain that to expect companies to be accountable to a range of stakeholders, whose interests and expectations are different and potentially in conflict, would make the directors' task impossible. The interests of stakeholder groups should be met by free-market competition, backed by legislation and legal controls that protect customers (monopoly and competition law), employees (employment law, health and safety law), consumers (product safety law, consumer protection law), suppliers (contract law, credit payment law) and society (environmental law, health and safety law, taxation law).

Corporate social responsibility (CSR) has become one of the important elements in contemporary corporate governance thinking. CSR accepts a company's responsibility to the wider range of stakeholders beyond shareholders and calls for boards to report how their activities affect them. CSR reporting has become an important feature of many companies' corporate governance activities, and after years of floss and gloss listed companies do seem to be taking genuine steps to be more "green" and "socially responsible" – even if their annual reports are using more paper than before to trumpet their "goodness". Sponsored by a UN effort, sustainability has added a further dimension to CSR reporting. The UN Global Reporting Initiative (GRI) produced a sustainability reporting framework, in which business, civil society, labour, investors, accountants and others collaborate. The GRI is based on the underlying belief that reporting on economic, environmental, and social performance by all organisations should be as routine and comparable as financial reporting.

Principles or prescription?

As the 21st century dawned many felt that corporate governance was well developed. Codes of best practice in corporate governance were in place in many countries. The importance of sound corporate governance is well recognised. In the United States markets were being satisfied, wealth created, and directors were apparently doing a good job at governing their companies.

Corporate governance commentators used to speak of the Anglo-American approach to governance, contrasting the unitary board, common law and markets for corporate control with the continental European two-tier board, Napoleonic law and illiquid, protected markets. But a fundamental dichotomy has emerged between the United States and the UK and Commonwealth countries such as Australia, Canada, Singapore, Hong Kong and South Africa since the passing of the Sarbanes-Oxley Act. The UK and Commonwealth countries base their corporate governance on voluntary compliance with principles in the codes ("follow the code or explain why not"), whereas the American approach is based on legal compliance ("obey the law or risk the penalties").

Convergence or differentiation?

A decade ago there was little doubt that corporate governance principles and practices were converging on the Anglo-American model with its unitary board, independent directors and transparency. Today that view is on hold. The American and British Commonwealth approaches to corporate governance have diverged, as stated above. Moreover, approaches to corporate governance in other parts of the world have shown the significance of, for example, cultural influences in East Asia and legal and political aspects in China and Russia. Certainly there are forces encouraging convergence, including the widespread acceptance of international accounting standards, which now includes the United States, and the activities of global corporations, the big four international auditing firms and international investors. But global standards, principles and processes are a long way off.

Chairman or chairman and CEO?

A further difference between the British Commonwealth and the American approaches to corporate governance is in attitudes towards the most significant managerial and board positions in a company. The codes of corporate governance are unambiguous in their recommendation that the roles of the chairman of the board and the chief executive of the business should be held by different people, thus providing checks and balances against domination of decision-making and overenthusiastic risk-taking by a single all-powerful individual. The UK Combined Code does, however, recognise that in some circumstances a single leader may be inevitable, but in that case calls for a strong group of non-executives on the board with their own appointed leader.

By contrast, in the United States, the roles of chairman and CEO are typically combined in a single, powerful individual, arguing that companies need single-minded leadership. Calls for the adoption of the approach to board and executive leadership adopted in the rest of the world are strongly resisted by the Business Roundtable, the body representing chairmen/CEOs in the United States. The question is which is preferable: a dominant leader who enhances performance or shared responsibility? Which reduces risk? This issue is sometimes called the duality question.

Society's new expectations of directors

The 19th century saw the foundations laid for modern corporations: this was the century of the entrepreneur. The 20th century became the century of management. Now the 21st century has become the century of governance, as around the world the focus swings towards the legitimacy and effectiveness of directors and boards and the way power is exercised over corporate entities. The original concept of the company was based on directors' duty. Subsequently, the emphasis swung from duty to power. The challenge to directors today, whether governing a global listed company, a subsidiary company, or a family firm, is to rediscover the need for professionalism, integrity and trust.

A-Z

A and B shares

Normally, each share in a company has one vote. Indeed, "one share, one vote" is a basic tenet of SHAREHOLDER DEMOCRACY. But some companies do create various classes of share with different voting rights. One reason is to increase capital, while keeping control in the hands of a few dominant shareholders. The WAL-LENBERG family in Sweden maintain control over their companies by such dual class shares. Another reason for issuing different classes of share is to give one class different terms, such as preferential rights on winding up or prior claims on profits. On the opening of the Chinese stockmarkets, "A" shares were available only to Chinese citizens resident in China. (See CHINESE CORPOR-ATE GOVERNANCE and DUALITY.)

❝❝ *Shareholder democracy is a farce. Proxies are ineffective. Annual general meetings are a sound and light show, and the slate of directors is re-elected.*

A director speaking to Richard Leblanc and Jim Gillies, *Inside the Boardroom*, 2005

ABI

See ASSOCIATION OF BRITISH INSURERS.

Accountability

Under company law the directors of a company are accountable to their SHAREHOLDERS. Such accountability is normally achieved through the regular DIRECTORS' REPORT AND ACCOUNTS and the ANNUAL GENERAL MEETING of the shareholder members of the company. In many jurisdictions, however, there has been a tendency to call for wider accountability from boards, particularly in a PUBLIC COMPANY. REGULATORS demand wider DISCLOSURE of financial and other information. Employees' representatives expect information on matters that could affect their interests. In the UK, the 2006 Companies' Act calls for boards to recognise a broader responsibility to other STAKEHOLDERS. In Germany, the Netherlands and Sweden employees have statutory rights to board-level accountability. Customer and other interest groups also call for greater transparency of company activities. STAKEHOLDER THEORY argues that public companies have a duty to be accountable to all interest groups that could be affected by the company's actions (including customers, distributors, employees, financial institutions and suppliers, as well as local, national and international public interests).

" *The directors of companies, being managers of other people's money than their own, cannot be expected to watch over it with the same anxious vigilance with which they watch over their own.*
Adam Smith, *Wealth of Nations*, 1776 (adapted)

Accountancy and Actuarial Discipline Board

The Accountancy and Actuarial Discipline Board (AADB) is an independent, investigative and disciplinary body for accountants and actuaries in the UK. It is responsible for operating and administering an independent disciplinary scheme covering members of the following UK accountants' professional bodies: the Association of Chartered Certified Accountants, the Chartered Institute of Management Accountants, the Chartered Institute of Public Finance and Accountancy and the Institute of Chartered Accountants in England and Wales; the Institute of Chartered Accountants of Ireland; and the Institute of Chartered Accountants of Scotland. The AADB is part of the UK's FINANCIAL REPORTING COUNCIL.

Accountancy Foundation

The REGULATOR of the UK accountancy profession, launched in 2002. Its responsibilities were subsequently transferred to the FINANCIAL REPORTING COUNCIL. Funded by the six UK accountancy professional bodies, delays and difficulties arose from the outset and the propriety of professional self-regulation was questioned. (Compare with the American regulator, the PUBLIC ACCOUNTABILITY BOARD.)

Accounting Oversight Board

See PUBLIC COMPANY ACCOUNTING OVERSIGHT BOARD.

Accounting Standards Board

The Accounting Standards Board (ASB) issues UK accounting standards, as its name suggests. It took over the task of setting standards from the Accounting Standards Committee (ASC) in 1990. The ASB also collaborates with accounting standard-setters from other countries and the INTERNATIONAL ACCOUNTING STANDARDS BOARD to influence the development of those standards and to make sure that its standards reflect international ones. The ASB is part of the UK's FINANCIAL REPORTING COUNCIL.

Added-value chain

Businesses must add value to their products or services if they are to satisfy their customers, make a profit and grow. In the food industry, for example, the farmer grows wheat, the flour mills turn

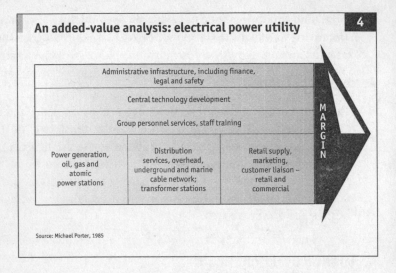

An added-value analysis: electrical power utility   4

Administrative infrastructure, including finance, legal and safety

Central technology development

Group personnel services, staff training

| Power generation, oil, gas and atomic power stations | Distribution services, overhead, underground and marine cable network; transformer stations | Retail supply, marketing, customer liaison – retail and commercial |

MARGIN

Source: Michael Porter, 1985

it into flour, the transport company carries it to the baker, where it is baked, or to the supermarket, where it is sold to the end user. Each link in the chain adds value. A business may be integrated with operations at each link of the chain or it might outsource all but a CORE COMPETENCE. Reebok, a shoe company, has hardly any manufacturing and no retailing outlets, only a highly profitable managerial and marketing function. Analysing the elements of the added-value chain in a business can provide some valuable strategic insights. Figure 4 illustrates a value chain analysis for an electricity supply utility.

Each of the boxes in Figure 3 can, obviously, be expanded into a whole set or hierarchy of more detailed diagrams that show just where value is being added in a company's processes. If associated with the related costs, a value chain analysis can highlight just what elements of the processes are driving costs and which are adding value. This information can be important in STRATEGY FORMULATION, because it can pinpoint what gives the business its strategic advantage and how its activities are differentiated from those of competitors. It can suggest new strategic options for improving existing activities and developing new strategies such as outsourcing, growth by acquisition, mergers or STRATEGIC ALLIANCES to obtain scale economies, share risk or enhance development.

Adjournment of meetings

See MEETING MANIPULATION.

Advisory boards

Companies operating internationally sometimes create advisory committees or boards in different parts of the world to give advice to the HOLDING COMPANY directors. Typically, prominent business leaders, politicians and other influential figures from the region are invited to serve. But they are seldom given executive powers. Advisory boards were prevalent in the 1970s and early 1980s. Subsequently, companies found that the advice they needed could be obtained more cheaply from consultants, who need be retained only as long as their advice is wanted. Some also found that advisory boards created complications, by taking decisions that were inconsistent with group-wide needs, even though they had no formal executive authority. An advisory board might, for example, propose investment in a country, when the board's global strategy called for disinvestment there.

Age of directors

Three factors restrict the age of directors: company law, which in some countries puts an age limit (typically 70–75) on directors unless the SHAREHOLDERS approve an exception (but in countries such as the UK age discrimination legislation has removed such age ceilings); the company's own ARTICLES OF ASSOCIATION; and, for listed companies, the LISTING RULES of the relevant stock exchange. OUTSIDE DIRECTORS tend to be older than EXECUTIVE DIRECTORS.

 Once on the board, directors seem to stay for ever. I would like to see a "sell-by" date stamped on the head of every director.
David Norburn, 1993

Agency theory

A statistically powerful, theoretical approach to CORPORATE GOVERNANCE. As the proponents of agency theory, Michael Jensen and William Meckling, explained in an article in the *Journal of Financial Economics* in 1976:

Agency theory involves a contract under which one or more persons (the shareholders) engage another person (the directors) to perform some service on their behalf which includes delegating some decision-making authority to the agent. If both parties to the relationship are utility maximizers there is good reason to believe the agent will not always act in the best interests of the principal.

In other words, directors pursue their own interests and cannot be trusted to act in the interests of the SHAREHOLDERS. Checks and balance mechanisms are needed. Certainly there is ample anecdotal evidence to support this contention: directors who treat listed, PUBLIC COMPANIES as though they are their own property, like Robert MAXWELL, or who fail to act in the interests of their shareholders by overstating profits as in the WASTE MANAGEMENT case.

A lot of research on board-level activities has been published using agency theoretical methods. Typically, this work has been based on aggregated, published data, and has been done by researchers who have no need to meet a company director. In the field of financial economics, agency theory offers a statistically rigorous insight into corporate governance processes. Reality, unfortunately, is more complicated. Board behaviour does not consist of contractual relationships, but can be influenced by inter-personal behaviour, group dynamics and political intrigue. Nor do all directors act in a way that maximises their own personal inter-ests; they can be trusted to act responsibly with independence and integrity, as envisaged by the alternative STEWARDSHIP THEORY.

❝❝ *No man, acting as agent, can be allowed to put himself into a position in which his interest and his duty will be in conflict.*
Lord Cairns, giving judgment in the London High Court in 1874

❝❝ *It is clear that the relative merits of agency theory and stakeholder theory will be debated for some time to come – one based on shareholding the other on stakeholding – although it is important to remember that in the real world governance is likely to lie somewhere between these two extreme positions.*
Robert Wearing, *Cases in Corporate Governance*, 2005

Agenda

The items of business to be covered in a meeting. Three approaches to agenda design can be distinguished:

1 The routine approach, in which each meeting follows the pattern of the previous (apologies, approval of the minutes, matters arising, the usual substantive items and any other business).

2 The chairman-led approach, in which the chairman determines the agenda, allocating appropriate time to each to optimise discussion.

3 The professional chairman approach, in which the chairman seeks advice on the agenda, perhaps from the COMPANY SECRETARY, or as some chairmen do by asking each director

whether there are items they wish to have discussed. Lord Caldecote, when chairman of Delta Group, wrote to each of his directors periodically to ask whether there were matters they felt that the board should be discussing for the future benefit of the firm.

Which approach is adopted depends on the BOARD STYLE.

❝❞ *Life is a constant struggle between honour and inclination*
Anon

AGM

See ANNUAL GENERAL MEETING.

Alliance building

See GAMES DIRECTORS PLAY.

Alternate director

The ARTICLES OF ASSOCIATION of some companies allow the board to nominate alternates for directors. This can be useful if board members have to travel a lot or are based abroad and cannot attend every meeting. When serving in the alternate capacity, the alternate director has all the rights to INFORMATION and all the duties and responsibilities of the other directors.

Amakaduri

See DESCENT FROM HEAVEN.

American Depositary Receipt

A vehicle for a foreign company to be listed on an American stock exchange. An American Depositary Receipt (ADR) is a security issued, for a fee, by an American investment bank that holds a matching number of real shares in the company. (See also GLOBAL SHARES.)

American Institute of Certified Public Accountants

See TREADWAY COMMISSION.

Annual general meeting

A properly convened meeting of the voting SHAREHOLDERS of a company. The annual general meeting (AGM) is part of the formal machinery of CORPORATE GOVERNANCE, at which the directors demonstrate their ACCOUNTABILITY to the owners. Certain decisions, such as the approval of the annual accounts and dividend, the appointment of directors and the confirmation of the auditors, are statutorily required to be taken by the AGM. The detailed rules, such as the amount of notice required and for voting (including proxy votes), are usually contained in the company's ARTICLES OF ASSOCIATION. Some jurisdictions allow small, CLOSELY HELD COMPANIES to forgo their AGM, because all members can be presumed to know about and be able to influence the situation.

In the United States, and increasingly in the UK, directors of LISTED COMPANIES expect to be extensively questioned at their AGMS. Indeed, they are often briefed, even rehearsed, on possible inquiries. INSTITUTIONAL INVESTORS as well as private investors now demand answers to questions on matters such as DIRECTORS' REMUNERATION and the company's (and by implication the board's) performance. In the past, PUBLIC COMPANY AGMS were often brief, formal and entirely predictable, with any sign of critical questioning thwarted from the chair and the only shareholder comment being a vote of thanks to the chairman and the board. Recently, however, that complacency has been challenged by active shareholders. In Japan the AGMs of nearly all listed companies are held on the same day to prevent the disruption of the meeting by paid troublemakers from the YAKUZA.

ARTHUR ANDERSEN

Arthur Andersen was one of the big five global accounting practices. Operating around the world, the firm provided audit and consultancy services to its clients and pioneered some original accounting practices. Its reputation, and certainly the partnership's self-image, was as an international leader of the profession. Then in the early years of the 21st century some of its major American clients – WASTE MANAGEMENT, WORLDCOM and ENRON – became spectacularly insolvent and the auditor was said to be less than blameless. Claims for damages from disgruntled creditors and shareholders of the failed companies threatened the financial viability of the Andersen firm. The American part of the firm was also found guilty of destroying evidence, although that verdict was quashed on appeal. But the damage was done. Clients changed auditors, Andersen partners moved to other firms, and the Arthur Andersen partnership came to an end.

Articles of association

The formal set of rules by which a company is run. Registered with the company regulatory authorities at the time of incorporation, in accordance with the company law in that jurisdiction, the articles are an important part of CORPORATE GOVERNANCE mechanisms. Articles can be amended by a resolution formally approved by a meeting of the company's members. Directors should always study the articles of their company. Occasionally non-standard drafting can have unexpected effects on director powers and board decisions. For example, an owner-manager of a company incorporated in the UK, which was in a joint venture with a Japanese SHAREHOLDER, was thwarted in his attempt to bring in new capital. He believed he had control because he held 61% of the voting shares, only to discover that to exercise such powers, the articles required the approval of 75% of the shareholders. (See STRATEGIC ALLIANCE.)

" *Boards are far from perfect institutions. They are struggling and will likely continue to do so. What is needed is a concerted effort in many board rooms and around the globe to improve this important institution.*
Colin Carter and Jay Lorsch, *Back to the Drawing Board: Designing Corporate Boards for a Complex World,* 2004

ASB

See ACCOUNTING STANDARDS BOARD.

Asian values

One of the explanations offered to explain decades of economic success throughout East Asia Pacific: business and governance practices rooted in a strong work ethic, a commitment to saving and a family-centric culture. Following the financial and economic collapses of countries such as Indonesia, Malaysia, Thailand and South Korea in 1997/98, CRONY CAPITALISM was offered as an alternative governance insight.

Associate director

Some companies give the title of director to senior managers, even though they are not formally members of the board. The reason may be to reward managerial performance with recognition and status, or to give prestige to an executive who is required to represent the company with clients, customers or government. Sometimes such employees are called associate directors. Even though they have not been appointed by the SHAREHOLDERS, or recognised as directors by the filing requirements of companies' acts and stock exchange listing agreements, such people could find themselves held as responsible as other directors if those with whom they had dealt reasonably thought they were directors. (See TITLES OF DIRECTORS.)

Association of British Insurers

An organisation representing the collective interests of the British insurance industry, including those of INSTITUTIONAL INVESTORS in the industry. The Association of British Insurers (ABI) has taken a higher profile in CORPORATE GOVERNANCE issues in recent years, monitoring company activities against codes of good corporate governance conduct, occasionally advising on SHAREHOLDER activism and PROXY VOTING options (see SHAREHOLDER POWER). It has issued guidelines on the information its members would like to receive from companies in which they invest. Research by the ABI in 2008 demonstrated a positive link between good corporate governance and company performance. (See also NATIONAL ASSOCIATION OF PENSION FUNDS.)

www.abi.org.uk

Audit

In most jurisdictions companies are required to have an audit by external, independent AUDITORS, who report to the SHAREHOLD-ERS that the annual report and accounts presented to them by the directors show a true and fair view of the state of the company's affairs. Although the exact wording varies by jurisdiction, the intention is to provide an independent verification of the direct-ors' financial report. In some places quarterly accounts are required, which also have to be audited; in others, private CLOSELY HELD COMPANIES may dispense with the audit if the sharehold-ers agree; and in a few, such as the British Virgin Islands, there is no audit requirement at all.

Audit committee

The relationship with the external, independent AUDITORS is crucial to board-level effectiveness. All directors need to know what issues have arisen during the AUDIT. The board must avoid the possibility of powerful EXECUTIVE DIRECTORS, such as the finance director or the CEO, becoming too close to their auditors and resolving issues before they reach the board. An audit com-mittee, which is a subcommittee of the main board, can avoid such problems. These days the members of audit committees are all independent OUTSIDE DIRECTORS, whose role is to act as a bridge between the external auditors and the board. Typically, audit committees meet three or four times a year to discuss the details of the audit, to consider any contentious points that have arisen on the accounts and to receive the auditor's recommenda-tions on audit-related matters such as management controls. The audit committee will often negotiate the audit fee.

All the CODES OF BEST PRACTICE in CORPORATE GOVERN-ANCE around the world call for audit committees, and the New York Stock Exchange requires one as a condition of listing.

Following corporate scandals, such as ENRON and WORLDCOM, there have been calls for the role of audit committees to be enhanced, making them responsible for various corporate governance functions. Some see this as a move towards the European-style TWO-TIER BOARD; others see problems if an audit committee interferes in management's legitimate responsibilities. The GREAT WESTERN RAILWAY COMPANY case shows that in the early days a group of shareholders fulfilled this function. (See also RISK MANAGEMENT.)

❝ Audit committees will fall short of their potential if they lack the understanding to deal adequately with the auditing or accounting matters that they are likely to face.
Cadbury Report, 1992

❝ It's not my responsibility to train directors on audit committees.
A chairman speaking to Richard Leblanc and Jim Gillies, *Inside the Boardroom*, 2005

Auditing Practices Board

The Auditing Practices Board (APB) was established in April 2002. It is committed to leading the development of auditing practice in the UK and the Republic of Ireland by establishing high standards of auditing, meeting the needs of users of financial information, and ensuring public confidence in the auditing process. The APB is part of the UK's FINANCIAL REPORTING COUNCIL.

Auditors

The independent, outside auditors fulfil a crucial role in CORPORATE GOVERNANCE. Usually appointed formally by the SHAREHOLDERS, on the recommendation of the board or its AUDIT COMMITTEE, the auditors report on the truth and fairness of the

financial report and accounts. Should the AUDIT throw up disagreements which cannot be reconciled with the company's
directors, the auditors may qualify the audit report. In recent years,
auditors of major PUBLIC COMPANIES around the world have
found themselves the subject of LITIGATION from dissatisfied
shareholders, challenging the validity of the audited accounts.
Sometimes this is because the company has failed and the auditors are a last resort because they are insured – the so-called DEEP-
POCKET SYNDROME.

Following the collapse of ENRON and other companies, the
independence of some auditors has been questioned, particularly
where the audit firm generated more from consulting work than
from the audit. The practice of accountants who had been involved
in an audit leaving the audit firm and joining the finance staff of
the client has also been challenged. The European Union has recommended that partners involved in performing audits should
not join the audit client before the end of a two-year cooling-off
period. Guidelines from the Institute of Chartered Accountants in
England and Wales require an assessment of threats to independence through self-interest, self-review, advocacy, familiarity or
intimidation. They also call for the partner responsible for an audit
to be rotated periodically, to avoid the danger of overfamiliarity
with the client. The audit partner of MAXWELL had never
changed.

66 *Auditors owe external loyalty, consultants internal.*
Allen Sykes, *Capitalism for Tomorrow: Reuniting Ownership and Control*, 2002

66 *Auditors are like the cuckoos in cuckoo clocks: they come out, comment
briefly and nip back inside. Ticking is what they do best.*
Robert Hodgkinson, when chairman of the Financial Reporting Council,
London

Aufsichtsrat

The upper SUPERVISORY BOARD of the German TWO-TIER BOARD. Large companies in Germany are seen as a form of "partnership" between capital and labour. Reflecting this approach to worker CO-DETERMINATION, half the members of the *Aufsichtsrat* represent the SHAREHOLDERS and the other half the employees.

Bb

B shares

See A AND B SHARES and DUAL VOTING RIGHTS.

Backdoor listing

See SHELL COMPANY.

Big four

The four global accounting firms, which audit the vast majority of global corporations: Deloitte, PricewaterhouseCoopers, Ernst & Young and KPMG. There were more, but following mergers and the collapse of ARTHUR ANDERSEN, only four major firms now remain. In 2006 the big four had 2,300 partners and a fee income of £6.3 billion. The next largest firm had 336 partners and a fee income of under £250m. A number of government and regulatory bodies have been reviewing the implications of the big four for competition policy and the possible effect if one of them went out of business.

BLACK, CONRAD

Conrad Black, a Canadian who took British citizenship to enter the British House of Lords, was an international media mogul, famous for his pugnaciousness and intellectual arrogance. He controlled an empire of publications, including the *Chicago Sun-Times*, the *Daily Telegraph* in the UK and the *National Post* in Canada, through an OWNERSHIP CHAIN of companies. Black held 65% of Ravelston Corporation, a Canadian company, which owned 78% of Hollinger, a company listed in Toronto, which owned 30% of the equity, but through shares with DUAL VOTING RIGHTS 73% of the votes, in Hollinger International, a company listed in New York. He filled his boardroom with prestigious names, including Henry Kissinger, a former US Secretary of State, Lord Wakeham, a former British government minister, and other friends, mainly directors of significant public companies.

Black was known for his ostentatious lifestyle, with corporate jets, a fleet of vintage cars, apartments and domestic staff paid for by the company. His wife memorably commented to *Vogue* that she had "an extravagance that knows no bounds", which prompted some INSTITUTIONAL INVESTORS and the CHAIRMAN of the AUDIT COMMITTEE to look more closely at the Black empire. Eventually, Black appeared in a Chicago court charged with diverting to himself over $80m from Hollinger International from the sale of newspapers. Further, his company Ravelston had charged Hollinger International multimillion-dollar fees for management and for agreeing not to compete with regional newspapers that had been sold. Allegedly the directors had approved these payments without question or independent advice. Nor had they queried the personal use of company assets, allowing Black to treat the company as his private empire. As Black said: "This is my company and I decide what the board knows, and when they know it." Black was sentenced to over six years in prison and fined $125,000. Protesting his innocence to the end, he claimed that he was the victim of "CORPORATE GOVERNANCE zealots".

BLACKSTONE GROUP

Peter Peterson and Stephen Schwarzman founded The Blackstone Group in 1985 with a shared secretary and a balance sheet of

$400,000. Today, Blackstone is a private equity company listed on the New York Stock Exchange with nearly US$100 billion assets under management. The private equity operation, established in 1987, is a global business with 98 investment professionals and offices in New York, London, Mumbai and Hong Kong, and manages five general PRIVATE EQUITY FUNDS as well as one specialised fund focusing on communications-related investments. In the early years Blackstone concentrated on leveraged buy-out acquisitions of US-based companies. Today it operates around the world and is also involved in start-up businesses, turnarounds, minority investments, corporate partnerships and industry consolidations.

www.blackstone.com

Board assessment

Management assessment is a routine practice in most large companies. Yet the most significant organ of the company – the board – was seldom assessed until recently. In 1998, the HAMPEL REPORT called for formal procedures to "assess both the board's collective performance and that of individual directors". Today, the UK COMBINED CODE and the CORPORATE GOVERNANCE codes of most countries call for formal assessment of boards and their committees, as well as of the performance of individual directors. The Corporate Governance Research Centre of the US Conference Board published *Determining Board Effectiveness* (1999), which offered a set of questions that go to the heart of board assessment:

- How does the board define its role and duties?
- How does the board prioritise its responsibilities?
- How effectively does the board monitor company performance?
- Does the board have sufficient independence to perform its duties properly?

- Does the board have the right mix of skills to achieve its goals?
- Does the board have the right size and structure?
- How does the board oversee auditing functions to minimise risk?
- How does the board best structure and use its NOMINATION COMMITTEE?
- What is the board's role in determining director and executive compensation?
- How does the board conduct CEO appointment and succession planning?
- Are the board's decision-making processes effective?
- Does the board have a process for evaluating whether it is achieving its goals?
- Can the board make course corrections if necessary?
- Does the board communicate effectively to investors?

(See also BOARD DEVELOPMENT.)

❝ *It is a useful though often painful exercise for a board to ask: How did we do? What lessons can be learned? How can we do better?*
Daniel Hodson, Gresham College, London

❝ *This corporate governance stuff has been all blown out of whack.*
A director speaking to Richard Leblanc and Jim Gillies, *Inside the Boardroom*, 2005

Board corporate governance policies

The increasing focus on CORPORATE GOVERNANCE has caused some boards to articulate their corporate governance policies, and in some cases to publish them. General Motors, for example, has extensive guidelines for the board. These include guidance on:

- Selection and composition of the board
  - board membership criteria

- selection of new directors
- extending the invitation to a potential new director to join the board
- resignation policy relating to majority voting for directors
- director orientation and continuing education
- Board leadership
  - selection of CHAIRMAN and chief executive officer
  - chair of the directors and corporate governance committee
- Board composition and performance
  - size of the board
  - mix of management and INDEPENDENT DIRECTORS
  - board definition of what constitutes independence for directors
  - former chairman and chief executive officer board membership
  - directors who change their present job responsibility
  - limits on outside board membership
  - meeting attendance
  - term limits and retirement age
  - board compensation
  - loans to directors and executive officers
  - stock ownership by non-employee directors
  - executive sessions of independent directors
  - role of the presiding director
  - access to outside advisers
  - assessing the board's performance
  - ethics and conflicts of interest
  - confidentiality
  - board's interaction with advisers, institutional investors, press, customers, etc
- Board's relationship to senior management
  - regular attendance of non-directors at BOARD MEETINGS
  - board access to senior management

- Meeting procedures
  - selection of AGENDA items for board meetings
  - board materials distributed in advance
  - board presentations
- Committee matters
  - board committees
  - committee performance evaluation
  - assignment and rotation of committee members
  - frequency and length of committee meetings
  - committee agenda
- Leadership development
  - formal evaluation of the chairman and chief executive officer
  - succession planning
  - management development

Adopted 1994 Revised 2008 www.gm.com/corporate/investor_information/docs/corp_gov/cg_guidelines.pdf

Many other major companies have now produced their own corporate governance codes, guidelines and policies.

 The most important factor governing a successful board is the quality of the board itself ... Board meetings must not be solemn affairs ... There is no absolute magic formula. Every company has its own culture and metabolism, and different types of business require separate types of management style and approach from the board.
Sir Richard Greenbury

Board development

Businesses have a tendency to outgrow their boards. A successful board in the past does not guarantee continuing success in the future. As the strategic situation facing a company changes new thinking and, perhaps, new faces are needed. Yet few boards have plans for director succession and development. Even fewer have a strategy for board development to make sure that the board evolves in line with proposed changes in the overall corporate strategy.

❝❝ *If a board can motivate managers, it will get the best out of them. If it cannot stand up to the chief executive and his cronies over their pay, then it will struggle to control them when they want to buy this dud rival or diversify into that dead-end business.*
The Economist, June 14th 2008

Board meeting

Boards of directors can meet when and where they want, subject to anything in the ARTICLES OF ASSOCIATION. Some boards have few meetings, either because the directors meet regularly on an informal basis so that the board meetings become an occasion for formalising decisions taken, or because the activities of the company do not require more meetings. Professional boards, however, usually have a regular schedule of meetings (often monthly). (See also BOARD STYLES.)

❝❝ *It is impossible to conceive of the corporation's [General Motors] board of directors having intimate knowledge of, and business experience in, every one of the technical matters which require top level consideration or action. Nevertheless the board can and should be responsible for the end result.*
Alfred P. Sloan, My Years with General Motors, 1963

Board performance

Board performance is under the spotlight as never before. SHARE-HOLDERS, particularly INSTITUTIONAL SHAREHOLDERS, have much higher expectations of the boards of companies in which they invest than in the past. Boards need to establish criteria for their own performance, monitor their achievements, and take remedial action when necessary. (See also COMMONWEALTH PRINCIPLES FOR CORPORATE GOVERNANCE, NEW YORK STOCK EXCHANGE LISTING RULES and the UK COMBINED CODE.)

> ❝❝ Coote got me in as a director of something or other. Very good business for me – nothing to do except go down into the City once or twice a year to one of those hotel places and sit around a table where they have some nice new blotting paper. Then Coote or some clever Johnny makes a speech simply bristling with figures, but fortunately you needn't listen to it – and I can tell you, you often get a jolly good lunch out of it.
>
> Agatha Christie, The Seven Dials Mystery, 1929

Board structures

At its simplest, board structure distinguishes those directors who hold management positions in the company and those who do not. Those with management positions are often referred to as EXECUTIVE DIRECTORS and those who do not as NON-EXECUTIVE DIRECTORS or OUTSIDE DIRECTORS. A further distinction can be drawn between those non-executive directors who are genuinely independent of the company (other than their directorship and, perhaps, a non-significant shareholding) and those who, though not employees, are in positions that might affect their independence and objectivity. (See INDEPENDENT DIRECTOR.)

Figure 1 on page 4 distinguishes management from governance by representing the GOVERNING BODY as a circle superimposed on the management triangle. This model can be applied to other broad structures.

First there is the board made up entirely of executive directors (Figure 5). In the all-executive board, every director is also a managerial employee of the company. Many start-up and FAMILY COMPANIES have this structure, with the founder, close colleagues and other family members all working in the business and being members of the board. The boards of some subsidiary companies

The all-executive board

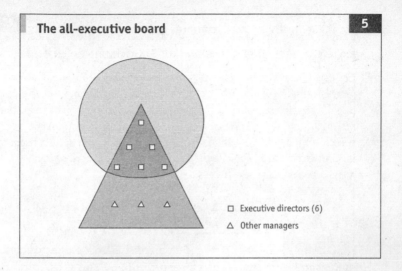

□ Executive directors (6)
△ Other managers

operating in groups also choose the all-executive board, which is, in effect, the senior management team of the business with no outside members. The boards of major Japanese companies are typically large and effectively comprise executives from the company. (See JAPANESE CORPORATE GOVERNANCE.)

" *Q. What is your ideal board? A. My chief executive and myself.*
Sir Terence Conran, founder of Habitat, 2001

A potential problem of a board which is dominated by executive directors is that they are, in effect, monitoring and supervising their own performance. One solution, other than to appoint independent non-executive directors, is for the CHAIRMAN to discuss with newly appointed executive directors what is expected of them. Executive directors have to wear two hats, one as the manager of a part of the business, the other as a director responsible for the governance of the company. The important thing is not to be wearing the manager's hat in the boardroom

Then there is the board with a majority of executive directors

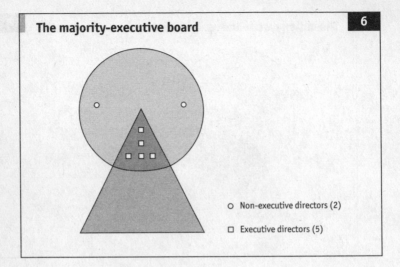

The majority-executive board   6

○ Non-executive directors (2)

□ Executive directors (5)

(Figure 6). In the evolution of companies and their boards, non-executive directors get appointed to boards for various reasons. Sometimes, in a developing PRIVATE COMPANY, the executive directors feel the need for additional expertise, knowledge or skills to supplement their own. Non-executive directors can also be appointed as nominees for those investing equity or debt in the business, or to secure relationships with suppliers, customers or others in the ADDED-VALUE CHAIN of the business. Another reason can be on succession in a family company when shareholdings are split between branches of the family.

However, the practice of leading PUBLIC COMPANIES in Australia, the United States and the UK is to have boards with a majority of non-executive directors. Indeed, in American LISTED COMPANIES the outside directors usually heavily outnumber the inside executive directors (Figure 7).

❝❝ *What matters is not only the structure of boards but how they work.*
Sir Adrian Cadbury, 1993

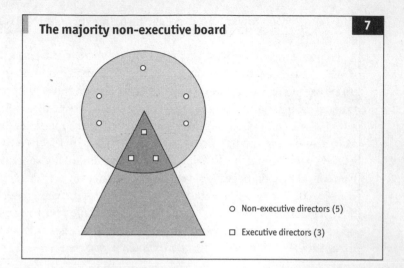

The majority non-executive board   7

○ Non-executive directors (5)

□ Executive directors (3)

Some argue that, if the outside members dominate the board, the governance process has really ceased to be a UNITARY BOARD

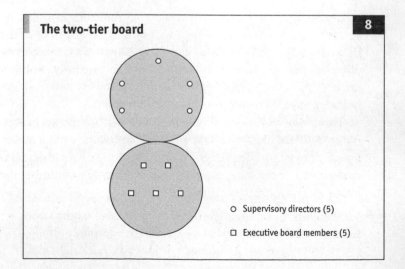

The two-tier board   8

○ Supervisory directors (5)

□ Executive board members (5)

and has moved towards the power structure of a TWO-TIER BOARD (Figure 8).

In the Anglo-American traditions of CORPORATE GOVERN-ANCE, the unitary board is the norm; that is a single board made up of executive and non-executive directors in whatever proportion is thought appropriate. The continental European model adopts the two-tier board in which an upper board supervises the executive board on behalf of STAKEHOLDERS. In the two-tier model the members of the supervisory board are totally separate from the senior management team and no common membership is allowed. The two-tier board is the basis for corporate governance in Germany and the Netherlands, and is allowed in some other countries in Europe, South America and Africa. (See GERMAN CORPORATE GOVERNANCE and EUROPEAN COMPANY.)

" *Corporate performance depends upon what boards do and how their members behave, not upon whether they have a particular committee structure.*
Colin Coulson-Thomas, 2002

Board styles

The CHAIRMAN of the board inevitably has an effect on the way that the board goes about its business. Boards vary enormously in their style. Figure 9 shows various board styles, depending on the extent of the directors' concern for their interpersonal relationships at board level, on the one hand, and their tough-minded concern for the work of the board, on the other.

- **The rubber-stamp board** shows little concern for either the tasks of the board or the interpersonal relationships among directors. Examples of such boards can be found in the "letter-box" companies registered in many offshore tax havens. The meetings of the board are a formality. Indeed, decisions are often minuted without a meeting actually

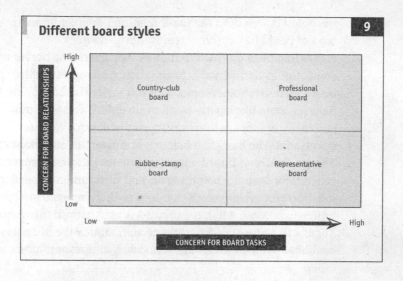

Different board styles 9

High

CONCERN FOR BOARD RELATIONSHIPS

Country-club
board

Professional
board

Rubber-stamp
board

Representative
board

Low

Low ⟶ High

CONCERN FOR BOARD TASKS

taking place. The boards of some private CLOSELY HELD
COMPANIES also treat their BOARD MEETINGS as a formality;
perhaps because one individual is dominant and takes the
decisions, or because the key players see each other
frequently and decisions are taken in the management
context.

■ **The country-club board,** in contrast, is very concerned with
interpersonal relations at board level and the issues before
the board may take second place. The boards of some old-
established companies that have been successful in the past
fit this model. Some FAMILY COMPANIES adopt a country-
club board style. Board meetings often have rituals. The
boardroom may be beautifully furnished, complete with
sepia pictures of previous chairmen. Legends and myths
surround board affairs. Meetings always follow the same
pattern. Following long-established traditions is revered.
Innovation is discouraged.

■ **The representative board** places more accent on the tasks of the board than it does on board relations. Frequently, this type of board has directors representing different SHAREHOLDERS or STAKEHOLDERS. The governing bodies of some non-governmental organisations with representative board members sometimes adopt this style. The board behaves more like a parliament of diverse interests. Issues can easily become politicised. Board discussions can be adversarial. The basis and balance of power are important.

■ **The professional board** adopts a style that shows a proper concern for both the board's tasks and directors' interpersonal relationships. A board with a successful professional style will have sound leadership from the chair. There will be tough-minded discussion among the members combined with a mutual understanding and respect for each other.

❝ *...there was no attempt to make management accountable to anyone. On the contrary boards of directors – legally the governing body of the corporation – became increasingly impotent rubber stamps for a company's top management."*
Peter Drucker, *Post-Capitalist Society*, 1993

❝ *Boards should pay greater attention to the calibre as well as the mix of directors, recognizing that effective board membership requires high levels of intellectual ability, experience, soundness of judgement and integrity."*
Hilmer Report, *Strictly Boardroom*, Australia 1993

❝ *Until the 1990s the executives dominated boards in both the US and the UK. Non-executives were mainly compliant cheerleaders.*
The Economist, November 2nd 2002

BOESKY, IVAN

Ivan Boesky was a securities dealer in the United States who epitomised the money and growth culture of the 1980s. He told a Business School commencement meeting in the University of California: "I want you to know that I think that greed is healthy. It is the basis of the capitalist system." He received a standing ovation: such was the business climate in the mid-1980s. Subsequently, he went to jail on insider dealing charges. The character Gecko in *Wall Street* owes much to his experience. (See DREXEL BURNHAM LAMBERT.)

BP: DIRECTORS' REMUNERATION

BP chairman Peter Sutherland said it was not a SHAREHOLDER revolt, but everyone knew that it was. In 2007 nearly a quarter of the voting shareholders showed their disapproval of the remuneration package of the outgoing CEO, Lord Browne. The board had to take notice of such a large protest. Browne had been with the company for over 40 years. As chief executive he had pursued an aggressive acquisitions strategy and built up the business to over £100 billion in revenues, making BP the largest company in the FTSE 100 index. But recently, Browne's leadership had been criticised, performance had been poor and there had been safety disasters. Browne decided to retire early, nearly three years before the end of his contract. The REMUNERATION COMMITTEE approved a remuneration package worth £72m. But it was a three-year performance-related bonus that caused most shareholder anger, because it included the period after he had left the company.

Bullock Report

When Sir Alan Bullock (now Lord Bullock) was Master of St Catherine's College, Oxford, in 1976, he was asked to chair an inquiry into industrial democracy by Harold Wilson, then prime minister and leader of the Labour Party. This was a response to the European Community's proposals in the fifth draft directive on company law harmonisation that major companies in all EC countries should adopt the German TWO-TIER BOARD structure, in which one half of the members of the SUPERVISORY BOARD represented capital (elected by the SHAREHOLDERS) and the other half represented employees (elected through trade union representation). The inquiry produced some of the first research into corporate governance in the UK (though the subject had yet to be given that title). The Bullock Report recommended the continuation of the British UNITARY BOARD, but with a proportion of the directors elected, through the trade union machinery, to represent employee concerns. Business interests were highly critical of both the Bullock proposals and the EC draft fifth directive. Neither was enacted. However, worker representation on WORKS COUNCILS was gradually achieved in the European Union under the Social Chapter of the Maastricht treaty.

66 *Boards have an unlimited capacity for self-delusion. The way they work is a black box.*
Andrew Pettigrew, 1997

Business roundtable

An association of CEOs in the United States which had been interested in CORPORATE GOVERNANCE matters for many years. In 2002, following the ENRON debacle, the Business Roundtable published new *Principles of Corporate Governance*. These suggested that successful governance needed a CEO of integrity and a strong ethical "tone at the top" set by senior management. It also recommended that there should be a code of conduct, which would enable employees to report potential misconduct without fear of retribution (see WHISTLE-BLOWING). The principles were largely superseded by the SARBANES-OXLEY ACT.

66 *Boards are a conundrum. Take a group of part-time directors and present them with an extremely difficult job, but give them limited time together. And then charge this institution with ultimate responsibility for ensuring that the nation's most important economic assets are well managed. How can such an unlikely arrangement work?*

Colin Carter and Jay Lorsch, *Back to the Drawing Board: Designing Corporate Boards for a Complex World,* 2004

Cadbury Report

Prominent institutions in the City of London, concerned about AUDIT and regulatory issues following a number of dramatic company collapses in the 1980s, set up a committee chaired by Sir Adrian Cadbury. To avoid the potential domination of companies by overpowerful chief executives or overenthusiastic executive management, the committee's 1992 report, *The Financial Aspects of Corporate Governance*, advocated the following checks and balances at board level:

- wider use of independent NON-EXECUTIVE DIRECTORS;
- the introduction of an AUDIT COMMITTEE;
- a separation between chairman and CEO;
- the use of REMUNERATION COMMITTEES;
- and adherence to a detailed code of best practice.

Under the code, all UK LISTED COMPANIES were required to report to shareholders on their governance practices, with the ultimate threat of delisting for non-compliance.

Reactions to the Cadbury Report varied. Some argued that it lacked teeth, claiming that delisting, being the ultimate sanction, would disadvantage the very SHAREHOLDERS who the report set out to protect, and that nothing short of legislation would stop abuses by dominant company leaders. Others feared that giving non-executives more power (Cadbury recommended that they appoint their own leader, have access to legal advice and meet separately if necessary) would erode the concept of the UNITARY BOARD, creating the continental European TWO-TIER BOARD by the back door. The Cadbury proposals were subsequently incorporated into the UK COMBINED CODE.

CalPERS

The Californian State Employees Pension Fund (CalPERS) has been the most proactive INSTITUTIONAL INVESTOR in the United States, setting a trend in SHAREHOLDER activism throughout the country. Now its attention has turned to CORPORATE GOVERN-ANCE in the international arena. It published a set of global prin-ciples for corporate governance in December 1996:

All markets should develop an appropriate code of best practice, by which directors can regulate themselves ... Such a code should be representative of the best governance practice in the market.

CalPERS has also proposed principles for good governance in Germany and Japan, arguing that changes are necessary if those countries are to attract overseas capital. However, CalPERS lost money on its investment in ENRON. (See SHAREHOLDER POWER.)

www.calpers.ca.gov

CARNIVAL CORPORATION AND CARNIVAL PLC

Carnival Corporation and Carnival PLC are DUAL LISTED COMPAN-IES, with listings in New York and London. This British-American corporation is the only group in the world to be included in both the S&P 500 and the FTSE 100 indexes. It is the world's largest cruise operator, with 12 cruise brands, including Carnival Cruise Lines, Princess Cruises, Holland America Line, Windstar Cruises and Seabourn Cruise Line in North America; P&O Cruises, Cunard Line, Ocean Village Holidays and Swan Hellenic in the UK; AIDA and A'ROSA in Germany; and Costa Cruises in Southern Europe. Carnival Corporation, incorporated in Panama, is the larger of the two holding companies and is listed on the New York Stock Exchange. Carnival PLC is listed on the London Stock Exchange and was formed from the P&O (Peninsular and Orient Steam Navigation Company) cruise business.

Catalyst

One of the roles a director can play (see CONFORMANCE ROLES).

Cecil King clause

Acting in line with the company's ARTICLES OF ASSOCIATION, the board of the International Publishing Corporation in 1968 removed their CHAIRMAN, Cecil King. Since then such provisions in company's articles have been called Cecil King clauses. Many company articles now include such clauses, sometimes requiring unanimity from the other board members, sometimes only a majority. Despite such provisions, some argue that it is still difficult to remove an underperforming director. To achieve the necessary support other directors have to declare their position, which could put their own tenure in jeopardy.

CEO

Short for chief executive officer, the top member of the management hierarchy. The term originated in the United States and is now widely used around the world in place of the British alternative, the managing director. In a UNITARY BOARD, the CEO is typically a member of the board. In the United States, contrary to the advice of many CODES OF BEST PRACTICE in CORPORATE GOVERNANCE, the CEO is often also the CHAIRMAN of the board (see DUALITY).

❝ *Britain's captains of industry are programmed early in life with a powerful need to achieve, high levels of resentment and a hunger for others' approval. Reared by dominant mothers who lavish them with tenderness and withdraw their love at the first sign of failure, [they] are brimming with repressed anger and driven by an unconscious craving for affection.*

Cyril Levicki, Reading University, in a study of directors of leading UK companies, 2001

CfD

See CONTRACT FOR DIFFERENCE.

Chaebol

Large conglomerate groups of companies in South Korea, dominated by family interests, formed after the second world war with close government involvement. Even though it only had a small shareholding, a family could maintain control by using cross-OWNERSHIP in subsidiary companies. In recent years the South Korean government has sought to reduce the power of the *chaebol* by requiring them to divest some of their interests. It had little success before the financial and economic crisis of 1997. Subsequently, the *chaebol*, finding it difficult to compete with other Asian producers because of their tradition of lifetime employment and militant trade unions, had such changes forced on them.

❝ *The role of chairman c 400 AD:*

The Abbot shall call together the whole congregation of the brethren to take council. He shall himself explain the questions at issue. And having had the advice of the brethren, he shall think it over himself, and shall do what he considers most advantageous.

Saint Benedict: *Rules for Monks*

Chairman

Many people speak loosely of the chairman of the company, whereas his or her role is, strictly, that of chairman of the company's board of directors. Subject to anything in the company's ARTICLES OF ASSOCIATION, the directors appoint one of their number to take the chair at their meetings; there are few statutory requirements for the role. Consequently, a range of styles is found. At one extreme the chairman does no more than manage the meetings, arrange the AGENDA, steer the discussions and make sure they reach a conclusion. At the other extreme is the powerful chairman who acts as a figurehead for the company, influences its strategic direction and manages the board, being concerned with its membership, committees and overall performance as well as chairing BOARD MEETINGS. In the UK, the Institute of Directors believes that holding multiple chairmanships is undesirable (see www.iod.co.uk).

The era of political correctness has caused many organisations to reconsider the title of the chairman of their GOVERNING BODY and its committees. Lady chairman, chairwoman, chairperson, or even the name of a piece of furniture, chair, is used. Worldwide, the number of women chairing the boards of major companies is minimal; but in many charitable and other non-profit companies women play a significant board role.

Whether the role of chairman should be combined with that of the CEO is much debated. Most CODES OF BEST PRACTICE recommend separation; in the United States the roles are often combined (see DUALITY).

❝ Every chairman brings a different style to the boardroom, ranging from the Napoleonic to the decisive, the pedantic to the humourless.
Patrick Dunne, Running Board Meetings, 1999

❝ Sir Roland Smith, chairman of Manchester United Football Club and many other companies, explained his role: "I just help to develop strategies and advice on improving company performance." Asked how Smith contributed to board meetings, Garry Weston, chairman of Associated British Foods, once said: "By asking the right questions. He is very impressive and has a lot of business experience and judgment."

Chairman's casting vote

Some ARTICLES OF ASSOCIATION provide for the chairman to have an additional vote should votes at a meeting of members or directors result in a tie. This can be particularly important where companies, particularly joint-venture companies, or boards have an even number of members.

Chinese corporate governance

In a country influenced by Marxist philosophy, OWNERSHIP is not the obvious basis for power. Yet many state enterprises have been turned into corporate entities and floated on China's stockmarkets in Shanghai and Shenzen. Many of these STATE-OWNED ENTER-PRISES (SOEs) have also been listed in Hong Kong and some in Singapore, New York, London and other stockmarkets. Typically, a minority of the shares are floated with the state holding the majority.

Oversight of the state's stake is the responsibility of the State-owned Assets Supervision and Administration Commission (SASAC) of the State Council. In 2008, total assets were worth over $1.56 trillion. So the SASAC is the largest institutional shareholder in the world, with eight in the *Fortune* list of the world's top 500 companies. It sometimes acts in the interests of the state to avoid unacceptable economic and social stresses such as unemployment, bankruptcy, corruption, financial pressures on the state economy and undesirable competition with state enterprises. The SASAC also exercises some control over the appointment of senior executives and INDEPENDENT DIRECTORS in SOEs. In some industries, the state also regulates prices.

The China Securities Regulatory Commission (CSRC) regulates CORPORATE GOVERNANCE in the SOEs and the securities market. The CSRC has developed a unique form of corporate governance, requiring a main board with at least one-third independent directors and an AUDIT COMMITTEE, as well as a SUPERVISORY BOARD with employee, SHAREHOLDER and state representatives. The CHAIRMAN of the supervisory board is usually a member of the relevant Communist Party committee. However, in practice, supervisory boards do not wield much power over the decisions of the main board of directors.

Although Hong Kong is now a Special Administrative Region of China, its corporate governance regime remains distinct, having developed from British company law and being among the most advanced in Asia. Most companies listed on the Hong Kong Stock Exchange, other than the mainland China companies, are FAMILY COMPANIES with control kept within the family. Although the Hong Kong regulatory authorities require a minimum of three independent NON-EXECUTIVE DIRECTORS, the heads of some family companies see little value in them. Their secretive, authoritarian, family-centric approach to business does not lend itself to OUTSIDE DIRECTORS who might disagree with their decisions.

" *People who defend bad corporate governance on the grounds of Asian values or some cultural difference are talking nonsense. Yes, there is a different structure of ownership; it's somewhat Victorian in that most companies are family controlled, but had I been around in Victorian times in England I think I would have seen similar bad corporate governance.*

David Webb, www.webb-site.com

Circuit breaker

After the 1987 stockmarket crash, some stock exchanges introduced trading breaks. These are points at which trading would be suspended should the market fall a certain distance to give time for reflection, avoid panic selling and prevent prices going into free-fall. Subsequent experience has led to alternative forms of triggering the circuit breaker being proposed, such as when the market falls a by certain percentage.

Classified boards

See STAGGERED BOARDS.

Closely held company

A PRIVATE COMPANY in which the SHAREHOLDERS and directors are effectively the same people. Consequently, many of the CORPORATE GOVERNANCE checks and balances that are needed to protect the rights of shareholders, where there is a separation between OWNERSHIP and management, are unnecessary. In some jurisdictions such companies are exempt from some AUDIT, DISCLOSURE and filing requirements. (See FAMILY DIRECTOR.)

Coalition building

See GAMES DIRECTORS PLAY.

Codes of best practice

CORPORATE GOVERNANCE practices came under review in the late 1980s, following corporate collapses around the world which were blamed on poor board-level practices. Various reports appeared, recommending best practices in corporate governance. The first was the UK's CADBURY REPORT, followed by Australia's HILMER REPORT, France's VIÉNOT REPORT, the Netherlands' PETER REPORT, South Africa's KING REPORT and others. Most proposals were based on perceived good practice, rather than rigorous research into their likely effect. In the UK, the Cadbury Report was followed by the Greenbury Report on DIRECTORS' REMUNERATION, a subsequent review called the HAMPEL REPORT and the TURNBULL REPORT on risk assessment. These reports were co-ordinated in the UK COMBINED CODE (see Appendix 2).

Subsequently, the Commonwealth Secretariat and the World Bank published a set of international principles for corporate governance (see COMMONWEALTH PRINCIPLES FOR CORPORATE GOVERNANCE). The OECD also produced a set of principles of corporate governance for the governments of member states (see Appendix 3).

For details of some codes, visit www.ecgi.org

❝❝ *The difficulty lies, not in the new ideas, but in escaping from the old ones.*
John Maynard Keynes, 1936

Co-determination

A governance process adopted in some continental European countries to make sure that significant corporate decisions are taken in partnership between labour and capital. For example, the SUPERVISORY BOARD in the German TWO-TIER BOARD model has equal numbers of SHAREHOLDER and employee representatives. Under the Social Chapter of the Maastricht treaty, large multinationals have had to establish WORKS COUNCILS to inform and consult with their employees about strategic changes affecting employment. This has applied in the UK since 1997. From 2008, any firm with 50 or more employees has to inform and consult about employment prospects.

Combined Code

The CODE OF BEST PRACTICE now adopted in the UK, combining the recommendations of the CADBURY REPORT, the Greenbury report and the HAMPEL REPORT; the subsequent TURNBULL REPORT has also been incorporated (see Appendix 2). Adopted by the London Stock Exchange as a listing requirement, firms must either comply or report the reasons for non-compliance. Criticisms of the Combined Code include its alleged lack of effectiveness and transparency criteria, failing to set targets for directors, and not requiring board CHAIRMEN to have relevant knowledge and experience of their company's industry.

Commonwealth Principles for Corporate Governance

The Commonwealth Secretariat and the World Bank published a set of principles for CORPORATE GOVERNANCE in 1999 intended to improve the quality of corporate governance in member states of the Commonwealth.

The 15 principles state that the board should:

- exercise leadership, enterprise, integrity and judgment in directing the corporation so as to achieve continuing prosperity for the corporation and to act in the best interests of the business enterprise in a manner based on transparency, ACCOUNTABILITY and responsibility;
- ensure that through a managed and effective process board appointments are made that provide a mix of proficient directors, each of whom is able to add value and to bring independent judgment to bear on the decision-making process;
- determine the corporation's purpose and values, determine the strategy to achieve its purpose and to implement its values to ensure that it survives and thrives, and ensure that

procedures and practices are in place that protect the corporation's assets and reputation;

- monitor and evaluate the implementation of strategies, policies, management performance criteria and business plans;
- ensure that the corporation complies with all relevant laws, regulations and codes of best business practice;
- ensure that the corporation communicates with SHAREHOLDERS and other STAKEHOLDERS effectively;
- serve the legitimate interests of the shareholders of the corporation and account to them fully;
- identify the firm's internal and external stakeholders and agree a policy, or policies, determining how the corporation should relate to them;
- ensure that no one person or block of persons has unfettered power and that there is an appropriate balance of power and authority on the board which is, *inter alia*, usually reflected by separating the roles of the chief executive and CHAIRMAN, and by having a balance between executive and NON-EXECUTIVE DIRECTORS;
- regularly review processes and procedures to ensure the effectiveness of its internal systems of control, so that its decision-making capability and the accuracy of its reporting and financial systems are maintained at a high level at all times;
- regularly assess its performance and effectiveness as a whole, and that of the individual directors, including the chief executive officer;
- appoint the chief executive officer and at least participate in the appointment of senior management, ensure the motivation and protection of intellectual capital intrinsic to the corporation, ensure that there is adequate training in the corporation for management and employees, and a succession plan for senior management;

■ ensure that all technology and systems used in the
corporation are adequate to properly run the business and
for it to remain a meaningful competitor;
■ identify key risk areas and key performance indicators of the
business enterprise and monitor these factors;
■ ensure annually that the corporation will continue as a going
concern for its next fiscal year.

Company

See JOINT STOCK LIMITED LIABILITY COMPANY.

Company limited by guarantee

A type of CORPORATE ENTITY in which the guarantors agree to
subscribe, should the company be wound up, to the extent of
their guarantee given on incorporation. This form of company
is adopted by not-for-profit organisations, such as academic and
educational bodies, cultural and sports organisations or welfare
and other charitable bodies. Network Rail Limited, the company
that took over from Railtrack, the insolvent owner of the UK's
railway infrastructure, was incorporated as a "not-for-dividend"
company limited by guarantee. Often the amounts guaranteed
are nominal and do not expose the members to significant
financial exposure. In the JOINT STOCK LIMITED LIABILITY
COMPANY, by contrast, SHAREHOLDERS' liability is limited to
the extent of their equity stake. However, like all corporate entities, companies limited by guarantee need governing – and governing well.

Company secretary

An officer of the company who can, potentially, make an important contribution to the board. As the CADBURY REPORT
suggested:

The company secretary has a key role to play in ensuring that board
procedures are both followed and regularly reviewed. The chairman
and the board will look to the company secretary for guidance on
what their responsibilities are under the rules and regulations to
which they are subject and on how those responsibilities should be
discharged. All directors should have access to the advice and
services of the company secretary and should recognise that the
chairman is entitled to the strong support of the company secretary
in ensuring the effective functioning of the board.

In the United States, the company secretary is known as the
corporate secretary. The American Society of Corporate Secretaries suggests that their duties and responsibilities include organising meetings of the board, board committees and SHAREHOLDERS,
maintaining the corporate records and stock (shareholder) records
and liaising with the securities markets. It further states that the
company secretary should be "the primary liaison between the
corporation's directors and management". The company secretary
need not be an employee of the company: he or she may work for
an outside agency or partnership. Indeed, in some jurisdictions,
another corporation can fulfil the function. In other countries,
including Australia, the company secretary must be a real
person.

The evolution of the company secretary's role highlights their
current contribution. When the JOINT STOCK LIMITED LIABILITY
COMPANY was developed in the UK in the mid-19th century, the
directors needed someone to keep their records. This was the job
of the secretary to the board. The function was largely clerical,
with the directors holding the power.

Changing attitudes to company secretaries can be seen in the contrasting comments of two senior British judges. In 1887, Lord Esher, Master of the Rolls, said:

A secretary is a mere servant. His position is that he is to do what he is told and no person can assume that he has the authority to represent anything at all, nor can anyone assume that statements made by him are necessarily accepted as trustworthy without further enquiry.

A century later things had changed. Corporate life had become complicated. Many companies ran diverse enterprises through complex groups of subsidiary and associated companies. Legislation affecting companies has become substantial. Now the role of the company secretary calls for professional knowledge and skill. In 1971, Lord Denning, Master of the Rolls, said:

Times have changed. A company secretary is a much more important person nowadays than he was in 1871. He is an officer of the company with extensive duties and responsibilities. This appears not only in modern Companies Acts but also in the role which he plays in the day-to-day business of companies. He is no longer merely a clerk. He regularly makes representations on behalf of the company and enters into contracts on its behalf ... so much so that he may be regarded as held out to do such things on behalf of the company. He is certainly entitled to sign contracts connected with the administrative side of the company's affairs, such as employing staff, ordering cars and so forth. All such matters come within the ostensible authority of a company secretary.

In most company law jurisdictions, companies are required to have a company secretary who is an officer of the company, although since 2006, in the UK, PRIVATE COMPANIES need not have one at all.

www.icsa.co.uk, www.icsasoftware.com

Confidante

One of the roles a director can play (see next entry).

Conformance roles

There are two principal sets of roles that every UNITARY BOARD of directors and governing body must fulfil (see Figure 3 on page 8): the conformance roles, involving EXECUTIVE SUPERVISION and ACCOUNTABILITY, and the PERFORMANCE ROLES, involving strategy formulation and policymaking. Many of the CODES OF BEST PRACTICE in CORPORATE GOVERNANCE emphasise the conformance roles; indeed, the HILMER REPORT specifically criticises the underemphasis on the performance roles.

The main conformance roles can be thought of as follows:

- **Judge.** Directors playing this role are able to make an objective assessment of a situation. This can be a vital contribution of OUTSIDE DIRECTORS, who, obviously, have the opportunity to see board matters from an external and independent point of view. Such an objective evaluation of senior management performance can overcome the tunnel vision sometimes found in those too closely involved with the situation, or the myopia brought on by being personally affected by the outcome.
- **Catalyst.** This role is played by a director who is capable of questioning the board's assumptions, causing change in others' thinking. Catalysts point out that what appears to be an incontrovertible truth to some board members is, in fact, rooted in questionable beliefs that others have about the company, its markets, its competitors and so on. They highlight inferences that are masquerading as facts and indicate when value judgments, rather than rigorous analysis, are being used in board deliberations. Most valuably, catalysts

stimulate the board's discussions with new insights and ideas.

- **Supervisor.** The whole board is responsible for the monitoring and supervision of executive management. But the call for NON-EXECUTIVE DIRECTORS, for a separation of the role of CHAIRMAN from that of CEO, and for the use of AUDIT, NOMINATION and REMUNERATION COMMITTEES emphasises the value of the supervisor role of outside directors.

- **Watchdog.** Directors who cast themselves in this role see themselves as the protector of the interests of other parties, such as the SHAREHOLDERS or, more often, a specific interest group. REPRESENTATIVE or NOMINEE DIRECTORS inevitably find themselves in this position, as they look out for the interests of the party who put them on the board. This might be a major investor for a director on the board of an American or British LISTED COMPANY, the employees for a director on a German SUPERVISORY BOARD, or the *keiretsu* group interests for a director on the board of a major Japanese company (see JAPANESE CORPORATE GOVERNANCE). Every director has a duty to be concerned with the interests of the company as a whole (that is with the interests of all the members without discrimination), so the watchdog role should be applied with care.

- **Confidante.** Some directors may find themselves acting as a sounding board for other directors, the chief executive or the chairman; a trusted and respected counsellor in times of uncertainty and stress; someone to share concerns with about issues (often interpersonal problems) outside the boardroom. The political process at board level inevitably involves the use, and sometimes abuse, of power, so the confidante can make a valuable contribution. But it is vital that he or she commands the trust of all the directors, otherwise the problem may be reinforced rather than resolved.

■ **Safety valve.** It is a legitimate role for directors to act as safety valves at a time of crisis to release the pressure, prevent further damage and save the situation. A classic example would be when the company has run into financial problems, management performance has deteriorated and the chief executive has to be replaced. Another example might be if the company faced an unexpected catastrophe. The sensible and steadying counsel of a wise member of the board could save an otherwise disastrous situation.

Contact person

One of the roles a director can play (see PERFORMANCE ROLES).

Contract for difference

A form of equity derivative that allows speculation on the movement in a share's price without owning the share. The contract for difference (CFD) requires payment of the difference between the current price and the price at some future date. CFDs carry no voting rights, although there have been cases where owners of CFDs tried to influence a company's board as though they did carry such rights.

Cooking the books

Once the preserve of overenthusiastic accountants, the falsification of records and the manipulation of financial results have reached the boardroom in some prominent companies. Directors of the following companies were all involved in what some of them, euphemistically, called "aggressive earnings management" and others saw as financial manipulation:

■ ENRON, apparently a highly successful American energy trader, engineered a set of special purpose entities, which took massive debts off its balance sheet.

■ WORLDCOM, a massive American telecoms firm, capitalised $3.8 billion of maintenance costs, which should have been charged against profits, as fixed assets to be written off over time.

■ Elan, an Irish pharmaceuticals group, sold the rights to royalties to companies it had created, with the option to buy them back at inflated prices.

■ Schroders, a respected financial institution in the City of London, overstated profits by £11m by incorrectly recording fee income on bills to clients of its fund management firm.

Boards can come under pressure to misrepresent their results from INSTITUTIONAL INVESTORS looking for profit growth and executives wanting share price rises to cash in their SHARE OPTIONS.

Core capabilities

See next entry.

Core competence

The hidden strengths of a business that the directors can call on during STRATEGY FORMULATION. Unlike the more obvious resources that a company has, such as its product portfolio, its finances and its organisational characteristics, core competencies reflect the knowledge in the organisation and its learning capability. A core competence in a financial institution might be its strength in handling derivatives, in a software house its experience in networking applications, or in an automobile manufacturer its knowledge of electronic controls. Some refer to core competencies as core capabilities, broadening the definition to include, for example, the ability of an entertainment company to deliver its video product over cable television, or of a retail chain store to access its suppliers directly by satellite-based electronic data interchange.

Strategic thinking in western companies in recent years has emphasised the benefits of identifying the core competencies and capabilities of the firm and building on them to the exclusion of all else. This includes not only the divesting of conglomerate businesses, unrelated to the core activities, but also outsourcing other functions so that both financial and managerial resources can be concentrated on the activities that are crucial to the company's strategic performance. Asian companies, by and large, do not share this enthusiasm for concentration, seeing business more as a series of trading opportunities, which enable transient networks of intertrading entities to be created, often with cross-holdings and cross-directorships.

Core values

A statement, typically approved at board level, of the underlying beliefs that a company has about itself and its relations with those involved with it. The core values of a passenger transport company, for example, might include statements that it is dedicated to safety, customer service and cost-effective travel, while providing rewarding career opportunities and job satisfaction for its staff and a reasonable reward for its investors. The articulation of core values can influence the process of STRATEGY FORMULATION and POLICYMAKING, not least because it defines the playing field, the games that are to be played and the rules by which the company intends to operate. (See also MISSION STATEMENT and SUSTAINABLE DEVELOPMENT.)

Corporate entity

The development of the corporate concept in the middle of the 19th century enabled massive capital formation, dramatic industrial development and untold wealth creation around the world. Previously, the only way to organise business was as a sole trader or partnership, in which, if the business failed, the debtor went to prison and his family to the poorhouse. The JOINT STOCK LIMITED LIABILITY COMPANY enabled a legal entity to be incorporated with an existence separate from its owners, whose liability for the company's debts was limited to their equity stake. Such a corporate entity can contract, sue and be sued independently of those who have provided the capital. A dramatically simple and superbly successful concept originally, the notion of corporate entity has now become complex, with many different types of corporate structures, many forms of financial instruments and complicated international corporate networks.

> The rise of the modern corporation has brought a concentration of economic power, which can compete on equal terms with the modern state – economic power versus political power, each strong in its own field. The state seeks in some aspects to regulate the corporation, while the corporation, steadily becoming more powerful, makes every effort to avoid such regulation.
>
> Adolf Berle and Gardiner Means, *The Modern Corporation and Private Property*, 1932

Corporate governance

The exercise of power over a CORPORATE ENTITY and the overall subject of this book. The process by which companies are directed and controlled, according to the CADBURY REPORT. All corporate entities need to be governed as well as managed. The structure, membership and processes of the governing body, typically the board of directors in a JOINT STOCK LIMITED LIABILITY COMPANY, are central to corporate governance. So is the linkage between the board and senior management. The relationships between the board and the SHAREHOLDERS, the AUDITORS, the REGULATORS and other STAKEHOLDERS are also crucial to effective corporate governance.

The word "governance" is ancient: Chaucer used it, although he spelt it in two different ways. But the phrase "corporate governance" is relatively new. The first book with the title *Corporate Governance* was published in 1984, the same year that the American Institute published a report on the *Principles of Corporate Governance. Corporate Governance: An International Review*, an academic journal, was launched in 1993.

www.thecorporatelibray.com, www.ragm.com, www.corpgov.net, www.worldbank.org/html/fpd/privatesector/cg/index.htm, www.oecd.org

❝ *Cycles of crisis and reform in corporate governance are becoming a worldwide phenomenon.*
Thomas Clarke, International Corporate Governance: A Comparative Approach, 2007

❝ *If I hear one more thing about corporate governance I think I'm going to puke.*
A chairman speaking to Richard Leblanc and Jim Gillies, *Inside the Boardroom*, 2005

❝ *The corporate governance debate has done little to improve the contribution of many boards. If anything the attention has been switched from building larger and better corporate cakes to applying the boardroom icing to existing cakes in recommended ways.*
Colin Coulson-Thomas, 2002

Corporate governance and corporate performance

See ASSOCIATION OF BRITISH INSURERS.

Corporate governance policies

See BOARD CORPORATE GOVERNANCE POLICIES.

" *The proper governance of companies will become as important as the proper governance of countries.*
James D. Wolfensohn, when president of the World Bank

Corporate governance ratings

Various organisations have rating systems and keep scorecards on companies' performance. These include INSTITUTIONAL INVESTORS such as CALPERS and HERMES INVESTMENT MANAGEMENT and investigating firms such as Davis Global Advisors in the United States, PIRC (PENSIONS INVESTMENT RESEARCH CONSULTANTS) and Déminor in Europe and CLSA for emerging markets. Broadly, markets pay a premium for shares that are well rated on their CORPORATE GOVERNANCE policies and practice.

www.clsa.com, www.davisglobal.com, www.deminor.org, www.pirc.co.uk

" *Governance ratings are becoming the leading edge of the corporate governance movement. Ultimately such ratings will play a similar role in the equity market as credit ratings currently do in the bond market.*"
Steven Davis, Davis Global Advisors, 2001

Corporate monitoring

Proposals for making corporate management more accountable to a company's SHAREHOLDERS, to increase stock returns, control CEO pay, and balance profits with social goals by encouraging minority shareholders to use their VOTING RIGHTS. Following warnings about self-serving company directors, financial analysts pushing shares and less than independent auditors, the founder of this project, Mark Latham, proposes the use of proxy advisory firms, paid for by the company, that would give independent voting advice to shareholders.

www.corpmon.com

Corporate planning

An analytical and professional approach to the board's PERFORM-ANCE ROLES. Growing competition around the world during the 1960s meant that firms could no longer sell all they could produce. A market-oriented professionalism began to emerge. Management consultants offered analytical tools such as PORTFOLIO ANALYSIS, product mapping, scenario building, SWOT ANALYSIS and value-chain analysis (see ADDED-VALUE CHAIN). Corporate planning departments were created. Directors were drawn into the strategic thinking process.

Corporate senate

Modelled on the successful Spanish Mondragon worker co-opera-tives, Shann Turnbull has applied the concept to public companies that he has formed in Australia. He suggests that "most corpor-ations in the English-speaking world are essentially corrupt because their UNITARY BOARD structures concentrate on conflicts of interest and corporate power". His alternative is a dual board structure with a corporate senate with not more than three members, elected on the basis of one vote per SHAREHOLDER, not per share. The senate has no proactive power, just the right to veto where it feels the board has a conflict of interest. (See also SHARE-HOLDER DEMOCRACY.)

Corporate social responsibility

Recognising the social and environmental impact of corporate activities when making decisions, sometimes called "corporate citizenship". Some companies report social and environmental indicators, as well as the traditional financial performance measures, to indicate the full impact of the company's activities. This is known as the triple bottom line. (See also ETHICS, EXXON, HSBC and SUSTAINABLE DEVELOPMENT.)

www.AccountAbility.org.uk, www.betterworld.com, www.bsr.com, www.corpwatch.com, www.eiris.org, www.globalreporting.org, www.iccr.org, www.keidanren.org, www.profitwithprinciple.co.uk, www.unglobalcompact.org, www.uksif.org

❝ Whatever the social responsibility gurus may say, business is a force for good in itself: its most useful contribution to society is making profits and products. Philanthropy no more canonises the good businessman than it exculpates the bad.
The Economist, June 25th 2008

Corporate strategy

See STRATEGY FORMULATION.

Corporate veil

A legal phrase emphasising that a veil effectively surrounds a company whose SHAREHOLDERS have limited liability which creditors cannot pierce in pursuit of their debts. In common-law jurisdictions this even applies to subsidiary companies that are wholly owned by a parent company, which controls their activities. In other words, the HOLDING COMPANY may walk away from its subsidiary's debts. In some other jurisdictions, including Germany, creditors may pursue their debts up the corporate chain of dominating companies in a group, thus piercing the corporate veil.

Corporatisation

See PRIVATISATION.

COSO Report

See TREADWAY COMMISSION.

Country-club board

A BOARD STYLE in which directors are more concerned with board rituals, their interpersonal relationships and the board culture than with tough-minded decision-making.

Crony capitalism

The economic shocks that hit East Asia in late 1997 were caused by CORPORATE GOVERNANCE based on close links between directors and members of government, the ruling elite or business associates, rather than on sound business logic, it was suggested. This contrasted with the alternative explanation of previous business success based on ASIAN VALUES.

Cronyism

See GAMES DIRECTORS PLAY.

Cross-directorship

See INTERLOCKING DIRECTORSHIP.

Cross-holding

The holding of voting shares by one company in another. The practice is prevalent in East Asia, where many companies build networks of alliance and share risk. Cross-directorships are often found where there are cross-holdings of shares. Some jurisdictions prohibit a SUBSIDIARY COMPANY holding shares in its parent, so that the device cannot be used to prevent a hostile takeover bid and thwart the MARKET FOR CONTROL. (See also JAPANESE CORPORATE GOVERNANCE.)

Crown jewels

A takeover defence used by some boards of companies targeted in a hostile takeover bid, in which they contract with another party to license or acquire a right in significant company assets. The aim is to reduce the attractiveness of the company to predators. The terms of such an arrangement often allow the other party to buy out the company at a predetermined price should the takeover materialise, or obtain damages in lieu.

D&O insurance

See DIRECTORS AND OFFICERS INSURANCE.

Deep-pocket syndrome

When a company is in financial difficulty or has become insolvent, there may be little point in SHAREHOLDERS or creditors suing the company because it has no money. Instead, their best option has been to take legal actions against those who are covered by indemnity insurance, such as directors and, particularly, the company AUDITORS, to pay them what they are legally owed by the company. (See DIRECTORS AND OFFICERS INSURANCE and LITIGATION.)

Dematerialisation

The process of replacing the title to shares traditionally recognised with hardcopy share certificates by electronic means. Dematerialisation enables the electronic transfer of title without the cumbersome tracing, handling and exchanging of pieces of paper. In an electronic share transfer system, SHAREHOLDERS give their authority to a company-sponsored share nominee.

Descent from heaven

Amakaduri, literally in Japanese a descent from heaven, refers to the practice, which was prevalent in some major Japanese companies, of appointing retiring bureaucrats from the regulatory bodies to well-paid sinecures, including directorships, when they retired. The same process can be seen in some other countries, including France, where members of the *grandes écoles* fraternity move readily from government to corporate service. (See REGULA-TORY CAPTURE.)

Dictum meum pactum

"My word is my bond", the motto of the old London Stock Exchange. A quaint reminder of a world now gone, replaced by one in which weasel clauses are written into contracts to avoid responsibility, agreements are ignored or renegotiated, and parties are sued as necessary.

Director

A member of the board of directors formally nominated and appointed by the shareholders in a properly convened meeting of the company in accordance with its ARTICLES OF ASSOCIATION. Some people may have a title including the word director – marketing director, director of administration, regional director and so on – without necessarily being formal members of the board. Such titles are sometimes given as rewards or to add status to executives in their dealings with the outside world. Such directors, unless they hold themselves out to be actual directors, have none of the responsibilities nor any of the rights of legally appointed directors. (See ASSOCIATE DIRECTOR.)

Directors and officers insurance

The need for personal indemnity by directors against the threat of LITIGATION has become important in many parts of the world as directors find themselves the subject of legal challenges. Legal action by SHAREHOLDERS and others alleging malfeasance, breach of duty, negligence or other actions in damages against companies, their boards, their AUDITORS and, particularly, against individual named directors has been increasing. Directors and officers insurance policies provide some protection against claims for damages, including the costs of fighting such actions. Typically called D&O insurance, these policies should not be confused with E&O insurance, which protects against errors and omissions in contracts. In some jurisdictions directors have to pay their own premiums since, it is argued, a company may not use its own funds to protect its directors from their own negligence.

Directors' contracts

The Greenbury Report criticised the practice of giving directors rolling contracts of three or more years and proposed that they should run for no more than a year. This meant that directors who performed poorly and were replaced did not receive a massive GOLDEN HANDSHAKE on the termination of a long-term contract. However, the basis of contracts for CEOs remains a subject of debate in the United States and the UK, particularly when incompetence sometimes seems to be richly rewarded. (See DIRECTORS' REMUNERATION.)

 The pleasant but vacuous director need never worry about job security.
Warren Buffett, chairman, Berkshire Hathaway Fund

Directors' duties

The British government's company law review, published in 2002 (and obviously drafted by a lawyer), proposed the following set of functions for directors.

1   *Compliance and loyalty*

a   A director must exercise his powers honestly and for their proper purpose, and in accordance with the company's constitution and decisions taken lawfully under it.

b   Subject to that requirement, he must (so far as he practically can) exercise his powers in the way he believes in good faith is best calculated in the circumstances, taking account of both the short- and the long-term consequences of his acts, to promote the success of the company for the benefit of its members as a whole.

c   The circumstances to which he is to have regard for that purpose include, in particular (as his duties of care and skill may require):
   - the company's need to foster its business relationships, including those with its employees and suppliers and the customers for its products and services;
   - the impact of its operations on the communities affected and on the environment; and
   - its need to maintain a reputation for high standards of business conduct.

2   *Independence of judgment*

a   A director must not (except as lawfully permitted under the company's constitution) restrict his power to exercise an independent judgment.

b   But this does not prevent him doing anything to carry out an agreement entered into in accordance with his duties.

3   Conflict of interest

A director must not:

- authorise, procure or permit the company to enter into any transaction in which he has an interest unless the interest has been disclosed to the relevant directors to the extent required under the Companies Act; or
- use any property, INFORMATION or opportunity of the company for his own or anyone else's benefit, nor obtain a benefit in any other way in connection with the exercise of his powers, unless he is allowed to make such use or obtain such benefit by the company's constitution, or the use or benefit has been disclosed to the company in general meeting and the company has consented to it.

4   Fairness

A director must act fairly as between the company's members.

5   Care, skill and diligence

A director must exercise the care, skill and diligence which should be exercised by a reasonably diligent person with both (sic) the knowledge, skill and experience which may reasonably be expected of a director in his position and any additional knowledge, skill and experience which he has.

www.dti.gov.uk/cld/review.htm

"" When all is said and done, the board's key focus is on the straight forward concept that its role is to drive the business ahead while keeping it under prudent control. In the end, being a board member is that simple – and that profound.

Bob Garratt, Thin on Top, 2003

Directors' liability

Misunderstanding about the liability of directors abounds. Unlike SHAREHOLDERS', directors' liability is not limited by the incorporation of a JOINT STOCK LIMITED LIABILITY COMPANY. Directors are not automatically liable for the debts of their company, provided they have not acted negligently or made it appear that they accepted personal liability. But a director can be personally liable for the firm's debts if he or she knew that the company was insolvent and allowed it to continue to trade. Disqualification from serving as a director can result (see DISQUALIFICATION OF DIRECTORS). Directors can also be fined if they mislead AUDITORS or fail to file various documents with the companies' registrar.

www.companieshouse.co.uk

Directors' remuneration

This remains a hot topic. INSTITUTIONAL INVESTORS in the United States and the UK have, for some years, been challenging the remuneration packages available to some directors, particularly when they seem to reward failure. In the Netherlands, Norway and Sweden, SHAREHOLDERS have a binding vote on directors' remuneration; in the UK, the shareholders' vote is advisory and non-binding; in the United States, shareholders struggle to have the issue included on the proxy form. In 1995 a group of City of London institutions commissioned Sir Richard Greenbury, then CHAIRMAN of Marks & Spencer, to look into board-level pay. The Greenbury Report provided a Code of Conduct, which has now been incorporated in the UK COMBINED CODE. The main recommendations were:

■ that companies should create REMUNERATION COMMITTEES consisting solely of independent NON-EXECUTIVE DIRECTORS;

- that the chairman of the remuneration committee should respond to shareholders' questions at the AGM;
- that annual reports should include details of all director rewards, naming each director;
- that directors' contracts should run for no more than a year to avoid excessive GOLDEN HANDSHAKES;
- that SHARE OPTION schemes for directors should be linked to long-term corporate performance.

66 *Performance and Integrity – How We Reward Our Leaders" (title of a booklet published by pharmaceutical giant GlaxoSmithKline). A title such as this, that seeks to justify astonishing increases to an already astonishingly generous pay package, echoes Orwell's Ministry of Truth.*
Sunday Times, November 2002

However, the code has not reduced claims of excessive remuneration, sometimes for failure on a massive scale. The ASSOCIATION OF BRITISH INSURERS and the NATIONAL ASSOCIATION OF PENSION FUNDS have issued guidelines on directors' remuneration:

- The responsibility for setting directors' contracts lies primarily with the remuneration committee.
- In line with the Combined Code, contracts should be set with reasonable notice periods.
- Boards should make sure that executives show leadership by aligning their financial interests with those of the company.
- The level of remuneration received by senior executives already factors in the risk associated with their role. Boards should make sure that contracts do not include any additional financial protection in the event of poor performance leading to termination.
- The remuneration committee should carefully consider what commitments (including pension contributions and all other elements) their directors' terms of appointment would entail in the event of early termination.

- Directors' contracts should ensure that severance payments arising from poor corporate performance should not extend beyond basic salary.
- Companies should clearly disclose key elements of directors' contracts on their website and summarise them in the remuneration report.
- Companies should fully disclose in their remuneration report the constituent parts of any severance payments and justify the total level and elements paid.

(See DIRECTORS' REMUNERATION REPORT and REMUNERATION RACHETING.)

❝ We need to bury the myth that executive incentives align managers' interests with those of their shareholders. Incentives always reward exceptional performance or exceptional deception: in most cases deception is the easier route.
David Creelman, Canada, 2002

❝ Business executives who fail are packed off with 40 or 50 million dollars for the road.
John McCain, Republican presidential candidate, 2008

❝ British Airways chief executive, Willie Walsh, waived his bonus in 2008 after the debacle on opening Heathrow Terminal 5, but in 2009 he was entitled to a bonus worth 100% of his 2008 £700,000 salary plus 150% of his 2009 £735,000. To take home the potential £1.8 million windfall, Mr Walsh would have to meet airline targets on profitability, ensure that enough flights were on time, and that customers were satisfied.
The Times, June 11th 2008

Directors' remuneration report

Legislation in the UK, applicable from the start of 2003, requires quoted companies to publish directors' remuneration reports and put them to SHAREHOLDER vote at the AGM. The report must contain:

- details of the members of the REMUNERATION COMMITTEE and anyone who advised that committee;
- a statement of the company's policy on directors' remuneration for the future;
- details of individual DIRECTORS' REMUNERATION, giving details of the performance criteria in incentive schemes, pensions and retirement benefits, their service contracts; and
- a line graph for the past five years showing how the company's performance has compared with competitors'.

Although shareholders vote on the report, the outcome remains advisory. However, the withdrawal of exceedingly generous remuneration proposals, following opposition from a significant body of shareholders (GlaxoSmithKline and Prudential in the UK, for example), suggests that the idea of shareholder influence can work.

6 6 *The hundreds of millions of dollars in compensation claimed each year by the leading US business and financial leaders has to be put into the perspective that although the United States is the most prosperous society on earth it is typified by mounting severe and very visible inequality. While CEO salaries inflated through the roof, in recent years average earnings in America actually went down.*

Thomas Clarke, *International Corporate Governance: A Comparative Approach*, 2007

Directors' report and accounts

Almost all company law jurisdictions now require directors to submit regular reports and accounts to all SHAREHOLDERS (the exceptions are generally tax havens such as the British Virgin Islands). The form and content of such reports and accounts have been progressively widened and sharpened through company law and by regulatory requirements, such as those of America's Securities and Exchange Commission, Australia's Securities Commission and Hong Kong's Securities and Futures Commission.

Disclosure

Directors have a FIDUCIARY DUTY not to make a SECRET PROFIT out of their position as a director. For example, a director or a close member of his family might be involved with another company which was bidding for a contract or have a personal interest in a company being considered for acquisition. Any such interest must be disclosed before the director takes part in any board decision-making on the matter. The CHAIRMAN and fellow directors can then decide on the appropriate action, such as asking the director to leave the meeting, not participate in the discussion or, having noted the interest, allowing participation in the decision-making. Directors should make sure that any interest declared is minuted, in case there is a subsequent legal challenge.

❝ *Transparency and good corporate governance do not come naturally to people.*
Frances Reid, European Bank for Reconstruction and Development, 2002

❝ *Cleverness, high salaries and impressive job titles do not guarantee full and fair disclosure.*
Colin Coulson-Thomas, 2002

Disqualification of directors

Most company law jurisdictions provide for the disqualification of directors if they are unfit to serve. Causes include theft, fraud, failure to meet the requirements of companies' legislation, or running a company that has traded while insolvent and without a reasonable chance of paying its creditors.

www.uk.experian.com

❝ *You cannot legislate for honesty in the boardroom.*
Cahal Dowds, president, Institute of Chartered Accountants of Scotland, 2002

Divide and rule

See GAMES DIRECTORS PLAY.

Dominant director

Sometimes a company reflects the entrepreneurial drive of one person, often the founder. In such cases, the dominant director often overshadows the board, though directors are able to offer advice, which might be heeded. (Bill Gates of Microsoft and Richard Branson of Virgin Airlines are examples of highly successful dominant corporate leaders.) But although dominant directors may take their companies to the highest levels of achievement, unless they can cope with the succession problem they ultimately fail. The list of those who failed to provide for their succession is endless and includes Henry Ford, "Tiny" Rowland of Lonrho and Robert MAXWELL. Unfortunately, experience suggests that dominant directors have great difficulty in working with a potential successor – "nothing grows under an oak tree". (See also DUALITY.)

❝ *The board's real role is to support the leader – whoever he is, chairman or CEO. If my board was absolutely divided I would put the matter to a vote: but all those who vote against me should resign.*
The opinion of one dominant director

DREXEL BURNHAM LAMBERT

This Wall Street securities trading firm was at the heart of the predator takeover market in the 1980s, using high-return, high-risk "junk" bonds. It provided the base for the insider dealing activities of Ivan BOESKY and provided the setting for the nefarious activities of Dennis Levine and Michael Milken. Levine, then in his 20s, discovered that insider trading was easy and apparently foolproof.

In his job he had access to information about prospective financial deals. Exchange that knowledge with an executive at another bank who knew about that bank's deals, trade the shares under a fictitious name in the Bahamas, open an account in a Swiss bank and, bingo, the compliance authorities would never know. Later, he grew overconfident – some might say greedy. He took a position in a company for which his own company was preparing a bid and made $1.3m. But he underestimated the capabilities of government investigators, acting with the co-operation of securities regulators (see INTERNATIONAL ORGANISATION OF SECURITIES COMMISSIONS). Levine pleaded guilty, gave evidence against his colleagues, and was sentenced to two years' imprisonment and a fine of $362,000. He also had to make restitution to the SECURITIES AND EXCHANGE COMMISSION of $11.6m in insider-trading profits and was barred from employment in the securities business for life. Milken was charged with racketeering and securities fraud. He agreed to plead guilty to six felonies, paid $600m in restitution and was sentenced to ten years in prison. One of the effects of these activities was a growing interest in CORPORATE GOVERNANCE. In 1988, Drexel pleaded guilty to six securities felonies and paid a record $650m in restitution. In 1990 it filed for the protection of the Bankruptcy Court.

❝ *Failed leaders were being revealed in every walk of life ... sad examples of excess, greed, and cynicism ... I was profoundly disappointed at how frequently the graduates of some of our finest business and law schools were involved, in one way or another, in the cases being brought before the SEC. Surely we could do better.*
John Shad, former chairman of the SEC

Dual listed company

Two companies, each of which is separately listed, linked by agreement into a group (see CARNIVAL CORPORATION AND CARNIVAL PLC).

Dual voting rights

Some jurisdictions forbid companies issuing classes of share with different VOTING RIGHTS. Some stock exchange LISTING RULES also forbid them. Where they are allowed, shares with different voting rights can be used to preserve the overall power of a founding family or other incumbent interests when issuing additional shares threatens to dilute their control of the company. (See A AND B SHARES.)

Duality

One of the continuing debates about the UNITARY BOARD is whether the roles of CHAIRMAN and CEO should be separate or combined. In the United States most LISTED COMPANIES combine the roles, giving considerable power to the head of the company. In the UK the CADBURY REPORT advocated separation. In Australia, the roles in public companies are usually separated. The arguments in favour of splitting the roles are that two heads are better than one and, more importantly, that duality provides essential checks and balances. SHAREHOLDERS, particularly if there are minority interests, may find that a dominant leader who is both chairman and CEO has no one to keep him under control. The alternative view is that single-minded leadership can produce better performance. Research into the alternatives seems to show that under single leadership a company can do better, at least for a while, but that where the subtle relationship between the chairman and the CEO works well, major companies thrive better in the longer term. An extension of the duality argument is whether a chief executive should ever be appointed chairman of the board after retirement. It often happens. Proponents talk of retaining his experience, but newly appointed chief executives more typically fear that their predecessor may not be able to let go of the managerial ropes when he occupies the chairmanship.

❝ *The basis for a reliable system of corporate governance is the current CEO-dominant paradigm. The only credible alternative is for large – primarily institutional – shareholders to exert far more control over corporate affairs than they appear willing to exercise. I prefer the benevolent despot.*
Alan Greenspan, 2002

❝ *In battle only one person can ride the white horse and lead the charge, shouting: follow me, men, this way victory lies.*
An experienced director on the chairman/CEO question

Due diligence

The process of making sure that a company's prospectus or similar description of a company's worth is accurate, not misleading and prepared with care. Usually carried out by a firm of accountants, due diligence is an essential prerequisite of issuing shares, PRIVATISATION and valuing companies.

Duty of care

Most legal systems impose on directors a duty to exercise reasonable care, diligence and skill in their work, through statute, case law or regulation. Directors are expected to bring to their director-level responsibilities the degree of care that could reasonably be expected, given their qualifications, know-how and experience. The interpretation of what constitutes reasonable care obviously depends on the background of the individual. If a director were a qualified accountant, engineer or lawyer, the degree of care would take these qualifications into account. But even if directors have no such qualifications, the standard of professionalism now expected of them throughout the world is significantly higher than it was a few years ago. Courts can act if fraudulent or negligent behaviour is alleged or where there are apparent abuses of power or suppression of the interests of minority shareholders. For example, courts will give a ruling if it is alleged that the directors have negotiated a contract that is detrimental to the interests of the minority. But, broadly, courts will not act to second-guess board-level business decisions taken under circumstances of normal commercial risk, should they subsequently prove to have been ill judged.

ECGI

See EUROPEAN CORPORATE GOVERNANCE INSTITUTE.

Empire building

See GAMES DIRECTORS PLAY.

Employee director

See WORKER DIRECTOR.

Employee representation

See WORKER DIRECTOR.

Employee Retirement Income Security Act

In the United States the Employee Retirement Income Security Act (ERISA) of 1974 lays down fiduciary responsibility rules for all those who exercise control over the assets of employee retirement benefit plans. The Pension and Welfare Administration, which administers and enforces the act, has laid down criteria (in the frequently referred to "Avon letter") which require the fund managers to act in the best interests of SHAREHOLDERS and plan beneficiaries, and not to use their proxy votes in companies in any way that is not in the beneficiaries' interests. This legislation also prevents directors calling on the proxy votes of shares held by their company's pension funds to promote or protect their own positions.

Employee share ownership

Employee share ownership is sometimes advanced as a means of ensuring employee commitment. Instead of capital hiring labour, the argument runs, employees use capital. The governance processes of such companies typically involve employee nominated members. Employee share ownership plans (ESOP) are most advanced in the United States, partly because US tax laws allow ESOPs generous tax relief. In the UK, the John Lewis Partnership is the most frequently cited example of employee ownership.

ENRON

The merger of Houston Natural Gas and InterNorth in 1985 created a new Texas energy company called Enron. In 1989, Enron began trading in commodities, buying and selling wholesale contracts in energy. By 2000, turnover was growing at a fantastic rate, with the increased revenues coming from energy commodities. Enron's share price rocketed and senior executives benefited from SHARE OPTIONS. The company's bankers, who received substantial fees from the company, also employed the analysts who encouraged others to invest in Enron. But the cash flow statement in 2000 included an unusual item: other operating activities $1.1 billion. These were the last accounts Enron would publish.

Enron's CEO, Joseph Skilling, believed that the company's business model – trading the output of the other old-fashioned asset-based businesses – was the way of the future. Enron was credited with "aggressive earnings management". To support its growth hundreds of SPECIAL PURPOSE ENTITIES (SPES) were created. These were separate partnerships that traded with Enron, often based in tax havens. Enron made long-term energy supply contracts with these SPES at market prices, taking the profit in its own accounts immediately. The SPES also provided lucrative fees for some of Enron's senior executives. Further, they gave the appearance that Enron had hedged its financial exposures with third parties, whereas the third parties were, in fact, contingent liabilities on Enron. The contemporary US accounting standards (GAAP) did not then require such SPES to be consolidated with partners' group accounts, so billions of dollars were kept off Enron's balance sheet.

In 2000, Enron's annual revenues were $100 billion and the stockmarket valued it at nearly $80 billion. It was ranked seventh in *Fortune*'s list of the largest American firms. By then Enron was the largest trader in the energy market created by the deregulation of energy in the United States.

Warning signs

Enron's auditor was ARTHUR ANDERSEN, whose AUDIT and consultancy fees from Enron were $52m a year. Enron also employed several former Andersen partners as senior financial executives. In February 2001, partners at Andersen discussed dropping their client because of its accounting policies, including accounting for the SPES, and the apparent conflicts of interest of Enron's chief financial officer, Andrew Fastow, who had set up and was benefiting from the SPES. In August 2001, Skilling resigned "for personal reasons". Kenneth Lay, the CHAIRMAN, took over executive control. Lay was a close friend of President George W. Bush and was his adviser on energy matters. In 2000, Lay made £123m from the exercise of share options in Enron.

A week after Skilling resigned, Chung Wu, a broker with UBS Paine Webber (a subsidiary of Swiss bank UBS), e-mailed his clients advising them to sell Enron. He was sacked and escorted out of his office. UBS Paine Webber received substantial brokerage fees from administering the Enron employee stock option programme. The same day Lay sold $4m of his own Enron shares, while telling employees of his high priority to restore investor confidence, which "should result in a higher share price". Other UBS analysts were still recommending a "strong buy" on Enron. Lord Wakeham, a former British cabinet minister, was a director of Enron and chairman of its NOMINATION COMMITTEE. Wakeham, who was also a chartered accountant and chairman of the British Press Complaints Council, was paid an annual consultancy fee of $50,000 by Enron, plus a $4,600 month retainer and $1,250 attendance fee for each meeting.

In mid-2001, Lay was given a warning about the company's accounting techniques by Sherron Watkins, an Enron executive, who wrote: "I am nervous that we will implode in a wave of accounting scandals." She also advised Andersen about potential problems. In October 2001 a crisis developed. The company revised its earlier financial statements, revealing massive losses caused by hedging risks taken as energy prices fell which had wiped out $600m of profits. An SEC investigation into this restatement of profits for the previous five years revealed massive complex derivative positions and the transactions between Enron and the SPEs. Debts were understated by $2.6 billion. Fastow was alleged to have received more than $30m for his management of the partnerships. Eventually, he was indicted on 78 counts involving the complex financial schemes that produced phantom profits, enriched him and doomed the company. He claimed that he did not believe he had committed any crimes.

Lawsuits against Enron and Andersen followed. Many Enron employees held their retirement plans in Enron stock; some had lost their entire retirement savings. Enron's Employees' Pension Fund sued for $1 billion, plus $1m per week fees. In November 2001, Fastow was fired. Standard & Poor's, a credit-rating agency, downgraded Enron stock to junk-bond status, triggering interest-rate penalties and other clauses. Merger negotiations that might have saved Enron failed.

Bankruptcy

Enron filed for Chapter 11 bankruptcy in December 2001. This was the largest corporate collapse in American history to that time; WORLDCOM was to surpass it. John Clifford Baxter, a VICE-CHAIRMAN of Enron, who had seen the problems and had heated arguments about the accounting for off-balance-sheet financing, resigned in May 2001 and was found shot dead. Two OUTSIDE DIRECTORS, Herbert Weinokur and Robert Jaedicke, members of the Enron AUDIT COMMITTEE, claimed that the board either was not informed or was deceived about deals involving the SPES.

Why did it happen?

There are three principal reasons:

- Enron switched strategy from energy supplier to energy trader, effectively becoming a financial institution with an increased risk profile, which the board failed to understand.
- Enron's financial strategy hid corporate debt and exaggerated performance.
- American accounting standards permitted the off-balance-sheet treatment of the SPES.

What were the implications?

There were implications in four areas:

- CORPORATE GOVERNANCE in the United States, including the roles of the CEO and the board of directors and the issue of DUALITY; the independence of outside, NON-EXECUTIVE DIRECTORS; the functions and membership of the audit committee; and the oversight role of institutional SHAREHOLDERS.
- Regulation in American financial markets, including the regulation of industrial companies with financial trading arms like Enron; the responsibilities of the independent credit-rating agencies; the regulation of American pension funds; and the effect on the world's capital markets.

- Accounting standards, particularly the accounting for off-balance-sheet SPES; the regulation of the American accounting profession; and the convergence of American GAAP with international accounting standards.
- Auditing, including auditor independence; auditors' right to undertake non-audit work for audit clients; the rotation of audit partners or audit firms or government involvement in audit; the need for a cooling-off period before an auditor joins the staff of a client company.

The most dramatic effect, however, was the passing of the SARBANES-OXLEY ACT in 2002, which affected all companies listed on an American stock exchange and their overseas subsidiaries.

Before the event:

❝ *Few companies will be able to achieve the excitement extravaganza that Enron has in its remarkable business transformation, but many could apply some of the principles.*

Ed Michaels, Helen Handfield-Jones and Beth Axelrod, *The War for Talent*, 2001

After the event:

❝ *The company appeared not merely to gently grill its accounts – they were seemingly roasted to a cinder. Enron, it seems, was almost a virtual company, with virtual profits.*

John Stittle, chartered secretary, 2002

❝ *A core of Enron executives deceived everyone. Enron Corporation, formerly one of the world's largest and most profitable companies in the United States, imploded with revelations of improper accounting practices, and alleged inadequate audits, mismanagement, and the failure of the board of directors to perform its fiduciary duty to shareholders.*

CalPERS, reporting how much it had lost in the Enron collapse and why, www.calpers.ca.gov

On the subsequent 2007/08 financial crisis prompted by US sub-prime mortgages

&& *History will marvel at the delusory mechanics that kept the show on the road for so long: banks' lopsided balance sheets that included worthless mortgages as assets, yet omitted the liabilities that funded them; post-Enron placebos that continued to encourage off-balance sheet accounting treatment while government agencies turned a blind eye; investor governance based on hedge-fund morality that puts achievement of market-beating returns as priority; and an entrepreneurial reward system that imposes no effective downside for even patently culpable management.*
Emile Woolf, Accountancy, 2008

Enterprise risk management

See RISK MANAGEMENT.

ERISA

See EMPLOYEE RETIREMENT INCOME SECURITY ACT.

ESOP

See EMPLOYEE SHARE OWNERSHIP.

Ethical funds

Investment funds, such as mutual and unit trusts, run by INSTITU-TIONAL INVESTORS, dedicated to investing in companies that meet certain ethical criteria, such as providing environmental benefits or not trading in weapons, polluting processes or defor-estation. Thus far such funds wield little power, other than raising awareness.

Ethics

As markets and business have become global and more open to international scrutiny, more attention has been paid to corporate ethics. Well-publicised financial scandals around the world, such as ENRON, HIH INSURANCE and MAXWELL, have focused the spotlight on CORPORATE SOCIAL RESPONSIBILITY. Environmental tragedies, such as Union Carbide's plant explosion in Bhopal, which killed and maimed many people in India, or the Exxon Valdez oil spill in Alaska, sharpened the focus. Increasingly, public opinion demands that boards of directors exercise their considerable powers for good or harm with responsibility and in the interests of the many who can be affected, rather than solely in the interests of SHAREHOLDERS and the short-term bottom line. Understandably, some directors feel that their job is to make sure that the company is profitable, while obeying the law, and that if a society wants companies to behave in a specific way it must pass legislation to that effect. But ultimately a directorship is a position of trust, demanding absolute integrity, including the ability to make moral judgments, recognising the broader and longer-term societal interests that can be affected by board decisions, and distinguishing the company's interests from personal interests.

The European Union has rejected a regulatory approach to corporate social responsibility, emphasising instead its voluntary nature. But it does encourage companies to include social and environmental information in their annual reports through a set of voluntary guidelines. France was the first European country to require companies to disclose details of their social responsibility practices. From 2004, all French LISTED COMPANIES had to report on their adherence to the International Labour Organisation's core principles on energy, environment and social impact. The UK's 2006 Companies Act also required boards to be aware of the social and environmental impact of their decisions. (See also SUSTAINABLE DEVELOPMENT.)

Ethics codes

Some boards publish a formal code of ethics for their company, to supplement their CORE VALUES and reinforce more informal understanding that typically exists in companies about "the way things are done here". The UK-based Institute of Business Ethics provides guidelines (www.ibc.org.uk).

" *Our code of ethics rests on a conceptual framework of fundamental principles and an analysis of threats and safeguards, rather than an ever-increasing number of rules that inevitably fail to cover every eventuality.*
Neil Learner, chairman, ICAEW Ethics Group

European Company

The European Union permits companies that operate in more than one EU country to be incorporated in the EU rather than in a single state. Known by the Latin phrase *Societas Europaea* (SE), such companies may adopt either the UNITARY BOARD or the TWO-TIER BOARD model of CORPORATE GOVERNANCE.

European Corporate Governance Institute

The European Corporate Governance Institute (ECGI) aims to improve governance through fostering independent scientific research and related activities. Formerly the European Corporate Governance Network, it has academic, corporate and ordinary members. The ECGI board has 11 members: six academics and five non-academics.

www.ecgi.org

Executive chairman

Sometimes used to describe a board CHAIRMAN who works full-time in the post. More often the title discloses a combination of the chairman and CEO roles (see DUALITY).

Executive director

A member of the board who is also employed by the company in a management capacity. As executives such directors are employees of the company, with rights and duties under employment law. As directors, however, they are responsible like all other directors under company law, as the law makes no distinction between types of director. One of the major challenges to an executive director is to be able to separate the two roles: on the one hand, to perform as a member of the senior management team running the enterprise; on the other to be a member of the board, jointly responsible with the other directors to see that it is being run well and in the right direction.

Executive supervision

The monitoring of management performance throughout the company, one of the principal elements of the board's activities. With a UNITARY BOARD, particularly if the EXECUTIVE DIRECTORS are in the majority or dominate board proceedings, objective monitoring and evaluation of executive performance may be diluted. Strong chairmanship of the board is then needed. With the supervisory or TWO-TIER BOARD structure this responsibility falls to the upper, SUPERVISORY BOARD. However, many unitary boards devote the greater part of their time and effort to this function, with their board papers mainly reporting financial results and recent operating data. Consequently, such a concentration on the compliance and CONFORMANCE ROLE of the board allows less time for the PERFORMANCE ROLE and responsibilities.

❝ *One of the problems of a board dominated by executive directors is that they are marking their own examination papers.*

Lord Caldecote, when chairman of Delta Group. Had he been commenting today, he might have added:

❝ *... and worse, many of them are awarding themselves the prizes.*

EXXON EUROPE AND EXXON MOBIL: CORPORATE SOCIAL RESPONSIBILITY POLICIES

Exxon Europe publishes its CORPORATE SOCIAL RESPONSIBILITY (CSR) policies clearly:

We take our responsibilities very seriously – for our employees, shareholders, customers, communities, the environment and society at large. We strongly believe that the way we achieve results is as important as the results themselves. Therefore, we are working hard to embed CSR into the way we do business. We have integrated CSR policies and practices into our business, which help us to ensure that we meet standards of integrity, safety, health, environment and social responsibility day in and day out and across our worldwide operations. We believe that this approach is essential to achieving superior business results. Our focus is on helping Europe meet energy demand in an economically, socially and environmentally responsible manner. But we cannot be all things to all people. We must balance the needs of a wide variety of stakeholders. To do so sustainably is what the policies, actions and performance improvements behind CSR are all about.

But at the 2008 AGM of Exxon Mobil US, the great-granddaughter of John D. Rockefeller, the company's founder, called for the company to curb greenhouse gas emissions, increase renewable energy research and develop sources of alternative fuel. The board resisted the proposals. CHAIRMAN and chief executive Rex Tillerson said that he thought Exxon had to keep focused on its mission of developing more oil and gas reserves, and that oil and gas would remain the primary fuel source for decades to come:

The past year was an outstanding year and a record for our corporation by nearly every measure ... millions of people have benefited financially by holding Exxon Mobil shares either directly or indirectly through their pension, insurance and mutual funds.

Three resolutions asking Exxon to study the impact of global warming on poor countries, reduce company emissions of greenhouse gases and do more research on renewable energy sources were rejected by the SHAREHOLDERS.

Family company

A company in which members of a family exercise control, either because a majority of the voting shares are held by family members or because family interests exercise sufficient influence over affairs to control board membership. Many family companies are CLOSELY HELD COMPANIES. But a PUBLIC COMPANY can also be a family company: Coca-Cola, Ford Motor Company, Hewlett Packard, Microsoft and Wal-Mart are examples. Problems typically arise in family companies when professional managers have to be brought in to supplement family members or in succession to founder members, particularly if one branch of the family continues to run the company and another does not. To overcome inevitable differences of opinion, some authorities recommend the creation of a FAMILY COUNCIL, separate from the board of directors, to reconcile differences between family members before the matter is considered at a board or a SHARE-HOLDERS' meeting.

Family council

As noted in the previous entry, differences can arise among family SHAREHOLDERS on succession. Family members who are still involved in management typically want profits to be ploughed back into the business. But if some shares pass to members of the family who are no longer involved in management, they want dividends and may be concerned about expensive benefits available to the EXECUTIVE DIRECTORS. Another conflict can arise if the second and third generations of the family expect to provide the senior management, whereas the company really needs to recruit professional management.

❝❝ *We may not do much good, but at least we don't do any harm*

Fin Guinness commenting on the role of family directors at Guinness in *Requiem for a Family Business*, 1997

FASB

See FINANCIAL ACCOUNTING STANDARDS BOARD.

Fat cat

The label "fat cat" has been applied to directors in both the United States and the UK whose remuneration appears to be excessive in terms of their contribution to the company. GOLDEN HANDCUFFS, GOLDEN HANDSHAKES, GOLDEN HELLOS, GOLDEN PARACHUTES and SHARE OPTIONS have all been used as evidence of excessive rewards, particularly when seen as rewarding failure. (See DIRECTORS' REMUNERATION.)

Fiduciary duty

Directors in most jurisdictions are expected to act with honesty, integrity and candour towards their company, in particular towards the interests of its SHAREHOLDERS. This fiduciary duty is to the company as a whole, to both majority and minority shareholders, should they exist. This can be difficult for a NOMINEE DIRECTOR who has been elected to safeguard the interest of the nominating shareholder, or where a dominant parent company exercises power over its subsidiary even though there are minority outside shareholders. Common law based on the Commonwealth (in Australia, Canada, Hong Kong, India, New Zealand, Singapore, South Africa and so on) allows directors to determine the best interests of the whole company, subject to the right of appeal to the courts. Directors of companies incorporated in the United States owe specific fiduciary duties to any minority shareholders. In other words, the primary duty of a director is to act honestly in good faith, giving all shareholders equal, sufficient and accurate information on all issues affecting their interests. The underlying (and universal) principle is that directors should not treat a company as though it exists for their personal benefit. (See also DUTY OF CARE.)

The seven principles of public life, drawn up by Lord Nolan, chairing a committee of the great and the good, to guide the British government, are highly appropriate to directors fulfilling their fiduciary duty:

- Selflessness – holders of public office should serve the public interest, not seek gains for their friends.
- Integrity – they should not place themselves under financial obligation to outsiders who might influence their duties.
- Objectivity – they should award public appointments and contracts on merit.
- ACCOUNTABILITY – they should submit themselves to the appropriate scrutiny.
- Openness – they should give reasons for their decisions.
- Honesty – they should declare conflicts of interest.
- Leadership – they should support these principles by personal example.

Figurehead

One of the roles a director can play (see PERFORMANCE ROLES).

Filibustering

See MEETING MANIPULATION.

Financial Accounting Standards Board

The organisation that sets GENERALLY ACCEPTED ACCOUNTING PRINCIPLES in the United States. After the ENRON debacle, the Financial Accounting Standards Board (FASB) was attacked for insisting on standards that are too detailed, allowing companies to stay within the rules but evade the spirit of accounting principles to provide a true and fair view.

www.fasb.org

Financial analysts

See INVESTMENT ANALYSTS.

Financial engineering

See COOKING THE BOOKS.

Financial Reporting Council

The independent REGULATOR responsible for promoting confidence in corporate reporting and governance in the UK. The Financial Reporting Council (FRC) promotes high standards of CORPORATE GOVERNANCE by maintaining an effective COMBINED CODE on corporate governance and promoting its widespread application, influencing European Union and global corporate governance developments and encouraging constructive interaction between company boards and INSTITUTIONAL SHAREHOLDERS. The FRC has a number of constituent bodies: ACCOUNTANCY AND ACTUARIAL DISCIPLINE BOARD, ACCOUNTING STANDARDS BOARD, AUDITING PRACTICES BOARD, FINANCIAL REPORTING REVIEW PANEL, PROFESSIONAL OVERSIGHT BOARD.

www.frc.org.uk

Financial Reporting Review Panel

Makes sure that the annual accounts of PUBLIC COMPANIES and large PRIVATE COMPANIES comply with the requirements of the UK Companies Acts and applicable accounting standards. The panel can ask directors to explain apparent departures from the requirements and tries to persuade them to adopt a more appropriate accounting treatment. Failing voluntary correction, the panel has the power to seek revision of the accounts through a court order. It is part of the UK's FINANCIAL REPORTING COUNCIL.

www.frc.org.uk/frrp

Financial Services Authority

An independent non-governmental body given statutory powers by the Financial Services and Markets Act 2000 to regulate the financial services industry in the UK. The Financial Services Authority (FSA) claims to have a risk-based rather than a rules-based approach. In 2000 it took over responsibility for listing companies from the London Stock Exchange and publishes the LISTING RULES, originally called the *Yellow Book* – although the new rule-book has a purple binder. The FSA is a company limited by guarantee and financed by the financial services industry. The Treasury appoints the FSA board.

www.fsa.gov.uk

Fund management

In managing their mutual funds, unit trusts and other investment products, INSTITUTIONAL INVESTORS have the potential to play a significant role in CORPORATE GOVERNANCE. Some commentators (the HAMPEL REPORT, for example) have called on them to exercise their VOTING RIGHTS, acting as mediator on behalf of all the SHAREHOLDERS, policing recalcitrant boards, attacking excessive DIRECTORS' RENUMERATION when necessary and generally supporting the creation of SHAREHOLDER VALUE. Others are less sure that institutional investors should be involved in such shareholder activism, pointing out that fund managers do not form a homogeneous group (see SHAREHOLDER POWER). At one extreme are funds which have a purely short-term orientation; at the other are RELATIONSHIP INVESTORS, who often seek a seat on the board. Between these extremes are the majority of fund managers around the world.

> *The issues of power and accountability were raised at the outset in relation to corporate boards. They will increasingly be raised in the context of the growing power and relative lack of accountability of institutional investors. Their exercise of power over boards will only be seen as legitimate if it is open and reflects the views of those who have entrusted their money to them.*

Sir Adrian Cadbury, *Directors' Monthly*, 1998

GAAP

See GENERALLY ACCEPTED ACCOUNTING PRINCIPLES.

Games directors play

Although routinely presented as a serious, analytical and rational process, boardroom behaviour is often intensely political, involving interpersonal rivalries, corporate power plays and networking skills. The games include the following:

- **Alliance building** is a power game played outside the boardroom for ensuring mutual support within. It is closely allied to log-rolling.
- **Coalition building** involves canvassing support for an issue informally outside the boardroom so that there is a sufficient consensus when the matter is discussed formally inside the boardroom.
- **Cronyism** is supporting a director's interests even though they may not be in the best interest of the company or its SHAREHOLDERS. For example, a director declares a personal interest in a contract in a tender being discussed by the board; he might even leave the room for the discussion. However, board members support his bid because of their relationship, even though it is not the most worthy. Cronyism is sometimes alleged to be the basis of CORPORATE GOVERNANCE in Asia.
- **Deal making** is a classic game, usually involving compromise, in which two or more directors reach a behind-

the-scenes agreement to achieve a specific outcome in a board decision.

- **Divide and rule** is a dirty game in which the player sees the chance to set one director against another, or groups of directors against each other. An issue in the financial accounts might be used, for example, to set the EXECUTIVE DIRECTORS, the NON-EXECUTIVE DIRECTORS and the AUDITORS against each other to achieve an entirely different personal aim.
- **Empire building** is the misuse of privileged access to INFORMATION, people or other resources to acquire power over organisational territory. The process often involves intrigue, battles and conquests.
- **Half truths** occur if a director, while not deliberately lying, tells only one side of the issue in board deliberations.
- **Hidden agendas** involve directors' pursuit of secret goals to benefit their own empire or further their own career against the interest of the organisation as a whole.
- **Log-rolling** occurs when director A agrees, off the record, to support director B's interests for mutual support when it comes to matters of interest to A.
- MEETING MANIPULATION
- **Propaganda** is the dissemination of information to support a cause. Seen more in relationships with shareholders, stockmarkets and financial institutions than in board-level deliberations. The regulatory authorities are likely to act if propaganda becomes excessive or deliberately false.
- **Rival camps** is a game played when there are opposing factions on a board in which hostilities, spies and double agents can be involved.
- **Scaremongering** emphasises the downside risks in a board decision, casting doubts about the situation so that the proposal will be turned down.
- **Snowing** involves executive directors deluging an OUTSIDE

DIRECTOR seeking further information with masses of data, confusing the situation and papering over any cracks.

■ **Spinning** is an art form developed at governmental level which presents a distorted view of a person or a situation, favourable to the interests of the spinner. In corporate governance spinning can be carried out at the level of the board, the shareholders or the media.

■ **Sponsorship** is support by one powerful director for another, usually for their joint benefit.

■ **Suboptimisation** occurs when a director supports one part of the organisation to the detriment of the company as a whole. Some executive directors suffer from tunnel vision because they are too closely involved with a functional department or a SUBSIDIARY COMPANY, and from short-sighted myopia because they will be personally affected by the outcome. An independent evaluation of senior management performance by outside directors can help to overcome such problems.

■ **Window dressing** produces a fine external show of sound corporate governance principles while covering up failures. Window dressing can also involve showing financial results in the best possible light while hiding weaknesses.

Directors with integrity and strong chairmanship will reduce the opportunities for game playing.

❝ *In my experience ..." is one of the most over-used phrases in board level discussions. The question that should always be asked is whether that experience is relevant to the subject in hand.*

❝ *As they say in board meetings, "trust me on this".*
Peanuts

GAZPROM

Gazprom is the largest natural gas company in the world, supplying the entire needs of eastern Europe and a lot of western Europe. The third largest company in the world by market capitalisation, Gazprom is Russia's largest company. In the days of the Soviet Union Gazprom was part of the oil and gas ministry. In 1992 it became a company. In 1994 it was privatised, with 60% offered and the state retaining 40%. Workers and management received 15% and other shares were offered to all Russian citizens through a voucher system, but the balance was sold by investment tender, which management was able to control. Dubious trading was alleged with evidence emerging of abuse by controlling SHARE-HOLDERS including asset-stripping. In 1996 Gazprom successfully offered 1% of its equity to investors abroad in the form of London depository receipts and a large bond issue in the United States.

The company's close relationship with the government during the presidency of Boris Yeltsin was strengthened when Vladimir Putin took over (see YUKOS). In 2001 Gazprom acquired NTV, a Russian independent television station, and in 2005 it purchased *Izvestia*, an influential Russian newspaper. In the same year it acquired Sibneft, an oil and gas company, thus consolidating its position as a global energy giant.

The 11-member Gazprom board has as its chairman the first deputy prime minister of the Russian Federation. Its deputy chairman is head of the Gazprom Management Committee, whose 17 members are the heads of various group operating companies and functional sections.

GENERAL ELECTRIC

Under the leadership of Jack Welch, who was CEO from 1981 to 2001, General Electric (GE) became one of America's most successful groups, operating in the electrical appliance, power generation, aircraft engine and financial sectors. After Welch's retirement his retirement package, which included the use of a company jet, came under scrutiny. Interestingly, this information came from his divorce proceedings, not from SEC filings. Welch's successor, Jeffrey Immelt, proposed changes to GE'S CORPORATE GOVERNANCE designed to strengthen the board's oversight of management. DISCLOSURE and transparency would be improved. Two-thirds of the directors would be genuinely independent. The chair of the compensation committee would serve as presiding director and chair at least three meetings each year of the non-employee directors. Immelt claimed that these changes went well beyond the SARBANES-OXLEY ACT requirements. Furthermore, the CEO would discuss with the board annually issues of strategy, risk and integrity, which it would then consider over the year. Each director would visit two GE plants a year without senior management being present. OUTSIDE DIRECTORS could not serve on more than two other PUBLIC COMPANY boards, if they were also CEOS, and other directors could not serve on more than four other boards.

“ *The current system of disclosure is designed to avoid liability not to inform anybody. There is no true number in accounting, and if there were, auditors would be the last people to find it.*
Harvey Pitt, when chairman of the SEC

Generally accepted accounting principles

American generally accepted accounting principles (GAAP) provide a detailed, legally oriented set of rules for dealing with various accounting situations, including the valuation of leases, depreciation and SHARE OPTIONS. Before ENRON, the feeling in the United States was that American GAAP provided the best approach to measuring corporate financial performance. Since

ENRON, there have been moves towards convergence with international accounting standards, which emphasise basic principles of accounting rather than detailed and prescriptive rules and may be less amenable to different interpretations. In 2007, the SECURITIES AND EXCHANGE COMMISSION (SEC) announced that if foreign companies with SEC-registered securities used INTERNATIONAL FINANCIAL REPORTING STANDARDS (IFRS) issued by the INTERNATIONAL ACCOUNTING STANDARDS BOARD, they would no longer have to reconcile their accounts with American GAAP. The FINANCIAL ACCOUNTING STANDARDS BOARD has suggested that, in due course, American standards will move towards IFRS.

www.fasb.org, www.aicpa.org

❝❝ It is incontrovertibly clear that long-standing deficiencies in the system we employ to produce quality audits of financial statements have caused a serious threat to the efficacy of our capital markets: we're experiencing a significant loss of investor confidence in public companies, their audited financial statements and the accounting profession.
Harvey Pitt, when chairman of the SEC

Generic strategy

A description of the overall strategic stance of a business. For example, a company might focus on a specific niche in the market, adopting a high-price strategy based on products differentiated by brand characteristics, quality or service; or it might base its strategy on volume, cost-efficiency and market positioning to compete on price with a low-cost strategy. Furthermore, in assessing strategic options, a company might expand through internally generated growth and in local, regional or international markets, or adopt a genuinely global strategy locating procurement, manufacturing, assembly, sales and marketing, servicing and the provision of finance wherever commercially and strategically viable. Directors need to share a perception of their company's generic strategies.

German corporate governance

PUBLIC COMPANIES in Germany have a TWO-TIER BOARD governance structure: an upper, SUPERVISORY BOARD (the *Aufsichtsrat*) and the executive board or committee (the *Vorstand*). Common membership of both bodies is prohibited. The supervisory board requires the executive board to present its proposals and plans to it for comment and approval, then reviews and assesses subsequent managerial performance. The power of the supervisory board lies in its ability to appoint and remove executives from the executive committee. In the CO-DETERMINATION process a close relationship between capital and labour is thought to be essential. Consequently, supervisory boards have equal numbers of representatives of SHAREHOLDERS and of employees. Common membership of supervisory and executive boards is not permitted. In 2002, the German Corporate Governance Commission launched a code of best practice (Kodex), which provided supervisory boards with more powers over management and external AUDIT, required details of DIRECTORS' REMUNERATION (including the criteria for performance-based rewards) and called for more timely information for investors. Not more than two former executives are allowed on the supervisory board. German companies must issue an annual statement, published online, showing whether they have complied with the code and explaining any discrepancies.

Global Corporate Governance Forum

An initiative of the World Bank and the Organisation for Economic Cooperation and Development (OECD) to promote improved

CORPORATE GOVERNANCE. The forum arranges round-table discussions and promotes the OECD PRINCIPLES of corporate governance.

www.gcgf.org

Global Reporting Initiative

An international multi-STAKEHOLDER effort to create a common framework for voluntary reporting of the economic, environmental and social impact of organisation-level activity. The mission of the Global Reporting Initiative (GRI) is to elevate the comparability and credibility of sustainability reporting practices worldwide. Businesses, accountancy, human rights, environmental, labour and governmental organisations are active participants in the GRI. (See SUSTAINABLE DEVELOPMENT.)

Global shares

Invented by the New York Stock Exchange to facilitate the Daimler/ Chrysler "merger" in 1998. The advantage of global shares over AMERICAN DEPOSITARY RECEIPTS is that they can be traded electronically around the world in many markets and multiple currencies. The Daimler/Chrysler shares began trading on 21 exchanges in eight countries.

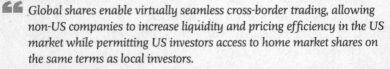 *Global shares enable virtually seamless cross-border trading, allowing non-US companies to increase liquidity and pricing efficiency in the US market while permitting US investors access to home market shares on the same terms as local investors.*

New York Stock Exchange, July 2002

Golden handcuffs

A term in DIRECTORS' CONTRACTS which binds them to the company for a given period for a substantial reward.

Golden handshake

A bountiful reward given to directors on the termination of their contracts, often negotiated when the contract was first signed. Such rewards are sometimes criticised because the extent of the handshake bears no relation to the contribution the director has made to the company – sometimes the reverse. (See also DIRECTORS' CONTRACTS and DIRECTORS' RENUMERATION.)

Golden hello

A one-off payment made to a director as an incentive to join a company, typically recognising some of the benefits forgone by leaving the previous company and acknowledging the additional costs and risk involved in the move.

Golden parachute

A device written into some DIRECTORS' CONTRACTS or offered on a potential takeover which enables them to float away from the company with exorbitant severance pay.

Golden share

A share in a company that gives overall voting power over that company to its owner, usually if something specific, such as a takeover bid, occurs. A typical case is a public-sector business, such as a power, transport or telecommunications company, which is privatised. The government holds the golden share to be able to prevent control passing to a foreign corporation. As business becomes more global, the use of golden shares is decreasing. Moreover, in 2002, the European Court of Justice issued a ruling limiting governments' use of golden shares on the grounds that such shares acted as a restriction on the MARKET FOR CONTROL.

Governing bodies

All CORPORATE ENTITIES need to be governed and the governing body fulfils that need. In the case of a JOINT STOCK LIMITED LIABILITY COMPANY the governing body is typically the board of directors. In other corporate entities it may be called the council, the senate, the executive committee, even the governing body. Most of the ideas and insights in this book can be applied to such bodies.

❝ *Every organisation from the humblest social club to the largest international company, needs a governing body to determine its strategic objectives and policies, to appoint and control its operational management, to monitor progress towards objectives and compliance with policies and to be accountable for its activities to parties to whom an account is properly due.*

Institute of Directors, London, *Guidelines for Directors*, 1991

Governing director

A phrase used mainly in Australia to describe a director with dominant powers in a PRIVATE COMPANY. Although the legislation requires such companies to have two directors, the statutes do not prevent companies framing their ARTICLES OF ASSOCIATION to give virtually all powers to one person: the governing director.

GREAT WESTERN RAILWAY COMPANY

Report of the Audit Committee

The auditors and Mr Deloitte attended the committee and explained the various matters concerned with the finances and other departments of the railway, which explanations were highly satisfactory. The committee considered the AUDITORS had performed their arduous duties with great care and intelligence and therefore confidently recommend that they be continued in office.

Paddington Station   Benjamin Lancaster
22nd February 1872   Chairman

Green mail

Arbitrageurs who buy shares on the possibility of a takeover bid with the intention of bidding up the price to sell at a profit, or acquiring a sufficient stake to block the bidder and force one side or the other to buy the shares at a premium to obtain control, are indulging in greenmail.

Greenbury Report

See DIRECTORS' REMUNERATION.

Hh

Hampel Report

This 1998 report from the Committee on Corporate Governance, chaired by Sir Ronnie Hampel, was a successor to the British CADBURY REPORT and Greenbury Report. It offered a set of "principles of CORPORATE GOVERNANCE", reflecting current conventional wisdom on corporate governance with three prevailing themes:

■ That good corporate governance needs broad principles not prescriptive rules. Compliance with sound governance practices, such as the separation of board chairmanship from chief executive, should be flexible and relevant to each company's individual circumstances and not reduced to what the report calls a "box-ticking" exercise. Self-regulation is the preferred approach; no more company legislation is needed.
■ That the board is accountable to the company's SHAREHOLDERS. There is no case for redefining directors' responsibilities to other STAKEHOLDER groups.
■ That the UNITARY BOARD is totally accepted in the UK. There is no interest in alternative governance structures or processes such as TWO-TIER BOARDS.

Predictably, perhaps, a committee predominantly comprising directors of major public companies and their professional advisers did not criticise contemporary corporate governance, nor did it advocate any measures which would further limit directors' power to make unfettered decisions or widen the scope of their ACCOUNTABILITY. Shortly after the report was published, the British government announced a fundamental review of UK company law. Many of the report's proposals are now enshrined in the UK's COMBINED CODE.

❝ *In corporate governance, we shall work for less regulation and against the idea of a permanent standing committee [on corporate governance], which would most likely look for ways of interfering with and regulating corporate activity.*
Tim Melville-Ross, formerly secretary-general of the Institute of Directors, London, 1997

Harmonisation of company law

A number of jurisdictions have tried to make their company laws converge. The European Union has had a company law harmonisation programme for many years, although that has largely been overtaken by social legislation affecting CORPORATE GOVERNANCE issues (see WORKER DIRECTOR). Australia and Canada have also developed business acts at the federal level, provoking adverse reactions from the states and provinces involved, which feared a loss of autonomy and tax revenue. In the United States, companies can only be incorporated in individual states; there is no federal companies' legislation, only federal securities legislation such as the SARBANES-OXLEY ACT. This is one reason why companies incorporate in the state of Delaware, which has relatively liberal company laws and a companies' court to settle disputes.

❝ *Corporations are truly getting to the same place as Church and nation state before them, where the position of the leader rather than the institution becomes paramount. This is the condition that precedes loss of legitimacy and collapse.*
Bob Monks, *The New Global Investors*, www.ragm.com

Hedge fund

An investment vehicle which seeks to provide investors with superior returns and which has great flexibility in what it invests in. A hedge fund manager might, for example, buy shares but to some extent "hedge" his bet by selling short an equivalent value of other stocks (that is, he sells shares he has borrowed for a fee, buying them back later). Hedge funds are typically heavily geared, thus increasing their potential return and their exposure to risk. Hedge fund investment has high risk and investors are usually rich individuals and INSTITUTIONAL INVESTORS, including other hedge funds, seeking to improve and hedge their overall performance. Hedge funds may take positions in commodities, buy equity shares, trade in debt and invest in futures, including energy futures, sugar prices, carbon emission prices, even the weather, while using all the tools in the contemporary financial-management tool box. Hedge fund investments are also illiquid; investors may only be able to sell their holdings every quarter and will often be required to give advance notice of their wish to do so; even then "gates" may restrict the proportion of an investor's holding that can be redeemed.

The most successful hedge fund managers earn over $1 billion a year. They like to stay out of the limelight as they do not want any political hassle when they influence exchange rates; nor do they want details of their salaries in the newspapers for fear that they may become a target of criminals. Criticisms of the governance of hedge funds include their secretiveness and lack of transparency, and the lack of DISCLOSURE on matters such as their investment strategies and profitability.

Helicopter vision

An essential requirement for every director: the ability to perceive issues at different levels of abstraction. When a helicopter is on the ground the pilot can see every blade of grass, but he cannot see very far. As the helicopter rises so more and more comes into the pilot's vision, but in less and less detail. At a considerable height it is possible to see to the distant horizon and scan all the ground in between; but the detail of individual elements has now been lost.

So it is with directors' thinking. Helicopter vision involves being able to think, for example, at the level of the personalities involved in a situation, at the level of departments, STRATEGIC BUSINESS UNITS or subsidiaries, or the company as a whole, or the industry, internationally or even globally. Some people, perhaps because of their professional training or earlier experience, think only at a single level. They do not make good directors. Those who can perceive issues at different levels have board potential.

But the greatest challenge to a director is not just to have helicopter vision – many people can achieve this with experience. The difficult part is to decide which level is appropriate to the matter at hand. Far too many decisions are made at an inappropriate level. A director may think a decision is an operational matter, failing to recognise the managerial or strategic aspects; or the reverse, that it is a strategic matter, failing to recognise the operational implications.

Hermes Investment Management

A major UK INSTITUTIONAL INVESTOR committed to shareholder activism with one of the largest CORPORATE GOVERNANCE teams in the world (see SHAREHOLDER POWER). The Hermes principles of corporate governance aim to make sure that UK LISTED COMPANIES are run in the long-term interests of SHAREHOLDERS. They include proposals such as companies should stick to their core business; managers should be given appropriate incentives;

companies should have an efficient capital structure and coherent strategies and should act ethically.

www.hermes.co.uk

❝ *Hermes' corporate governance programme is founded on a belief that companies with interested and involved shareholders are more likely to achieve superior long-term performance than those without. Tied closely with this is the belief that a company run in the interests of shareholders will need to manage [relations with] ... its employees, suppliers and customers, to behave ethically and have regard for the environment and society as a whole.*
www.hermes.co.uk

❝ *We are desperately keen to act as an owner, rather than as a spectator. There is too much gloss and not enough content on the fundamental economic basis of the business which is, after all, the prime reason for our investment.*
Tony Watson, chief executive, Hermes

Higgs Report

In 2002, the British government formed a committee chaired by Derek Higgs, a former corporate financier at Warburg, to consider the role of NON-EXECUTIVE DIRECTORS and how "more independent and more active non-executives, drawn from a wider pool of talent, can play their part in raising productivity". As *The Times* remarked at the time: "The mind boggles." Higgs produced a short and independent report, based on best practice, much of which has now been incorporated into the UK COMBINED CODE.

❝ *The review is ultimately about behaviour and interaction in the boardroom, and how boards can best operate. This involves trust, confidence, supportive behaviour and openness in debate – and it is not just about stopping risk.*
Derek Higgs

HIH INSURANCE

HIH Insurance Group was Australia's largest insurer. When it collapsed the £1.9 billion loss left many policyholders and investors bereft. Some lost their homes. A royal commission questioned the founder and chief executive, Ray Williams. Observers commented on a tale of "spectacular munificence", saying that "it was like the last days of Pompeii". Williams enjoyed a millionaire's lifestyle. His secretary travelled first class. A corporate adviser was given round-the-world air tickets for himself, his wife, four children and a nanny to compensate for working over Christmas. Rodney Adler, a director, whose FAI insurance company HIH had taken over for more than £200m in 1998, received a £2.3m termination payment and a £350,000 a year consultancy fee. Williams, a philanthropist who had donated millions to medical research, claimed that his own life savings were in the company and that he had not sold any shares. The problems, he claimed, were due to errors of judgment, in particular the failure to undertake DUE DILIGENCE on FAI, which had gaping holes in its finances. The underlying question is: what was the board doing while this saga was going on?

Hilmer Report

A report by Fred Hilmer, published in 1993 by the Sydney Institute with the title *Strictly Boardroom* (reflecting the film *Strictly Ballroom* in which competitive ballroom dancing had become so regulated that innovation was stifled). This, says the report, is what can happen to CORPORATE GOVERNANCE if it focuses on control and compliance. It advocated an emphasis on the PERFORMANCE ROLES of the board.

❝ *The board's key role is to ensure that corporate management is continuously and effectively striving for above-average performance, taking account of risk. This is not to deny the board's additional role with respect to shareholder protection.*

Hilmer Report, *Strictly Boardroom*, Australia, 1993

Holding company

The company at the top of a group of companies which holds all or a majority of the shares in its subsidiaries and thus controls their activities. Often called the parent company of the group.

HSBC: CORPORATE RESPONSIBILITY REPORT

HSBC calls itself the world's local bank. It is listed on five stock exchanges and has 200,000 shareholders spread over 100 countries. The following is taken from the corporate responsibility section of its annual report. Stephen Green, the group's chairman, wrote:

How a business like HSBC responds to the challenge of balancing the needs of people, planet and profit is part of our corporate responsibility strategy ... we want HSBC to be one of the world's leading brands for corporate responsibility.

At HSBC, we believe that corporate responsibility is critical to our long-term business success. In order to deliver enduring returns to our shareholders, we need to build lasting relationships with our customers that are based on the highest standards of personal integrity, transparency and fair dealing in all our business activities. This is the philosophy that underpins our approach to running our business responsibly. We are committed to treating all present and future stakeholders in an open and transparent way. This commitment to openness is vital, whether in relation to the products and services we provide to our 125 million customers, in the way we manage our global workforce of 312,000 employees, or in the assessment of sustainability risks in our lending and investment activities, which range from commercial banking loans to multi-million dollar infrastructure projects. Companies like ours must also share responsibility for addressing some of the formidable challenges currently facing societies across the globe, including the impact of climate change. We also provide support for educational and environmental projects worldwide through our charitable donations which totalled US$86.3 million in 2006.

We aspire to be one of the world's leading brands in corporate responsibility. An example of our strategy here is microfinance, which demonstrates the growing alignment between business and community investment. Our new microfinance strategy is based on commercial viability albeit with high social impact ... small-scale financial services for those without banking relationships largely in the developing world.

We believe financial institutions will be critical in minimising the impacts of climate change, playing a key role in financing the shift to cleaner energy and more efficient transport. HSBC itself aspires to be among the leading financial institutions in a low-carbon economy ... HSBC is supporting its clients to run environmentally responsible businesses ... As part of our long-standing commitment to the environment we have since 2003 measured energy usage and CO_2 emissions from our offices around the world, along with waste production and water usage ... In addition, since we became the world's first carbon neutral bank in 2005, we have purchased carbon dioxide "offsets" ... thereby bringing our own net impact to zero.

HSBC was overall winner in the first *Financial Times* Sustainable Banking Awards and the 2007 Hong Kong Institute of Certified Public Accountants Best Annual Report Competition.

www.hsbc.com/1/2/sustainability

IASB

See INTERNATIONAL ACCOUNTING STANDARDS BOARD.

IASC

See INTERNATIONAL ACCOUNTING STANDARDS COMMITTEE.

ICGN

See INTERNATIONAL CORPORATE GOVERNANCE NETWORK.

IFRS

See INTERNATIONAL FINANCIAL REPORTING STANDARDS.

Incorporation

The creation of a JOINT STOCK LIMITED LIABILITY COMPANY by a company registration authority. (See also OVERSEAS INCORPORATION.)

Independent director

An OUTSIDE DIRECTOR or NON-EXECUTIVE DIRECTOR with no interests in the company, other than the directorship, which might affect, or be seen to affect, the exercise of independent judgment.

Some company REGULATORS lay down detailed criteria to determine independence, such as whether directors have any significant business dealings with the company (for example, as a supplier, customer or banker), whether they are related to the CHAIRMAN or CEO, or whether they have been employed by the company in the past. Although there may be a good case for people with such connections or experience to be on the board, they cannot be considered to be fully independent, and hence cannot be part of the check-and-balance mechanisms enshrined in the AUDIT COMMITTEE, the NOMINATION COMMITTEE or the REMUNERATION COMMITTEE.

Some people serve on many boards and are effectively professional directors. This has been criticised by, for example, the UK's Institute of Directors, which has suggested that full-time executives should not hold more than two non-executive directorships and no director should sit on more than six boards. In reality, of course, independence is a state of mind. As well as meeting the independence criteria, a successful independent director needs to be capable of thinking independently, making a stand and, if necessary, being tough-minded.

www.independentdirector.co.uk

❝❝ *I think the whole idea of independence is bunkum – and dangerous too. It leads to a "them" and "us" approach with the independent directors feeling they carry the can for the executives and the executives leaving governance to part-timers.*
Prue Leith, cookery expert, business woman and non-executive director

❝❝ *In my view you can't have twenty non-executive jobs and pretend you are doing the job properly. My personal limit is three non-executive directorships, and I will not stay on the board for more than six years. I also think that the chairman shouldn't be there for too long. My limit is six years. You avoid the risk of excessive power.*
Sir John Collins, chairman, DSG International

❝❝ *The division of responsibility between directors, auditor and senior management is not sufficiently clear. The focus is almost entirely on defining the responsibilities of directors. Yet the commercial reality of the matter is that, in these days of conglomerates and perhaps trans-national conglomerates at that, the opportunity for non-executive directors to exercise meaningful control over management is as slight as the ability of ministers to control a vast bureaucracy.*
Justice Andrew Rogers in the AWA case, Australia, 1992

❝❝ *Non-executive directors need to act as a "loyal opposition" to management to challenge and check their proposals. However, NEDs can be inhibited from challenging management when management can determine or influence their tenure on the board.*
Shann Turnbull, Australia, 2002

Induction programme

A programme of visits, meetings and training to provide a new director with valuable INFORMATION and knowledge. Essentially, the programme introduces the incoming director to the board, the company and the business. A new NON-EXECUTIVE DIRECTOR may have little knowledge of the company or its industry. Conversely, an EXECUTIVE DIRECTOR, although often said to be "promoted" to the board for successful executive performance, may have little knowledge and no experience of board-level work. The purpose of a director induction programme is to speed up the time it takes for a new director to make a real contribution to the board.

❝❝ *I find that it takes a director up to a year before he really understands what is going on in board meetings, and another year before he really contributes anything worthwhile.*
Chairman of a major UK company

❝ *My orientation was one hour before the board meeting.*
A director speaking to Richard Leblanc and Jim Gillies, *Inside the Boardroom*, 2005

Industry analysis

STRATEGY FORMULATION has to be competitor and customer based and is often global in context. For many directors industry analysis is the starting point for thinking about corporate strategy. Michael Porter, a professor at Harvard Business School, has outlined five driving forces of competitive analysis (see Figure 10).

Taking an industry perspective has changed the strategic battlefield for many boards. No longer are they constrained by thinking primarily about their own products and services and how to market them. Now they focus on the needs of customers and potential customers. They review the strategies being pursued by their competitors. They identify potential new competitors and

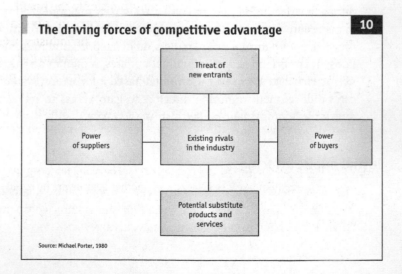

The driving forces of competitive advantage 10

Threat of new entrants

Power of suppliers

Existing rivals in the industry

Power of buyers

Potential substitute products and services

Source: Michael Porter, 1980

think about what barriers there are to entry into the field. They consider what developments, perhaps in technology, delivery systems or new products, might cause customers to change their allegiance. In other words, directors should think strategically before they get down to approving plans for their own company.

One of the difficulties of industry analysis is determining the boundaries of the industry. Industries overlap: telecommunications and computers, publishing and the internet, retail banking and financial services. STRATEGIC ALLIANCES increasingly cross the frontiers of traditional industries. Potential competitors may come from what appeared to be a non-competing industry.

Information

Directors have the right to all the information they feel necessary for them to fulfil their responsibilities as directors. In some companies, they are provided with no more than a standard pack of routine data before a BOARD MEETING. They start with inadequate information and cannot digest additional data tabled during the meeting. However, some CHAIRMEN make great efforts to make sure that the directors are provided with the information they need, with formal board papers, ad hoc reports and presentations, board briefings and individual updates, rooted in an initial INDUCTION PROGRAMME. Computer-based information systems can be developed to enable directors to gain access to relevant director-level information. (See also WAR ROOM.)

Initial public offering

The sale of newly issued shares by an investment bank, usually to large financial institutions, on behalf of the issuing company. Often abbreviated to IPO. (See also INVESTMENT ANALYST.)

❝❝ *I don't need to raise any capital, so why should I care about corporate governance?*
Director of a Russian company, 2002

Inside information

Confidential information about a company's affairs known only to those inside the company. Using such information to buy shares to make a profit or sell shares to prevent a loss is INSIDER DEALING, which is illegal in most jurisdictions.

Insider dealing

Trading in a LISTED COMPANY's shares on the basis of privileged, share-price-sensitive INSIDE INFORMATION would be a breach of a director's FIDUCIARY DUTY. It is also illegal in most countries. Japan, Hong Kong and Germany were among the last countries to make insider dealing a criminal offence, although thus far there have been few successful prosecutions. The problem is that it is often difficult to prove that a particular transaction was made as a result of inside information. The United States has the most severe penalties for insider dealing.

Insider dealing can involve either buying shares in the secret knowledge of events that would drive the price up, or selling shares to avoid a loss given secret intelligence on events that would cause the price to fall. The argument against the practice is not so much that it is unfair, or because it involves a misuse of information, but because insider dealing destroys the credibility and the integrity of the market. Directors have to be particularly careful not to trade in their company's shares when they are possession of inside information, such as the company results just prior to publication and before the stockmarket has that information. The COMPANY SECRETARY should inform directors when the window of opportunity for trading in the company's shares is open and, more importantly, when it is closed.

 Private information is practically the source for every large modern fortune.

Oscar Wilde, *The Ideal Husband*

Institutional investor

A financial institution with shareholdings in LISTED COMPANIES. Institutional investors include pension funds, investment trusts, mutual funds (or unit trusts), life and other insurance companies and banks running investment portfolios for clients. The proportion of shares held by institutional investors has been increasing throughout the world. In the UK it is now well over 50%. Often institutional investors show little interest in the CORPORATE GOVERNANCE of the companies in which they invest. The so-called "voice or exit" dilemma faces an institution deciding whether to take a short-term perspective and "vote with its feet", selling its shares if it is dissatisfied with a company's performance or potential, or to take a stand in specific cases, getting involved in the company's governance and voting its shares accordingly. A few institutional investors with large positions in a stock, or those tracking shares on a particular index, may find that they are locked in. Consequently, they do get involved in governance. Institutions that have been prominent in corporate governance include CALPERS and HERMES. (See also RELATIONSHIP INVESTING.)

I think public comment can be a very dangerous way of working for an institutional shareholder. We are here to enhance the value of people's money. We wouldn't in any way want to cause problems by making comments in public.

Lawrence Burr, managing director, NSW State Superannuation Investment and Management Corporation, Australia, 1993

❝ *The most important question raised by the emergence of the pension funds, and other institutional investors, as the main suppliers of capital and the majority owners of the large business is their role and function in the economy. Their emergence makes obsolete all traditional ways of managing and controlling large business. It forces us to think through and redefine the governance of companies.*
Peter Drucker, *Post-Capitalist Society*, 1993

Interlocking directorship

A term for directors who sit on each others' boards, sometimes called a cross-directorship. Studies in the UK and the United States have analysed the structure of cross-directorships, which can involve complex networks of linkages as well as direct links with A on B's board and B on A's board. In some circumstances, such as in a STRATEGIC ALLIANCE, there can be benefits in cross-directorships. But generally the practice is suspect because of the often- undisclosed concentration of power. (See also JAPANESE CORPORATE GOVERNANCE.)

International Accounting Standards Board

Founded in 1973 as the International Accounting Standards Committee, the International Accounting Standards Board (IASB) was created in 2001 as an independent body responsible for setting international financial reporting standards. Over 150 accounting bodies from over 100 countries are members. The national stand-ard-setting bodies in eight countries – Australia, Canada, France, Germany, Japan, New Zealand, UK and United States – have an IASB member resident in their jurisdiction. As Sir David Tweedie, the IASB's chairman, explained, the aim of IASB is to promote convergence on a single set of high-quality, understandable and enforceable global accounting standards, which will provide transparent and comparable information.

www.iasb.org.uk

International Corporate Governance Network

In 1995 a number of parties interested in CORPORATE GOVERNANCE formed the International Corporate Governance Network (ICGN) to co-ordinate their efforts. These included CALPERS and the Council of Institutional Investors in the United States, the ASSOCIATION OF BRITISH INSURERS and NATIONAL ASSOCIATION OF PENSION FUNDS in the UK, the Corporate Governance Forum of the Centre for European Policy Studies and others. Many leading pension funds and institutional investors have since joined. An estimated $10 trillion is under investment by member organisations. The ICGN secretariat is based in London.

www.icgn.org

❝ *Three quarters of institutional investors in Europe and America are prepared to pay a premium between 12 and 14 percent for stocks that demonstrate good corporate governance.*
McKinsey & Co study, 2002

International Financial Reporting Standards

Financial reporting standards published by the INTERNATIONAL ACCOUNTING STANDARDS BOARD. International Financial Reporting Standards (IFRS) are required throughout the European Union for publicly traded companies to remove barriers to cross-border trading in securities and to make sure that financial statements throughout the EU are compatible and transparent. They are recognised for cross-border reporting in 52 countries, although many still require local standards for local companies. The American SECURITIES AND EXCHANGE COMMISSION currently recognises IFRS only for foreign companies that are listed in the United States. (See also GENERALLY ACCEPTED ACCOUNTING PRINCIPLES and FINANCIAL ACCOUNTING STANDARDS BOARD.)

 Attacking the barriers to cross-border voting is a powerful new demand from US institutions to vote shares worldwide.
Stephen Davis, *Global Proxy Watch*, 1997

International Organisation of Securities Commissions

A voluntary organisation of financial regulators from over 50 countries whose members regulate the vast majority of securities traded worldwide. The International Organisation of Securities Commissions (IOSCO) holds regular meetings to exchange information, unite standard-setting efforts and provide mutual assistance to promote the integrity of markets. So the regulation of financial markets and the monitoring of abnormal trading in shares are now global. It is increasingly difficult for INSIDER TRADERS to bury dealings through transactions in overseas markets. IOSCO is based in Madrid, Spain, and looks to the INTERNATIONAL ACCOUNTING STANDARDS BOARD to provide acceptable international accounting and financial reporting standards.

www.iosco.org

Investment analyst

A supposedly independent provider of research on LISTED COMPANIES for potential investors. Unfortunately, many investment analysts in both the UK and the United States are employed by financial institutions which may have an interest in promoting the shares of client companies. So their objectivity has been questioned. At worst, analysts were seen as puppets of their employing finance house, ramping stocks before they were offered to the public. The problem was exemplified in a 1992 internal staff memorandum at Morgan Stanley:

> Our objective is to adopt a policy, fully understood by the entire firm, including the research department, that we do not make negative or controversial comments about a client as a matter of sound business practice.

So much for independence. Some US banks paid substantial penalties after the publication of incriminating evidence of biased research reports.

Some things never change. In 1934, Benjamin Graham and David Dodd wrote in their classic book *Security Analysis*:

> In the last three decades the prestige of security analysis on Wall Street has experienced a brilliant rise and an ignominious fall ... the new era involved the abandonment of the analytical approach [with] facts and figures being manipulated to support the delusions of the period.

IOSCO

See INTERNATIONAL ORGANISATION OF SECURITIES COMMISSIONS.

IPO

See INITIAL PUBLIC OFFERING.

Japanese corporate governance

Keiretsu are networks of Japanese companies connected through inter-trading, extensive INTERLOCKING DIRECTORSHIPS and CROSS-HOLDINGS. Typically, the network includes a financial institution. CHAIRMEN and senior directors of companies in the *keiretsu* meet regularly and have close, informal relationships. In the past, CORPORATE GOVERNANCE had a STAKEHOLDER, rather than SHAREHOLDER, orientation.

Boards are large and almost entirely executive. Traditionally, in *keiretsu* companies the board plays a formal, even ritualistic role; in effect it is the top four or five layers of the management organisation. Promotion to the board, as in the West, is a mark of distinction; but unlike in the West, interpersonal competition, which has been a feature of life throughout the organisation, continues on the board for promotion to the next level.

The commercial code calls for "representative directors" to be elected by the board. Whereas, from a western viewpoint, these might be expected to represent the interests of various stakeholders in the firm, their role is to represent the company in its dealings with outside parties such as the government, banks and other companies in the industry. Typically the representative directors include the chairman, PRESIDENT and other senior directors. The code also calls for the appointment of individuals as full-time statutory AUDITORS. They report to the board on any financial problems or infringements of the company code or the company articles. They can call for INFORMATION from other directors and company employees and can convene special meetings of the board. These internal board-level auditors, of course, liaise with the external professional auditors.

NON-EXECUTIVE DIRECTORS, in the western sense, are untypical. A few of the executives might have served with other companies in the *keiretsu* added-value network, and in that sense be able to represent the interests of suppliers or downstream agents; others might have been appointed to the company's ranks on retirement from the *keiretsu's* bankers or even from among the industry's government REGULATORS (known as a DESCENT FROM HEAVEN). Only recently have independent, OUTSIDE DIRECTORS been appointed, often under pressure from international sources of capital.

The Japanese do not see the need for such intervention "from the outside". Indeed, they have difficulty in understanding how outside directors function. How can outsiders possibly know enough about the company to make a contribution, they wonder, when they themselves have spent their lives working for it? How can an outsider be sufficiently sensitive to the corporate culture? Worse, might they not damage the harmony of the group by failing to appreciate the subtleties of their relationships?

The social cohesion within Japanese firms is well known, with high levels of unity throughout the organisation, non-adversarial relationships, lifetime employment, enterprise unions, personnel policies emphasising commitment, initiation into the corporate family, decision-making by consensus, cross-functional training and promotion based on loyalty and social compatibility as well as performance. Boards are still generally decision-ratifying bodies rather than decision-initiating and decision-taking forums, as in the West. Meetings of managing directors and the directors in their teams are crucial, as are the informal relationships between the top echelons of the board.

However, with the Japanese economy facing stagnation in the 1990s, traditional approaches to corporate governance were questioned. A corporate governance debate developed and the bank-based, stakeholder-oriented model came under scrutiny. The poorly performing economy had weakened many of the banks at the heart of *keiretsu*. Globalisation of markets and finance put further pressure on companies. The paternalistic relationship between company and lifetime "salaryman" slowly began to crumble. Some companies came under pressure from overseas INSTITUTIONAL INVESTORS. Company laws were redrafted to permit a more American style of corporate governance, but few firms have yet embraced them. In 2008, eight international investment funds called for greater shareholder democracy, and a report from the Japanese Council for Economic and Fiscal Policy proposed that anti-takeover defences be discouraged and the takeover of Japanese firms be made easier. In the same year, the Asian Corporate Governance Association provided a critique of corporate governance in Japan:

We believe that sound corporate governance is essential to the creation of a more internationally competitive corporate sector in Japan and to the longer-term growth of the Japanese economy and its capital markets. While a number of leading companies in Japan have made strides in corporate governance in recent years, we submit that the system of governance in most listed companies is not meeting the needs of stakeholders or the nation at large in three ways:

- By not providing for adequate supervision of corporate strategy.
- By protecting management from the discipline of the market, thus rendering the development of a healthy and efficient market in corporate control all but impossible.
- By failing to provide the returns that are vitally necessary to protect Japan's social safety net – its pension system.

> ❝❝ *The path to the Japanese board has changed little over the past forty years. There is only one route and it begins on the first day a new employee, fresh from university, arrives at the corporate offices ... Elevation to the rank of director [is] the supreme reward for competent service, but with little modification in managerial responsibilities ... Eventually many departmental heads are again promoted becoming simultaneously head of an operating unit and a "managing director". Even the "senior managing directors" are heads of divisions or important staff departments. These are masquerade boards in which managers briefly don the masks of directors.*
>
> Aron Viner, "The Coming Revolution in Japan's Board Rooms", *Corporate Governance*, Vol. 1, No. 3, July 1993

Joint stock limited liability company

A CORPORATE ENTITY formally incorporated under the company law of a given jurisdiction, with a legal existence separate from its owners, whose liability for the company's debts is limited to their shareholding. It was a brilliantly simple and superbly successful idea of the mid-19th century and it underpins CORPORATE GOVERNANCE. Without companies there would be no need for directors. However, it is the SHAREHOLDERS' liability that is limited, not the DIRECTORS' LIABILITY.

www.companieshouse.co.uk, www.hemscott.com, www.market-eye.co.uk

> ❝❝ *All hail astonishing fact,*
> *All hail invention new,*
> *The joint stock company act,*
> *of parliament, sixty two.*
> *And soon or late I always call*
> *for Stock Exchange quotation,*
> *No scheme too great, and none too small*
> *for companification.*
>
> Gilbert and Sullivan, *Utopia Ltd*, 1893

❝ *A corporation is a collection of individuals united in one collective body and possessing ... capacities which do not belong to the natural persons ... [including] perpetual succession and of acting by the collective vote or will of its members.*

Chief Justice Marshall in the Dartmouth College Case, 1819

Joint venture

See STRATEGIC ALLIANCE.

Judge

One of the roles a director can play (see CONFORMANCE ROLES).

Kk

Keiretsu

See JAPANESE CORPORATE GOVERNANCE.

King Reports

A South African Committee, under the chairmanship of Mervyn King, published a code of corporate practices and conduct in 1994, based on a broad consensus of the South African corporate community. The report included a "code of ethics for enterprises and all who deal with enterprises".

Recognising there was a move away from the single bottom line, which emphasised the interests of SHAREHOLDERS, a second report (King II) was published in 2002. It focused on the triple bottom line, which embraces the economic, environmental and social aspects of a company's activities (see CORPORATE SOCIAL RESPONSIBILITY). Boards' responsibility for RISK MANAGEMENT also featured.

Ll

Lead director

An independent NON-EXECUTIVE DIRECTOR or OUTSIDE DIRECTOR appointed to head the group of INDEPENDENT DIRECTORS on the board and, in some cases, to be spokesperson for the company with the SHAREHOLDERS. The potential for conflict with the duties of the board CHAIRMAN has to be carefully handled. Another use of the term can be found in companies with complex business interests, where individual directors are given a portfolio of interests on which they take the lead in BOARD MEETINGS. For example, one director might lead on new product development, marketing in a specific product group and management of one of the group's international regions.

Legal duties

Directors have two fundamental duties under the company law of almost all jurisdictions: a FIDUCIARY DUTY to act with honesty, integrity and candour towards the members of the company; and a duty to exercise reasonable care, diligence and skill in their handling of company matters.

Limited liability

See COMPANY LIMITED BY GUARANTEE and JOINT STOCK LIMITED LIABILITY COMPANY.

❝❝ *Just exactly whose liability is limited in the limited liability company?*
A member of the British Royal Family in 1981 on taking up a non-executive directorship. The answer was and still is the shareholders, not the directors.

Limited liability partnership

The UK Partnership Act of 1890 made partners personally liable for a firm's debts if it became bankrupt, but did not require partnerships to publish their accounts. When partnerships were small this seemed reasonable. But as partnerships grew, particularly in the accountancy profession, the personal exposure of individual partners to their share of the debts of a huge global firm became unacceptable. In a limited liability partnership (LLP), an entity is created that is distinct from its partners, who are known as members. The price of limiting the liability of partners is the need to publish accounts including profits and remuneration which conform to UK accounting standards, just like limited liability companies (see COMPANY LIMITED BY GUARANTEE and JOINT STOCK LIMITED LIABILITY COMPANY).

Listed company

A company whose shares are traded on a stock exchange. To be listed on the stock exchange board, the company must satisfy the LISTING RULES of that exchange.

Listing rules

The regulations that each stock exchange lays down governing the minimum requirements for having a company's shares listed on that market. Typical listing rules include requirements on the contents of prospectuses, on reports and accounts to members, and on matters of board membership, over and above the requirements of the company law in the jurisdiction of incorporation. For example, the London Stock Exchange requires each company's annual report to state whether the requirements of the UK COMBINED CODE have been fulfilled, and if not, why not. The ultimate sanction for failing to meet listing rules is delisting; but since this would disenfranchise public SHAREHOLDERS, which the listing rules are predominantly intended to protect, such sanctions are generally threats used in discussions rather than actions carried out in practice.

Litigation

A growing part of corporate life. AUDIT firms, companies, boards and individual directors are increasingly being exposed to claims for damages in actions brought by shareholders, bankers, customers and others, alleging losses arising through negligence, usually when a company has run into financial difficulties. The former NON-EXECUTIVE DIRECTORS of Equitable Life Assurance Society were sued for £3 billion. Courts will seldom second-guess the business judgment of boards; however, that does not prevent aggrieved parties bringing actions. In the United States, which has become the most litigious nation in the world, the threat of legal action sometimes deters people from serving as OUTSIDE DIRECTORS. Even if their DIRECTORS AND OFFICERS INSURANCE cover is adequate, directors can still face the aggravation and mental suffering of legal action, the personal embarrassment of media exposure and the loss of reputation even if found not guilty. Some companies, and particularly their AUDITORS, having faced massive claims for damages, can find indemnity insurance prohibitively expensive or even unavailable. (See also ARTHUR ANDERSEN and DEEP-POCKET SYNDROME.)

LLP

See LIMITED LIABILITY PARTNERSHIP.

Log-rolling

See GAMES DIRECTORS PLAY.

Long range planning

See BUDGETARY PLANNING.

LONG-TERM CAPITAL MANAGEMENT

Myron Scholes and Robert Merton, winners of the Nobel Prize in economics, were on the board of Long-Term Capital Management (LTCM), a HEDGE FUND founded in 1994 by John Meriwether, a Wall Street pioneer of fixed-income arbitrage. The company developed mathematical models to arbitrage deals in American, Japanese and European government fixed-interest bonds, buying some bonds and short-selling others as prices narrowed. Initially, LTCM was highly successful. As it prospered, it began trading in options and merger arbitrage. But the 1997 East Asian financial crisis produced significant losses, which were compounded by the Russian government's default on its bonds in 1998. Holders of European and Japanese bonds, fearing further defaults, transferred to American Treasury bonds and the previous arbitrage opportunities used by LTCM reversed. The firm lost nearly $2 billion of its capital. Fearing a chain reaction in the financial markets, the Federal Reserve Bank organised a bail-out by major creditor institutions of over $3.5 billion. The banks participating in the bail-out received 90% of LTCM and an independent SUPERVISORY BOARD was created. In the end LTCM was wound up in 2000 in an orderly fashion, but the fact that it had been bailed out made some think that other institutions might assume risks in the future believing that the Fed would rescue them if they ran into trouble.

Mm

MAN

The Man group was founded in London by James Man over 200 years ago as a brokerage business. It now runs HEDGE FUNDS to exploit market inefficiencies with low risk. Its clients include INSTITUTIONAL INVESTORS and corporations. Man Group is incorporated in the UK and quoted on the London Stock Exchange. In 2008 it had assets under management worth over $70 billion. Its website explains its managed futures investment programmes:

Trading takes place around-the-clock and real time price information is used to respond to price moves across a diverse range of global markets encompassing stock indices, bonds, currencies, short-term interest rates and commodities. The instruments traded are primarily futures and OTC [over-the-counter] foreign exchange forwards and metal contracts ... always underpinned by a strong research ethic. The Group has succeeded in developing a structured investment model in which investment selection, portfolio construction, risk management and investment service functions are modularised, which enables it to galvanise the full potential of alternative strategies as well as leverage the creativity and expertise of its highly qualified investment professionals. Drawing on extensive know-how in different investment disciplines and established relationships within the alternative investment community, the various teams are able to access high quality managers and practitioners.

www.mangroupplc.com

Market for control

The possibility of a hostile takeover bid for the control of a PUBLIC COMPANY supposedly keeps the incumbent directors on their toes. The market for control is well developed in the UK and the United States, but less so in continental Europe and elsewhere in the world. In these countries, legislators believe that aggressive takeovers produce undesirable social costs, and boards are allowed to protect their companies (and themselves) from successful bids by using a POISON PILL.

MARKS AND SPENCER

Marks and Spencer, a long-established and successful UK retailer, announced in 2008 that Lord Burns would stand down as CHAIR-MAN and Sir Stuart Rose (the current chief executive) would be appointed executive chairman. Investors, analysts and media commentators were aghast. The company was proposing to combine the roles of chairman and CEO, in breach of the principles of the UK COMBINED CODE and contrary to the London Stock Exchange LISTING RULES. The company would have to explain officially why it had not followed the code.

Sir Stuart had worked for the company for 17 years and was recognised as having done a remarkable job in improving the company's fortunes, warding off a hostile takeover bid and strategically positioning the company for the future. The retiring chairman explained that, although the company had a lot of talent, no one was yet ready to assume the role of chief executive. The board had considered bringing in a new chief executive from outside the organisation. But the retail environment started to deteriorate in the second half of 2007 and the business needed clear leadership. He explained that the company had consulted with its ten largest SHAREHOLDERS and the ASSOCIATION OF BRITISH INSURERS, who were concerned about succession. In response to concerns, he confirmed that the board was conscious of the governance arguments that companies should split the roles of chairman and chief executive, as it was undesirable to have too much concentration of authority in one person. Moreover, the board agreed that the move would be temporary and the company would revert to the conventional model in 2011. Sir David Michels, the senior INDEPENDENT DIRECTOR, would be appointed as deputy chairman, with a clear specification of the duties of chairman and deputy chairman. An additional NON-EXECUTIVE DIRECTOR would be appointed, together with two new EXECUTIVE DIRECTORS, and the responsibilities of the group finance director and operation director would be enlarged.

MAXWELL

Robert Maxwell was born in Slovakia in 1923, grew up in poverty, fought with the Free Czech army and received the British Military Cross. He became an international publishing baron. In the early 1970s, inspectors appointed by the UK government led an inquiry into his company Pergamon Press and concluded that he was not "a person who can be relied on to exercise stewardship of a publicly-quoted company". Nevertheless, he subsequently succeeded in building a media empire including two PUBLIC COMPANIES, Maxwell Communication Corporation and Mirror Group Newspapers. Following his death in 1991 in mysterious circumstances at sea, it was alleged that he had used his dominant position as CHAIRMAN of the trustees of the group's pension funds to siphon off funds to support his other interests and that he had been involved in an illegal scheme to bolster the price of companies in the group. Eventually, the lead companies were declared insolvent and the group collapsed. Investigators estimated that £763m had been plundered from the two public companies and their pension funds to prop up Maxwell's private interests.

There are many lessons for directors in the Maxwell affair. Maxwell's leadership style was dominant: he reserved considerable power to himself and kept his senior executives in the dark. An impressive set of NON-EXECUTIVE DIRECTORS, who added respectability to the public company boards, were ill informed. Maxwell threatened LITIGATION to prevent criticism of his corporate affairs; many investigative journalists and one doctoral student received writs. The complexity of the group's organisational network, which included PRIVATE COMPANIES incorporated in tax havens with limited DISCLOSURE requirements, made it difficult to obtain a comprehensive overview of group affairs. The failings of the AUDITORS, the trustees of the Maxwell group pension fund, and the regulatory bodies were all recognised.

Meeting manipulation

Many BOARD MEETINGS call as much for political acumen and interpersonal skill as for analytical ability and rational argument. There are a number of devices which the skilful meeting manipulator uses to advantage:

- The management of the AGENDA provides an ideal opportunity: who decides what is discussed and, more significantly, what is not controls the focus of the meeting.
- Lobbying people before the meeting is an obvious trait of the meeting manipulator.
- At the start of the meeting, challenging the MINUTES of the last meeting can be used to reopen discussion of an item that was resolved against your interests last time.
- Quietly taking over the meeting, in other words hijacking the chair, can work if the CHAIRMAN is weak.
- Should the tenor of the meeting not be running in your direction, there are a number of devices to stall or refocus the debate. Talking around the subject to shift the discussion to

favourable issues is a particular skill of the meeting manipulator. Profound irrelevance is his stock in trade. But filibustering to run the discussion out of time will seldom work at board level.

■ The put-down involves the skilful introduction of doubt when responding to a proposal before the board, as in: "We discussed this matter before you joined the board and decided against ..." or "The bank would never agree with anything like that ..." These are simple examples; good put-downs can be far more sophisticated.

■ Presenting ideas in the context of other people's can be powerful: "I was inclined to believe ... until I heard X, now I wonder whether we should ..." The fact that X was advocating something quite different is irrelevant.

■ Summarising the discussion thus far can be used to emphasise favourable points and downplay others: "What the meeting seems to be saying is ..."

■ An extension of the summarising device is to predetermine the decision, preferably in Latin. For example, "We seem to have reached the decision, chairman, NEM. CON." can be suggested, whether anyone is against or not.

■ Where a discussion seems to be flowing against your interests, a challenge usually works. "On a POINT OF ORDER, chairman" is a call that, if offered with sufficient challenge and conviction, will stop an orator in full flight. Strictly, points of order are only relevant if there are standing orders covering the running of meetings, but that should not deter a skilful meeting manipulator. Argue that the discussion has strayed from the point of the agenda item, that extraneous issues are being raised, or that this discussion would be more appropriate under another item – anything to deflect the discussion.

■ The concluding item on some agendas is "any other business", but the chairman may insist that only items previously notified can be discussed and that no papers can be tabled. No matter. Use the agenda item "date of the next meeting" to introduce a new topic, explain the issue, hand out the papers, express your opinion and suggest further discussion.

- The formation of a subcommittee or informal grouping to make recommendations can also be proposed to prevent the meeting reaching an adverse decision: "We need to look into this issue with the care and attention it deserves." Make sure that the subcommittee has a majority of those who favour your idea.

- Calling for a postponement of discussion until the next meeting, on the grounds of lack of INFORMATION, the need for more reflection, or until an absent member is present, can also be used to postpone a decision that seems likely to go against your interests. Calling for an adjournment of the meeting is a heavier version of the postponement device.

- If the ARTICLES OF ASSOCIATION or the rulebook of the CORPORATE ENTITY specify a QUORUM, keep your eyes on the number of people present. A lack of a quorum will totally stymie further debate. A devout meeting manipulator may claim the lack of a quorum even when there are enough people because no one else present knows how many are actually needed.

- Hidden agendas – things that individuals want to achieve to benefit themselves or for their part of the organisation, rather than that of the whole organisation – can significantly affect the running of meetings.

- Lastly, the management of the minutes provides a crucial opportunity to manipulate a meeting.

The meeting manipulator's advice to a new director would be:

- Forget rationality and what you learned in your MBA

programme; influence not analysis is what counts in directors' meetings.

- Ignore the apparent issue on the agenda, set out to discover the cliques and cabals, find out who wields what power over whom.
- Make your presence felt, but carefully: "I wonder whether we might consider ..." not "these financials are a load of rubbish". "In my experience ..." is a better start to a contribution than "Surely everyone knows that ...".
- Propose alternatives rather than attack proposals on the table: "Another alternative might be ..." rather than "That'll never work in a month of Sundays."

(See also GAMES DIRECTORS PLAY.)

66 *There are very few regulations in law which prescribe the manner in which meetings in general must be conducted.*
Lord Citrine, *ABC of Chairmanship*, 1939

Memorandum of association

The formal, legal constitution governing a company. Typically, the memorandum will state the company's name, the location of its registered office, its objectives, that the liability of its members is limited and the amount and type of shares. Since a JOINT STOCK LIMITED LIABILITY COMPANY has a legal existence separate from its members, it is important for there to be a formal document that enables anyone contracting with the company to know its precise legal status. The memorandum, duly agreed by the founding members of the company, is filed with the companies' registration authority at the time of incorporation and any subsequent change requires the approval of the shareholders.

www.companieshouse.gov.uk

Mentor

An experienced member of a board who accepts a responsibility, usually quite informally, to induct and guide a new member into the ways of the board and the company. The relationship can enable the new director to contribute more quickly and effectively.

❝ *If you don't have financial literacy, you shouldn't be on the board.*
A director speaking to Richard Leblanc and Jim Gillies, *Inside the Boardroom*, 2005

Minutes

The formal record of a meeting, often kept by the COMPANY SEC-RETARY. Although there are no specific rules governing the content or format of minutes of BOARD MEETINGS or board subcommittee meetings, they should provide a competent and complete record of what transpired and what was decided. Should there be any future challenge, the minutes, duly approved as a true and fair report at a subsequent meeting, can be used as strong evidence of what was decided. Companies develop their own style in minute-keeping; for example, some boards note the names of the main contributors to the discussion, others do not. In some cases, it has to be admitted, the minutes are no more than a staccato record of who attended and what was decided. At the other extreme, there are minutes that are almost a verbatim report of the proceedings, complete with stage directions. The ideal lies between the two. They should contain sufficient information to capture the principal threads of the discussion, the options considered, the agreement reached and plans for action. The person responsible for writing the minutes potentially wields considerable power. (See MEETING MANIPULATION.)

Mission statement

A statement of the underlying purposes of a company, usually approved at board level. Typically, a mission statement will include references to the various STAKEHOLDERS in the business process – for example, suppliers, customers, SHAREHOLDERS, employees and, sometimes, broader societal interests. A well-developed mission statement can help a company's directors in the PER-FORMANCE ROLES of STRATEGY FORMULATION and POLICY-MAKING because it establishes the desired relationship between the company and other parties that might be affected by board decisions. The danger in a mission statement is that it can become little more than a public relations exercise, exhorting the company to do well by all its stakeholders, despite inevitable conflicts of interest, and without establishing the company's actual mission. (See also CORE VALUES.)

MITTAL

Mittal's hostile takeover of steelmakers Arcelor in 2006, after a long battle, produced the world's largest steel company, with 330,000 employees and earnings of over $15 billion. Arcelor was incorporated in Luxembourg and adopted European governance with a supervisory, TWO-TIER BOARD. The founding family still played the dominant role in Mittal. During the takeover defence, Arcelor criticised Mittal because its UNITARY BOARD had many Mittal family members and few INDEPENDENT DIRECTORS.

In the merged Arcelor Mittal, the Mittal family retained 43.5% of the VOTING RIGHTS. The new board had 18 members, with Joseph Kinsch as CHAIRMAN (formerly chairman of Arcelor), Lakshmi Mittal as PRESIDENT, nine independent directors, as well as employee representative directors and nominee directors to reflect the interests of significant SHAREHOLDERS. The CEO and CFO were Mittal family members.

www.arcelormittal.com

Monitoring management

Monitoring and supervising executive management is one of the principal parts of a board's work. Indeed, many boards devote the majority of their time to this activity, sometimes to the detriment of the PERFORMANCE ROLES. A problem in monitoring management activity is striking the right balance between making sure that management is pursuing the policies and plans agreed by the board and avoiding domination of executive decision-making. Monitoring management activities is often financially oriented, using data generated by internal management accounting systems and executive information systems. But financial measures can overemphasise short-term performance to the detriment of the board's responsibility for the longer-term development of the business. Increasingly, boards are seeing that they need non-financial measures of performance on matters such as customer satisfaction, product development and employee morale. It is also important not to rely solely on routine and standard performance reports. Briefings and presentations from non-board executives can be valuable sources of orientation and INFORMATION for directors, particularly OUTSIDE DIRECTORS. Effective NON-EXECUTIVE DIRECTORS, a tough-minded CHAIRMAN and a professional BOARD STYLE can prevent the complaint that EXECUTIVE DIRECTORS are monitoring their own performance. (See also EXECUTIVE SUPERVISION.)

Myners Report

A report on British pension fund investment. Its author, Paul Myners, accused NON-EXECUTIVE DIRECTORS of failing to stand up to executives and suggested that they should meet formally with the five or six largest INSTITUTIONAL INVESTORS once a year, without company executives in attendance. The report called for a review of the role of the non-executive director, which led to the HIGGS REPORT.

NAPF

See NATIONAL ASSOCIATION OF PENSION FUNDS.

National Association of Corporate Directors

A non-profit membership organisation in the United States founded in 1977 to serve the CORPORATE GOVERNANCE needs of corporate boards and individual board members. The National Association of Corporate Directors (NACD) produces research and benchmarking data, publishes guides and has called for a common corporate governance code. It has identified ten core principles, including a split between CHAIRMAN and CEO (see DUALITY).

National Association of Pension Funds

The leading voice of workplace pensions in the UK, with over 1,300 INSTITUTIONAL INVESTOR members, between them providing pensions to over 10m working people, and with combined assets in excess of £800 billion. The National Association of Pension Funds (NAPF) has taken a higher profile in CORPORATE GOVERNANCE issues in recent years, monitoring company activities against codes of good corporate governance conduct, occasionally advising on SHAREHOLDER activism and PROXY VOTING options. (See ASSOCIATION OF BRITISH INSURERS and SHAREHOLDER POWER.)

www.napf.co.uk

❝ *Communication is key. In the past companies have not understood shareholders. They in turn have wondered why a company hasn't explained its actions adequately in its annual report.*
David Gould, NAPF

Nem. con.

Short for *nemine contradicente*, literally that no one is speaking against, or unanimous (see MEETING MANIPULATION).

NETWORK RAIL

In 1994, John Major's Conservative government privatised the railway system, which had long been run by the state enterprise British Railways, later British Rail. Companies were granted rights to run train services over various routes, and a public company, Railtrack, was incorporated to control the entire railway infrastructure (tracks, signals, bridges, tunnels and some stations). Over the next few years, Railtrack was criticised for its poor performance in maintaining and developing the rail infrastructure and the spiralling costs of new projects. The strategy of having a single company to run the rail network, which was used by all the train operators, was questioned. Its safety record was also poor. Following a second fatal crash, Railtrack's board of directors was said to have been near panic.

By 2001, Railtrack had reached a level of indebtedness which left it no longer financially viable without repeated subsidy from the taxpayer. But by now the government had changed. In October 2001 the secretary of state for transport, Stephen Byers, called for Railtrack to be put into administration on the grounds of its insolvency. Critics accused the government of deliberately bankrupting the company to partially renationalise the railway system, bringing the infrastructure back under state control. No compensation was offered to the SHAREHOLDERS, because the company was insolvent and the privatisation legislation administration called for such a move. A year later, the government created a new company to run Britain's rail infrastructure, Network Rail, which was incorporated as a private COMPANY LIMITED BY GUARANTEE, but with the governance standards of a public limited company. The company had over 100 guarantor "members" (not shareholders), who represented the rail industry, the Department for Transport and the public. The company explained that it was a "not for dividend company", that it operated as a commercial business directly accountable to its members, who received the annual report and accounts, attended the AGM, approved the appointment of directors and AUDITORS and could remove senior executives. However, some of the members complained that management was not really accountable to anyone. "There is a democratic deficit," wrote Lord Berkeley, a member representing the rail freight industry. He proposed a new board with fewer "governors" who would have wider powers to supervise management.

New York Stock Exchange Listing Rules

The CORPORATE GOVERNANCE debacles of ENRON and WORLDCOM shook the complacent view that the United States had corporate governance systems that the rest of the world could well emulate. The SARBANES-OXLEY ACT introduced some significant legislative changes. The New York Stock Exchange (NYSE) adopted the act's requirements and added further changes to corporate governance standards in its *Listing Manual*.

Some essential elements of the new requirements were:

- CEOs should certify each year that there are no violations of the NYSE listing standards.
- The board must have a majority of INDEPENDENT DIRECTORS.

- Boards must convene regular sessions for non-management directors to meet without executives present.
- A company must have an AUDIT COMMITTEE, NOMINATION COMMITTEE and REMUNERATION COMMITTEE consisting solely of independent directors.
- The CHAIRMAN of the audit committee must have an accounting or financial background.
- The audit committee must have sole responsibility for hiring and firing the company's outside independent auditors and for approving any non-audit work done by the audit firm.
- Independent directors must have no material relationship with the company; their companies must not do significant business with the company; and candidates may not join a board if they have worked for the company in the past five years.
- A five-year cooling off period is required before a former employee of the company or its auditor can be considered independent.
- Companies must adopt and disclose corporate governance guidelines on director qualifications, director responsibilities, director access to management, DIRECTOR REMUNERATION, director continuing education, management succession and provide an annual review of BOARD PERFORMANCE.
- SHAREHOLDERS must be given more opportunity to monitor and participate in the governance of companies .
- SHAREHOLDER approval is needed for SHARE OPTION plans.
- Companies should establish orientation programmes for new board members and encourage continuing director education

www.nyse.com

❝ *New directors should be equipped with an aggressive curiosity and a sensitive bullshit detector. They need a bit of scepticism that allows them to take unsentimental looks at the facts. They need their own data sources, access to information to get a realistic picture. They often get insulated and think they owe the CEO. They forget it is the shareholders they are supposed to represent.*
Jay Marshall, AlixPartners, 2002

Nomad

See next entry.

Nominated adviser

The rule book of the Alternative Investment Market (AIM) of the London Stock Exchange requires each company applying for listing to appoint an experienced firm as its nominated adviser (nomad). The nomad is responsible for making sure that the company is appropriate for the AIM and that it is compliant with the AIM's rules.

Nomination committee

A subcommittee of the main board, made up wholly, or mainly, of independent OUTSIDE DIRECTORS, which makes recommendations on new appointments to the board. It is an attempt to prevent the board becoming a cosy club, in which the incumbent members appoint like-minded people to join their ranks. A check-and-balance mechanism designed to reduce the possibility of a DOMINANT DIRECTOR, such as the CHAIRMAN or CEO, pushing through their own candidates. Nomination committees are required in British and American LISTED COMPANIES. Unfortunately, the supposedly independent outside directors forming the committee are sometimes themselves the choice of the chairman or CEO. Nevertheless, if the board is to work together as a tough-minded, effective team, it is just as well that they know each other. In the UK, although listed companies have adopted most of the requirements of the COMBINED CODE, the requirement to have a nomination committee has been resisted by a few. This is not surprising: the right to appoint to the board goes to the very heart of corporate power.

❝ *I am not happy with co-options to the board by the incumbent directors to fill casual vacancies that are put to the AGM merely for confirmation.*
John Charkham, formerly chairman of PRONED

Nominee director

A director who is acting as a nominee for a major SHAREHOLDER or other STAKEHOLDER, such as a venture capitalist or a bank investing in the company. The position of nominee directors can be fraught with difficulty, because all directors have a primary duty to act for the good of the entire body of shareholders and not to take the part of any particular interested party. Furthermore, directors have a duty not to disclose privileged INFORMATION unless it is available to the whole body of shareholders. In practice it is important for a director who has been nominated and appointed to represent specific interests that his position is understood by the other directors. A director who receives confidential information, which is not available to the shareholders, must respect that confidentiality. Should a seriously contentious situation arise, a nominee director would be well advised to seek legal advice.

Non-executive director

A member of the board who is not employed by the company as an executive. The term is widely used in the UK and other countries in the Commonwealth such as Australia, Hong Kong and Singapore. In the United States the term more frequently used is OUTSIDE DIRECTOR. A basic tenet of good CORPORATE GOVERNANCE is that the non-executive directors provide a check-and-balance mechanism on the EXECUTIVE DIRECTORS. To achieve that, however, the non-executive directors also need to be independent of the company. In other words, they should have no relationship with the company, other than the directorship, that could be seen to influence the exercise of objective, independent judgment. This means that a director acting as a nominee for a major SHAREHOLDER or a bank, or someone linked to a firm in the company's ADDED-VALUE CHAIN such as a supplier or a distributor, a family member of the chief executive, or a past employee of the company cannot be seen to be independent. There may be a good case for such people to serve on the board as non-executive directors, but they cannot be seen to be independent. Particular challenges for non-executive directors are finding enough time to devote to the affairs of the company and knowing enough about the company's business and board-level issues.

www.nonexecutivedirector.co.uk, www.uk.experian.com,
www.independentdirector.co.uk

“ Non-executive directors are the general manager's pet rocks.
Ross Perot

“ Non-executive directors are like bidets. No one knows what they are for but they add some class.
Michael Grade, prominent non-executive director

❝ What we want are non-executive directors who are geese not frogs. Frogs will sit motionless in water that is heated to boiling point, unaware of their situation, and taking no action until their ultimate demise. Geese, as in Rome, honk loudly at impending crisis.

Christopher (Kit) McMahon, when deputy governor of the Bank of England

❝ Relying on part-time outsiders is dangerous nonsense. The idea has come about that in some manner non-executive directors can second-guess the executives. Of course they can't. The commercial world would be in a far healthier state if all directors in listed companies worked within the business.

Lord Young, president, Institute of Directors, formerly a Conservative cabinet minister and chairman, Cable and Wireless

Non-profit entity

Non-profit enterprises, or as some prefer not-for-profit organisa-tions (recognising that enterprises for profit do not always make a profit), may be incorporated formally as COMPANIES LIMITED BY GUARANTEE. Almost all the material in this book will be relevant to their directors. Others may be created as trusts, when the requirements of trust law will apply, but again many of the insights and ideas will be relevant to members of the governing body. A particular challenge to boards of non-profit entities is determining what performance measures are appropriate, given that the bottom-line profit criterion, by definition, does not apply.

Non-voting shares

Shares which carry rights to contribute to and participate in the company's financial affairs but not the right to vote in company meetings. Such shares are not common and are usually offered to outside investors in companies in which existing SHAREHOLDERS want to retain their dominant control. Non-voting shares are not allowed under the LISTING RULES of most stock exchanges.

NORTHERN ROCK

The previous run on a British bank had been in the 19th century, but in September 2007 there was a run on Northern Rock. Formerly a British building society (savings and loan association), Northern Rock was incorporated in 1997 and floated on the London Stock Exchange. It grew dramatically, becoming the UK's fifth largest mortgage lender with around 800,000 home-owner borrowers and 1.5m depositors with savings of some £28 billion. In July 2007, Adam Applegarth, the CEO, wrote:

Operationally Northern Rock had a good first half in 2007. Mortgage lending has been particularly strong with a gross market share of 9.7% and a net market share of 18.9% ... Credit quality remains robust.

But he added, more ominously:

The outlook for the full year is being impacted by sharp increases in money market and swap rates ... This has resulted in a negative impact on net interest income as mortgage pricing in the market generally has lagged behind increases in funding costs in the year to date. [However] the medium term outlook for the company is very positive.

Within three months Northern Rock could not meet its financial obligations. The Bank of England provided an emergency facility to prop it up. The company urged its savers not to panic. Predictably, they did. Savers, many elderly, waited in line for hours to withdraw their savings. Northern Rock had been hit by the financial world's reluctance to lend short-term, as other institutions hoarded cash to cope with the fallout from defaulting subprime mortgage loans in the United States. Why did this happen? Where was the board of directors?

Classically banks lend long-term to house owners against mortgages on their property and borrow short-term from personal savers, who trust the bank to repay their funds with little or no notice. Northern Rock leveraged this classical model by borrowing additional funds from the money market. Some of its loans were then securitised and traded on the swap market. This worked well when interest rates were low and funds were readily available. As a result Northern Rock's business grew, until the funds famine produced a crisis. The board had 12 members: the CHAIRMAN, the chief executive, four EXECUTIVE DIRECTORS and six NON-EXECUTIVE DIRECTORS. The company had an AUDIT COMMITTEE, NOMINATION COMMITTEE, REMUNERATION COMMITTEE and risk committee. The CHAIRMAN was Mat Ridley, son of Viscount Ridley, who had previously been chairman. Educated at Eton and Oxford, he had a doctorate in zoology, had been a journalist on *The Economist* and is the author of several well-received books on science. The chief executive was Applegarth, who joined the company in 1980 as a graduate trainee.

The House of Commons Select Treasury Committee report into the Northern Rock affair commented:

> The non-executive members of the Board, and in particular the Chairman of the Board, the Chairman of the Risk Committee and the senior non-executive director, failed in the case of Northern Rock to ensure that it remained liquid as well as solvent, to provide against the risks that it was taking and to act as an effective restraining force on the strategy of the executive members.

In February 2008 Northern Rock was nationalised and the bank came under government control. A new chief executive was appointed. Shareholders were to be recompensed at a level set by an independent panel. Alistair Darling, the Chancellor of the Exchequer, insisted that the public OWNERSHIP was temporary, before "ultimately trying to return it to the private sector".

OECD Principles

In May 1999, members of the Organisation for Economic Co-operation and Development (OECD) adopted the OECD Principles of Corporate Governance (see Appendix 3). These non-binding principles do not offer a universal CORPORATE GOVERNANCE system but are intended to serve as a reference point for countries' own efforts to evaluate and improve their legal, institutional and regulatory framework. In essence, the OECD principles call for the corporate governance framework to:

- protect the rights of SHAREHOLDERS;
- recognise the rights of STAKEHOLDERS and encourage active co-operation between companies and stakeholders in creating wealth, jobs and sustainable firms;
- ensure timely and accurate DISCLOSURE on all material matters affecting the company, including the financial situation, performance, OWNERSHIP and governance of the company;
- require the board to direct the company's strategy, monitor management effectively and be accountable to the shareholders.

www.oecd.org

Outside director

A term used in North America to describe a member of the board who is not an executive employee of the company. The term NON-EXECUTIVE DIRECTOR is used in the UK and most

Commonwealth jurisdictions. An outside director should be a genuine outsider, that is, someone who is independent of the company, with no relationships (other than the directorship) that might be seen to affect the exercise of objective, independent judgment.

❝ *But what about the board? These guys were the illustrious guardians of the Ford Motor Company. They were supposed to constitute checks and balances to prevent flagrant abuse of power by top management. But it seems to me their attitude was: "As long as we're taken care of, we'll follow the leader." ... There's one mystery I want to unravel before I die: How can those board members sleep at night?*

Lee Iacocca in *Iacocca: An Autobiography*, with William Novak, 1984

❝ *The control of a large corporation is such a complex job and requires such constant attention that the outside board member, who has his own affairs to look after, can know very little about the business – too little on the whole to be useful as an outsider ... And an outside director in a large corporation cannot know enough to be specific, he must remain a figurehead.*

Peter Drucker, *Concept of the Corporation*, 1945

Overseas incorporation

Companies listed on a stockmarket are sometimes incorporated in another country. In Hong Kong, the majority of FAMILY COMPANIES that are listed are incorporated in tax havens such as Bermuda or the Cayman Islands. In London, over 100 companies on the Alternative Investment Market (AIM) are incorporated in the Channel Islands. Benefits of overseas incorporation include a lower tax burden, greater freedom to run the company, and relief from takeover and merger legislation. The requirement to disclose financial information and beneficial OWNERSHIP is typically less, and sometimes non-existent.

Ownership

Ownership is the basis of power in the Anglo-American concept of the corporation. Formally, the SHAREHOLDER members of the company nominate and appoint the directors, who have a duty to exercise stewardship over the corporation for the benefit of the shareholders and to be accountable to them. Reality can be rather different. In large, PUBLIC COMPANIES the membership is likely to be diverse, with both individual and institutional shareholders, whose objectives for dividend policy and capital growth differ and who are scattered geographically. The ability of owners to exercise power in such circumstances is severely limited. Various options have been suggested, such as TWO-TIER BOARDS with the SUPERVISORY BOARD reflecting, among other things, shareholder interests, or a CORPORATE SENATE providing an intermediary shareholder committee. Some commentators call for INSTITU-TIONAL INVESTORS to exercise their power on behalf of all the owners. STAKEHOLDER THEORY calls for a rethink of the essentially 19th-century concept of the corporation to reflect 21st-century societal needs.

" *In less than a century there is a serious question as to whether the modern corporate form has become obsolete ... How can one justify a system in which investors purchase shares in a company that is far too big and complex to permit any meaningful shareholder involvement in governance?*

Robert A.G. Monks and Nell Minow, *Power and Accountability*, 1991

Ownership chain

A string of companies, often including LISTED COMPANIES with other investors, which enables the SHAREHOLDERS at the top of the chain to exercise control over companies down the chain by leveraging their investment. The Agnelli family chain in Figure 11 on the next page enabled family interests to exercise control over Fiat.

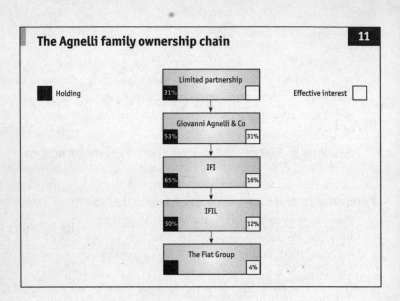

The Agnelli family ownership chain   11

Holding

Limited partnership
31%

Effective interest

Giovanni Agnelli & Co
53%   31%

IFI
65%   16%

IFIL
30%   12%

The Fiat Group
                            4%

PCAOB

See PUBLIC COMPANY ACCOUNTING OVERSIGHT BOARD.

Pensions Investment Research Consultants

A leading independent research and advice consultancy on CORPORATE GOVERNANCE and CORPORATE SOCIAL RESPONSIBILITY in the UK. Pensions Investment Research Consultants (PIRC) corporate governance services and shareholder voting guidelines provide a benchmark to INSTITUTIONAL INVESTORS, including pension funds, trade unions, banks and asset managers. PIRC has contributed significantly to shareholder activism and improved corporate governance in the UK. (See SHAREHOLDER POWER.)

www.pirc.co.uk

Performance roles

Every UNITARY BOARD is responsible for the performance of the organisation, involving STRATEGY FORMULATION and POLICY-MAKING, as well as fulfilling CONFORMANCE ROLES.

The main performance roles can be thought of as:

- **Wise man.** The board respects the wisdom of the director, who brings accumulated knowledge and experience in business and elsewhere to bear on issues facing the board. Long-serving directors may find themselves cast in this role by newer board colleagues. Accumulated wisdom can, of course, have limitations in fast-changing situations.

- **Specialist.** The director relies on his or her particular professional training, skills and knowledge to make a contribution. For example, the specialism could be in accountancy, banking, engineering, finance or law; or could stem from specialist knowledge of a particular market, technology or functional area, such as marketing, manufacturing or personnel. In some newer, growing companies OUTSIDE DIRECTORS are appointed to the board specifically to provide such specialist inputs until such time as the company can afford to acquire such skills in-house at the executive level. When a board is relying on such expertise, it is important to make sure that the director remains in touch with the subject, which can sometimes prove difficult for those operating at board level.
- **Window-on-the-world.** The director is being used as a source of INFORMATION on issues relevant to board discussions. Usually this will be on matters external to the company, such as insights into market opportunities, new technologies, industry developments, financial and economic concerns or international matters. Obviously, it is essential that the information is relevant, accurate and current. This is often a role specifically sought from outside directors, who are in a position to obtain such information through their day-to-day activities. A danger is that directors chosen because of their access to specific information lose touch with it.
- **Figurehead.** The director is called on to represent the company in the external arena; for example, in meetings with fund managers and financial analysts, or in trade and industry gatherings. The CHAIRMAN of the board often takes on this responsibility, perhaps being invited to join public committees, commissions and the governing bodies of important public institutions, as well as joining the boards of other, non-competing companies. A figurehead for the

company is also increasingly important for many companies in dealing with the media.

- **Contact person.** This is an important role often played by outside directors, who are able through their personal contacts to connect the board and senior management to networks of potentially useful people and organisations. For example, the director might be needed to forge contacts in the world of politics and government; link the company with relevant banking, finance or stock exchange connections; or make introductions within industry or international trade. This role typically supplements the window-on-the-world role, but adds a more proactive dimension. Politicians are sometimes offered directorships on the assumption that they have useful contacts and influence in the corridors of power.

- **Status provider.** In the past, eminent public figures were often invited to join boards just to add status, rather than any specific contribution they could make to board deliberations. A knighthood or elevation to the House of Lords in the UK, or service as a senator in the US, almost guaranteed invitations to join PUBLIC COMPANY boards. In today's business climate, business acumen, professionalism and the ability to contribute directly to board affairs are vital. Moreover, exposure to LITIGATION deters some public figures from accepting merely honorary directorships. But even today, if a company has been experiencing some high-profile problems, it can help restore confidence if a status provider with a reputation for integrity is appointed to the board.

Peters Report

A committee set up under the auspices of the Dutch Association of Securities-Issuing Companies and the Amsterdam Stock

Exchange Association, which reported in 1997 on CORPORATE GOVERNANCE in the Netherlands, a country that uses SUPERVISORY BOARDS. The report made some 40 recommendations on the composition, task, appointment, remuneration and method of working of both the supervisory and executive boards. Better accountability, increased transparency and a more professional way of working were recommended for the Dutch system of CORPORATE GOVERNANCE.

PIRC

See PENSIONS INVESTMENT RESEARCH CONSULTANTS.

POB

See PROFESSIONAL OVERSIGHT BOARD.

Point of order

Some organisations establish formal rules for the orderly conduct of meetings. Typically, such rules provide for participants in the meeting to appeal to the CHAIRMAN on a "point of order" should they feel the rules are not being followed. (See also MEETING MANIPULATION.)

Poison pill

A device for foiling a hostile takeover. For example, the terms of a company's ARTICLES OF ASSOCIATION may include provisions that:

- reduce the voting power of any shares once a holder acquires, say, 30%;

- provide a high-return security to existing SHAREHOLDERS should a bid not be recommended by the board;
- introduce convertible stock on which the conversion terms change on an unwelcome bid.

Some jurisdictions try to outlaw poison pills to make sure there is a free MARKET FOR CONTROL.

Policymaking

Policies enable strategies to be implemented. For example, a company may need a set of market policies that lay down the ground rules on matters such as pricing, service and customer relations. Without such policies, management might well take decisions that were contrary to the STRATEGIC INTENT. A company might need:

- product policies to cover issues such as product safety, innovation and quality;
- financial policies to cover credit and debt collection, borrowing limits and gearing, spending controls and management approval limits, inventory control and working capital management;
- employment policies to lay down the criteria for worker safety, pay and conditions, and the company's attitude towards trades unions;
- enterprise RISK MANAGEMENT polices – these play a particularly important role;
- CORPORATE SOCIAL RESPONSIBILITY policies, detailing the company's commitment, for example, to minority rights, pollution control or the environment generally.

Policymaking is one of the principal elements of the board's PERFORMANCE ROLES. In business circles it is usual to talk of policies stemming from strategies; for example, a company, having decided to pursue a strategy of product differentiation, will need appropriate pricing policies, customer relations policies and product safety policies. In government circles the terms may be reversed; for example, a government talks of pursuing a policy of tax reduction through various strategies such as cutting tax rates or through higher allowances.

Portfolio analysis

A professional CORPORATE PLANNING technique which enables directors to place their product portfolio in a matrix comparing market share (and thus the ability to generate cash flow) with market potential (the likelihood of growth). Portfolio methods generated jargon. Firms were enabled, for example, to identify and distinguish their products as "stars", "cash cows", "dogs" and those with "potential". Star products had high market share and continuing potential; cash cow products also had large market shares but their life cycle was in decline, so they could be milked to provide the funds to invest in products which had potential but as yet low market share; dogs had neither current market standing nor future potential and should be removed from the portfolio. Such methods were based on a belief that all products had life cycles which should be reflected in corporate strategies. Experience has shown that although portfolio analysis can give directors some useful insights, it does not produce strategies. The theory of product life cycles was found to be too simple and, organisationally, it proved difficult to find managers who were prepared to see the profits that they had created "milked" to feed other parts of the company.

Pre-emption rights

Whenever a company offers new shares for cash, existing SHARE-HOLDERS should be offered the chance to buy shares in proportion

to their existing holdings. This way existing shareholders are protected from an erosion of their capital and their VOTING RIGHTS.
Pre-emption rights stop directors issuing shares to third parties,
perhaps at a discount to the current market price, against the will
of their existing shareholders.

President

A title often held in conjunction with that of CHAIRMAN. The
precise responsibilities and powers vary considerably. It is used
more widely in American companies than elsewhere.

Président directeur-général

The powerful sole head of many French companies in which the
UNITARY BOARD is normal but not mandatory.

Presiding director

See BOARD CORPORATE GOVERNANCE POLICIES and GENERAL
ELECTRIC.

Principles-based corporate governance

CORPORATE GOVERNANCE in the UK and in Commonwealth
countries whose company law is rooted in British law (Australia,
Canada, India, Singapore, South Africa, for example) is based on
the principle of "comply or explain". In other words, companies
abide by a code of corporate governance principle or practice, but
where they do not, they must explain the reason in their corporate
governance report. By contrast, the American approach to corporate governance calls for obeying the law. (See RULE-BASED COR-
PORATE GOVERNANCE and SARBANES-OXLEY ACT.)

Private company

Many company law jurisdictions differentiate between a PUBLIC COMPANY and a private company. Private companies, typically, are not allowed to invite the public to subscribe for shares and have to limit the number of SHAREHOLDERS (50 in the UK). In recognition of their special status, the regulatory requirements for private companies, for example on the filing and DISCLOSURE of information, are less demanding. Some jurisdictions recognise a further subcategory of private company for small companies or CLOSELY HELD COMPANIES, in which the owners, directors and managers are closely related, giving further concessions such as relaxing AUDIT requirements if all the shareholders agree. The majority of private companies are small but there are a few large ones. Many are subsidiaries of other companies but some are private companies, including John Lewis (owned by the employees) and Virgin Atlantic (owned by Sir Richard Branson and Singapore Airlines). As a result of the activities of PRIVATE EQUITY FUNDS, delistings from the stockmarket have produced some large private companies in recent years, such as Boots in the UK.

Private equity funds

Private equity funds have significant capital to invest in the acquisition of limited companies, including LISTED COMPANIES, which may be taken private thus avoiding the PUBLIC COMPANY disclosure requirements. Private equity firms seek capital for their funds mainly from INSTITUTIONAL INVESTORS. Some states restrict investment in such funds to accredited investors who are able to shoulder the risk. Before the sub-prime lending crisis in 2007–08, mergers and acquisition in the United States and the UK reached an all-time high. Much of this growth was a result of private equity institutions acquiring control of previously listed companies. Some commentators have felt that the acquisition of listed companies by private equity interests could dilute stockmarkets through PRIVATISATION. However, such developments could be seen as a return to the earlier 19th-century model of joint stock companies, when a handful of external shareholders invested in a public company, elected the directors and held them to account for their stewardship.

Typically, private equity firms are unregulated, other than within the company and banking regulations and laws of the relevant jurisdiction, although the Sir David Walker voluntary code calls for equity firms in the UK to publish relevant information annually or as a regular update on their websites. Calls for more transparency and greater DISCLOSURE are sometimes heard on the grounds of potential conflicts of interest, finance market stability, or public interest, particularly when a well-known listed company disappears under the veil of private equity. The response of private equity firms is, predictably, that their responsibility is to the owners of their firm and the investors in their funds. Greater exposure of their funding, strategies, or portfolios, they say, would inhibit the private deals which enable private equity to generate impressive returns while shouldering significant risk. (See BLACK-STONE GROUP.)

Privatisation

There are two different meanings:

1   The decision by the directors of a LISTED COMPANY to take it
    private again by buying back the shares in the hands of the
    public. Fortnum & Mason, a superior food and speciality
    goods store in London, after 62 years on the stockmarket,
    returned to private hands in 2001. Many PRIVATE EQUITY
    FUNDS have acquired public listed companies which they
    have then privatised, possibly for restructuring, realising
    value in various assets and, possibly, floating again.

2   The privatising of enterprises that had previously been run as nationalised industries. This is sometimes referred to as corporatisation. Often this process starts with the creation of a CORPORATE ENTITY, with a board of directors to run the business on market-oriented, profit-driven criteria, followed by privatisation with the shares floated on the stockmarket. The UK and New Zealand pioneered the process, which has been followed in many other countries. Telecommunications, power utilities, water supply, airlines, railways and shipping companies have all been privatised. In the UK, some people have suggested that privatisation has gone too far, citing problems with Railtrack (which effectively went bankrupt) and other utilities caused by the investment needed to meet public expectations and the difficulties of providing universal service, for example supplying remote areas at below true market cost. Such challenges are usually tackled by establishing a REGULATOR and through government subsidy.

The largest instance of privatisation has been in China, where many state-owned enterprises have been corporatised. Typically, a minority of the shares have been listed, the majority remaining in the hands of the State-owned Administration and Supervision Commission (SASAC), which has become the largest institutional investor in the world.

Professional Oversight Board

Oversees the regulation of the auditing profession in the UK by recognised supervisory and qualifying bodies, monitors the quality of the auditing function of economically significant entities, and provides independent oversight of the regulation of the accountancy and actuarial professions. The Professional Oversight Board (POB) is part of the UK's FINANCIAL REPORTING COUNCIL.

Proxy voting

Under typical ARTICLES OF ASSOCIATION, SHAREHOLDERS have the right to appoint proxies to vote on their behalf on the resolutions before general meetings of shareholders. In earlier times this typically meant voting on the reappointment of directors and AUDITORS, accepting the annual accounts and agreeing the dividend to be paid. In recent years, particularly in the United States and increasingly in the UK, dissatisfied shareholders have used the proxy mechanism to promote their concerns, calling for the removal of CHAIRMEN and CEOS, attacking the level of DIRECTORS' RENUMERATION and introducing other critical resolutions. If the shareholder is a company, a representative can be appointed as proxy and can attend meetings and vote.

Public company

A company that is permitted to invite the public to subscribe for its shares. By definition all companies listed on a stock exchange are public companies; but a public company need not be listed and may attract its SHAREHOLDERS, such as venture capitalists, by other means. Recognising the benefits a public company enjoys, most jurisdictions require more extensive filing, DISCLOSURE and information access than is required of a PRIVATE COMPANY. In the 19th century, in the early days of the corporate concept, all companies were public companies. Today, although public companies are usually the more significant firms and some of them are huge, they account for less than 5% of all companies.

Public Company Accounting Oversight Board

The regulating body for the American accounting profession, created by the SECURITIES AND EXCHANGE COMMISSION in

2002 following the ENRON and WORLDCOM debacles. The Public Company Accounting Oversight Board (PCAOB) is independent of the accounting firms, thus effectively ending the American accounting profession's long-established system of self-regulation.

www.sec.gov

Quango

The move towards cost-effectiveness in government has led to developments such as corporatisation, PRIVATISATION and outsourcing. One result has been the creation of various quasi-governmental institutions to facilitate, monitor and regulate these activities. Quango is an acronym for quasi-autonomous non-governmental organisation. Typically, the organisation has its own facilitating legislation, which defines and creates the entity and determines its governance processes, including its mission and accountability, the form of its governing body and how the directors are appointed, which is often by the government or state agencies. Examples include the Federal National Mortgage Association (Fannie Mae), which was created by the US government to provide home financing for low- and middle-income families.

Quango is also used, particularly in the UK and Australia, as an acronym for quasi-autonomous national governmental organisation to describe organisations to which governments have devolved power, but in which they retain a direct influence. Examples include the UK's Vehicle Certification Agency of the Department for Transport and the Job Centres of the Department for Work and Pensions. Many of the issues of CORPORATE GOVERNANCE discussed in this book apply to the members of such boards, committees and councils, even though they may not have the formal title of director.

Quorum

The minimum number of members who need to be present, under the ARTICLES OF ASSOCIATION or other rules of a CORPORATE ENTITY, to make a meeting quorate, thus legitimising it (see MEETING MANIPULATION).

Rr

Regulator

Every company law jurisdiction needs a country or state-wide registrar to make sure that companies are properly incorporated, are listed on the company register, and continue to meet the various requirements to avoid being struck off, such as filing periodic returns and financial reports. The company registrar provides one of the basic controls in CORPORATE GOVERNANCE. PUBLIC COMPANIES listed on a stock exchange need a state financial regulatory body, such as the SECURITIES AND EXCHANGE COMMISSION in the United States and the FINANCIAL REPORTING COUNCIL in the UK. The listing committee of the relevant stock exchange also exercises a regulatory function ensuring compliance through their LISTING RULES. State regulators may also be necessary where state utilities and other state business enterprises have been privatised.

❝❝ *Federal law in the United States has much less to say on the duties of company boards than on day-care centres.*
Nell Minow, www.thecorporateboard.com

Regulatory capture

A too close relationship between a regulatory body and the profession, industry or company it is regulating, which can erode the independence and objectivity of the REGULATOR.

Related party transaction

A business transaction between a company and a party closely related to it, such as a director or a major SHAREHOLDER; for example, the purchase by the company of a property from one of its directors. The LISTING RULES of most stock exchanges require related party transactions to be disclosed and, often, approved by the other shareholders.

Relationship investor

An INSTITUTIONAL INVESTOR who takes a significant, long-term stake in a listed company with a view to being closely involved with a close relationship with the board. A good example is Warren Buffett, whose Berkshire Hathaway Fund invests in a handful of companies for the long term, intending to exercise some influence over the company. Sometimes the relationship investor will have a NOMINEE DIRECTOR on the board. Some might argue that relationship investing represents a return to the original concept of SHAREHOLDER democracy and power; others note that a relationship investor is able to influence the board while the other shareholders lack that INSIDE INFORMATION and influence.

66 *Relationship investing contrasts sharply with the stereotype of the American shareholder who is depicted as an off-track bettor with no interest in the horse beyond the results for the daily race. "Betting slip" shareholding is not a promising base for responsible ownership. The combined status of ownership and commercial relationship gives particular investors a sufficiently significant stake to ensure an effective presence.*

Robert Monks

❝ *I've always said my favourite time frame for holding a stock is forever. I don't buy stocks with the idea of selling them unless I'm in arbitrage ... I only invest in companies within my circle of competence: I don't mind missing opportunities from firms I don't understand.*

Warren Buffett, Berkshire Hathaway Fund

❝ *A good director is one who has a meaningful financial stake in the venture ... [as] there is nothing that makes a director think like a shareholder more than being a shareholder.*

Warren Buffett, Berkshire Hathaway Fund

Remuneration committee

A committee of the main board, consisting wholly or mainly of independent OUTSIDE DIRECTORS, with responsibility for overseeing the remuneration packages of board members and, possibly, members of senior management. DIRECTORS' RENUMERATION remains a concern around the world. The problem is how to provide sufficient incentive to directors, rewarding success, while avoiding the label FAT CAT. Even a remuneration committee, composed entirely of outside directors, may not be thought independent if its members were nominated by the CHAIRMAN or CEO and are themselves senior executives of other companies. Moreover, if the independent members on the remuneration committee are EXECUTIVE DIRECTORS in other companies they may have a personal interest in inflating the level of director rewards.

❝ *Shareholders should have access to details of directors' remuneration. This would end the charade of "you come on my board and I'll come on yours" – or rather "you come on my remuneration committee and I'll go on yours".*

Lord Young, president, Institute of Directors, formerly a Conservative cabinet minister and chairman, Cable and Wireless

Remuneration racheting

Directors can use a number of arguments to justify high board-level rewards. These include the following:

- **International comparator.** "To ensure that our company attracts and holds executive directors of the calibre we need against international competition, we have to give rewards that are broadly comparable to those they could obtain in the industry anywhere in the world." This argument is advanced even if the directors concerned have never been headhunted in their lives and whether or not they have any possibility of working abroad.

- **Headhunter.** "We have just recruited a new EXECUTIVE DIRECTOR and the headhunters assured us that he had to receive a package that is 30% more than that of the highest paid director. Of course, we all had to have an increase to maintain differentials." This argument conveniently overlooks the fact that the headhunter's fee is based on 30–35% of the first year's salary of the new appointee.

- **Top of the industry.** "Our firm prides itself on being one of the leaders in the industry, even though at the moment we are not among the most profitable. We expect to pay our directors in the upper quartile of the industry range as shown by the comparator pay research." This argument ignores the performance of the firm or the directors.

- **Fear of loss.** "We could lose our directors to the competition unless we pay competitive rates." This argument is sometimes advanced even though the directors concerned are within a year or two of retirement and would be of absolutely no interest to competitors.

- **Doubling up the bonus.** "We believe that it is important for directors' rewards to be performance-related. Moreover, we expect excellent performance in both the short and the long term. So we calculate bonuses on the annual profits, then we have a parallel three-year scheme which rewards directors if earnings per share grow by 30% over that period." This way the directors get rewarded twice on the same performance, inflation is ignored and there is no upside cap should there be exceptional circumstances. Moreover, directors do not get penalised for poor performance.

In the UK, the United States and some other countries there are now specialist consultants offering advice to companies on appropriate levels of reward. Some also advise the fund managers of INSTITUTIONAL INVESTORS who increasingly monitor DIRECTORS' RENUMERATION and take action when it seems out of line. (See also REMUNERATION COMMITTEE.)

Representative board

A board whose members are nominated by specific SHAREHOLDERS to represent their interests. In the case of a CORPORATE ENTITY without shareholders, such as a not-for-profit entity, the board may well be appointed to represent the interests of members; for example, the committee of a Canadian agricultural co-operative has members representing growers, buyers and sources of finance. Representative boards are frequently found in non-profit entities where the directors are elected to serve the interests of various interest groups – for example, in a UK hospital trust, to represent patients, doctors, nursing staff, the health authority and the local community.

Representative director

See NOMINEEE DIRECTOR and JAPANESE CORPORATE GOVERNANCE.

Responsibilities of directors

See FIDUCIARY DUTY and DUTY OF CARE.

Risk management

Successful business involves taking risks. Risk can arise at the strategic, managerial and operating levels. Most companies cover their operating-level exposure by insurance against fire, theft, accident and so on. At the managerial level a risk policy identifies and determines a response to risks such as product hazards, corporate fraud, environmental pollution, employee injuries, business interruption through fire or internet interference, as well as LITIGATION risk and reputation risk. Risks at the strategic level include exposure to challenges in the market, hostile takeover bids and significant economic, political or financial changes around the world. Every board has a duty to make sure that:

- significant risks facing the company are recognised;
- risk assessment systems operate effectively throughout the organisation;
- risk evaluation procedures are developed and work;
- risk monitoring systems are robust, efficient and effective;
- business continuity strategies and risk management policies exist, are regularly updated and applied in practice.

In establishing the company's risk policies, every board faces four possible responses to risk:

- **Avoid the risk.** Do not commit to the planned action and abandon the proposed project.
- **Mitigate the risk.** Make capital investments or incur regular expenditure by, for example, investing in standby equipment, duplicating or triplicating critical components, training staff, introducing risk policies, such as requiring senior executives

to travel in different cars and planes, or never building on flood plains or in typhoon/hurricane locations.

■ **Transfer the risk.** Spread the exposure among other parties. Insure against the risk, thereby transferring elements of risk to an insurance company, while recognising that some risks may be uninsurable. Create derivative instruments, or agreements with financial institutions that transfer risk to third parties.

■ **Retain the risk.** In other words, accept the risk. Self-insuring is an approach adopted by many governmental organisations. This risk strategy, what some commentators call the firm's risk appetite, needs to be made at board level.

The TURNBULL REPORT, now incorporated in the UK's COMBINED CODE on CORPORATE GOVERNANCE, and the 2002 SARBANES-OXLEY ACT recognise the board's responsibility for managing risk.

Rival camps

See GAMES DIRECTORS PLAY.

Roles for directors

Although all directors have the same responsibility to act for the good of the company, in practice different members of the board play different roles according to their knowledge, experience and expertise. A balanced board will have members appointed for the different qualities they can bring to the job, whether they are technical skills, knowledge or good contacts. (See CONFORMANCE ROLES and PERFORMANCE ROLES.)

Rubber-stamp board

A form of BOARD STYLE in which the directors act solely to confirm decisions taken by executive management or the HOLDING COMPANY in a group.

Rule-based corporate governance

Years ago, experts wrote about the Anglo-American (or Anglo-Saxon) model of CORPORATE GOVERNANCE. Indeed, there are still many similarities between the United States and the UK and Commonwealth countries: UNITARY BOARDS with independent OUTSIDE DIRECTORS, AUDIT COMMITTEES, NOMINATION COMMITTEES and REMUNERATION COMMITTEES, and company law based on common law. But in the United States, governance is regulated by legal statute and mandatory rules, which are inherently inflexible. LITIGATION levels are high. Directors face legal penalties for non-compliance. The 2002 SARBANES-OXLEY ACT strengthened this emphasis on governance under penalty of law. The American model has become rule-based, with the regulators asking "is this legal?", whereas the UK model remains principles-based, with the regulators asking "is this right?". (See PRINCIPLES-BASED CORPORATE GOVERNANCE.)

Safe harbour

A provision in a contract, regulations or law that protects a party that has performed its duties in good faith. Used, for example, in a company flotation when DUE DILIGENCE tests have been properly carried out, even though circumstances change and the flotation fails.

Safety valve

One of the roles a director can play (see CONFORMANCE ROLES).

Sarbanes-Oxley Act

A law rushed through in the United States in 2002 after a series of CORPORATE GOVERNANCE scandals including ENRON and WORLDCOM. The rules are regulated by the SECURITIES AND EXCHANGE COMMISSION and are incorporated into the listing requirements of American stock exchanges. They apply to all companies quoted in the United States, including overseas companies whose shares are available there. CEOs and CFOS are required to certify under oath that their financial statements neither contain an "untrue statement" nor omit any "material fact". AUDIT COMMITTEES must have totally INDEPENDENT DIRECTORS. AUDITORS are not allowed to undertake lucrative non-AUDIT work. The PUBLIC COMPANY ACCOUNTING OVERSIGHT BOARD was created.

The Sarbanes-Oxley Act (SOX) has been criticised as an over-reaction and condemned as extraterritorial legislation by overseas companies listed in the United States. The cost of compliance has proved to be much higher than expected, particularly compliance with s404, which requires director certification and independent confirmation that appropriate management control systems are in place. Lawyers and auditors may be the main beneficiaries of the act.

SASAC

See STATE-OWNED ASSETS SUPERVISION AND ADMINISTRATION COMMISSION.

SEC

See SECURITIES AND EXCHANGE COMMISSION.

Secret profit

A director must not make a secret profit out of dealings with the company, for example through private interests in a contract in which the company is involved. Directors have a duty to disclose any such interests to the board and to abide by their decision as to what is in the company's best interest.

Securities and Exchange Commission

An American body set up in 1934 to protect SHAREHOLDERS from overambitious company promoters and unscrupulously powerful, incumbent boards. Over the years the DISCLOSURE, regulatory and investigative processes of the Securities and Exchange Commission (SEC) have increased and the United States now has the most expensive (and the most litigious) corporate regulatory regime in the world. The belief of many Americans that their corporate regulatory system was the envy of the world and should be widely adopted elsewhere took a serious knock following the ENRON and WORLDCOM debacles. After the sub-prime lending crisis in 2007–08 consideration was given to reviewing and possibly amalgamating a number of regulators in the finance industry, including the SEC.

❝ *Q. How should America's securities law be reformed?*
A. By a simple two-part law.
Section one: it shall be unlawful.
Section two: the SEC shall have the power to define "it".
Harvey Pitt, chairman, SEC

Senate

See CORPORATE SENATE.

Shadow director

Occasionally, a person exercises power over a company's affairs but is not on the board. Although not formally a director, the other board members operate in his shadow. Often this is the founder and significant SHAREHOLDER, who remains in the shadows to escape the DISCLOSURE requirements of directorship. In some jurisdictions shadow directors can be held responsible for their actions as though they actually were directors.

Share option

The right to buy a share at a predetermined price some time in the future. Share options (stock options is the American term) are often awarded to directors as part of DIRECTORS' RENUMERATION to provide an incentive and reward for performance, enabling the recipient to exercise the right after the share price has risen. Options are typically given to EXECUTIVE DIRECTORS, although HERMES, one of the UK's largest fund managers, has suggested that NON-EXECUTIVE DIRECTORS in the UK should receive half their remuneration in shares. In the United States it is standard practice to issue stock options to OUTSIDE DIRECTORS. Consequently, there is a big difference in remuneration levels for non-executive directors in the UK and the United States. Share options can prove a strong incentive to directors, but that includes a strong incentive to bolster the firm's share price. Options played a part in the downfall of ENRON and WORLDCOM. Some disadvantages of options are as follows:

- **Reloading.** If a company gives new options, whenever they are exercised, executives can play the market, irrespective of their performance.
- **Resetting.** Share options are unattractive on a falling stockmarket, so some companies lower the bid price of their directors' options – hardly an incentive to perform.
- **Rewarding mediocrity.** A good incentive would reward better-than-average performance, but option prices include general rises in the market.

In the past some countries accounted for options as though they were free. However, as extra shares are issued other holdings are diluted. Options taken up by directors (and other employees) have a value, hence they have a cost, which should be reflected in the company's accounts. There is no respectable argument against this principle, which is now incorporated into most accounting standards, requiring the valuation of the discounted future value of options and charging the cost against profits.

❝ *Options are a one-way bet. If a company's share price goes up, the holder of the options can make a serious fortune. If the share price falls, the holder of the option doesn't lose a penny. Nothing risked, everything to gain.*
Sunday Times, November 2002

Shareholder

The owner of shares in a company. A company's ARTICLES OF ASSOCIATION may authorise various classes of share, including ordinary shares, preference shares (which give preferential rights to dividend and/or on winding-up) and other more specialised types of shares. The shareholder VOTING RIGHTS attached to each class of share determine the potential governance power in the company. Company law lays down the information that must be provided to all shareholders. Traditionally, this was delivered in printed prospectuses, regular directors' reports and financial accounts, and other required notices; but increasingly communication can be through electronic means. (See also DUAL VOTING RIGHTS.)

Shareholder activism

See SHAREHOLDER POWER.

Shareholder democracy

Traditionally, ownership of shares is the basis of power in a JOINT STOCK LIMITED LIABILITY COMPANY. Normally the ARTICLES OF ASSOCIATION provide SHAREHOLDERS, voting on resolutions before shareholder meetings, with one vote for each share they hold. Although many refer to this as shareholder democracy, in reality it is shareholder plutocracy – power exercised according to wealth. In a democracy the people (*demos*) have one vote each. There have been calls for power over companies to be exercised in this way. (See CORPORATE SENATE.)

However, despite having votes, shareholders in many LISTED COMPANIES, particularly in the United States, have limited power to determine membership of the board and affect corporate decisions. Some have called on INSTITUTIONAL INVESTORS to work together to exercise the proxy power of their votes. Others look to HEDGE FUNDS to acquire a stake sufficient to have a representative director on the board. Other ideas for improving SHARE-HOLDER POWER through shareholder watchdog boards have included a shareholder panel, proposed by the Auditing Practices Board in London, a CORPORATE GOVERNANCE board, proposed in the Australian Senate, and a conflicts board, proposed in the United States in the University of Michigan's *Journal of Law Reform.*

www.aph.gov.au/senate, www.corpmon.com, www.corpwatch.com, www.
shareholderaction.org

Shareholder power

In a private CLOSELY HELD COMPANY the SHAREHOLDERS and the directors are often close, even the same people, and consequently the shareholders can readily influence board decisions. However, individual shareholders in PUBLIC COMPANIES seldom have real power in governance matters. In the major LISTED COM-PANIES, shareholdings are widely dispersed and geographically spread. Even with shareholder interest groups and better opportunities to communicate with the other members, individual investors usually lack the position, prestige or power to influence an incumbent CHAIRMAN and his board. RELATIONSHIP INVESTORS seek to overcome this problem. But an INSTITUTIONAL INVESTOR, even with a small holding, may be able to influence boards, particularly if it acts in concert with others. However, the interests of different types of institutional investors do not necessarily coincide; for example, some may be looking for a quick profit while others want to take a longer-term view. There is also the potential problem if institutional investors get too close to the board that share-price-sensitive INSIDE INFORMATION may be obtained (see, for example, CALPERS, HERMES and PIRC).

www.corpmon.com, www.corpwatch.com, www.shareholderaction.org

❝ *Electronic reporting will become the norm for companies, enfranchising the ultimate owners of capital, leading to cheaper costs of capital and ultimately driving a democratisation of shareholder relations.*
Paul Myners, chairman, Gartmore Investment Management

Shareholder value

The boards of many LISTED COMPANIES are committed to maximising the value of their SHAREHOLDERS' equity, a commitment reinforced by the HAMPEL REPORT. But the measurement and management of shareholder value are not a straightforward accounting calculation. There are a number of methodologies used, including value-based management (VBM), economic value added (EVA) and shareholder value added (SVA). But, essentially, all measurements of shareholder added-value recognise that historical, profit-based measures fail to take into account the cost of the capital that has been used and offer variations on measures of the present value of future cash flows, discounted at the average cost of capital. Trends in share prices and dividend payouts are often taken as a short-term surrogate for shareholder value. Unfortunately, the result of efforts to enhance shareholder value can lead to board-level short-termism that limits vital research and development, strips out assets and employees to meet the company's long-term goals and outsources essential functions.

Shell company

A LISTED COMPANY whose shares are not currently traded on the stock exchange. On some exchanges, if control is obtained over such a company, the listing can be used to obtain a quotation for another business enterprise, without incurring the cost and exposure of a full prospectus by "backing" the other business into the shell. This is sometimes called a backdoor listing.

SIEMENS

Siemens is Europe's largest engineering group, manufacturing a diverse range of products from power plants to home appliances, computers to railway engines. Incorporated in Germany, the company has a TWO-TIER BOARD. In 2007 the chief executive, Klaus Kleinfeld, challenged the SUPERVISORY BOARD to renew his contract or accept his resignation. The supervisory board voted no: Kleinfeld left. Previously, he had successfully run Siemens's American operations, listing the company on the New York Stock Exchange in the process. He had also been an OUTSIDE DIRECTOR on the boards of Citigroup and Alcoa, an American aluminium company. Under his guidance the Siemens Group had reported a 10% increase in revenue and a 36% increase in profits. He was internationally recognised as successful. But both the union and the SHAREHOLDER representatives on the supervisory board disliked what they saw as his aggressive American management methods, which jarred with Germany's consensual style of corporate leadership.

Moreover, although Kleinfeld was not personally involved, a fraud investigation had begun in November 2006 involving senior managers and a massive slush fund held in banks outside Germany, which was used to pay bribes to win contracts. Interestingly, the company employed an independent ombudsman to act as a channel for employees who wanted to whistle-blow about what they knew.

Sources: *The Economist*, April 28th 2007; www.siemens.com

Snowing

See GAMES DIRECTORS PLAY.

Societas Europaea

See EUROPEAN COMPANY.

SOE

See STATE-OWNED ENTERPRISE.

Sokaiya

Members of YAKUSA gangster organisations in Japan which some-times disrupt ANNUAL GENERAL MEETINGS of companies. *Sokaiya* were originally employed to make sure that no one asked awkward questions (the average length of SHAREHOLDER meet-ings in Japan is short). But sometimes disputes arise over board remuneration and trouble ensues. A famous meeting of the Sony Corporation lasted 13 hours with chairs as well as abuse being thrown. Some companies pay off the *sokaiya* to avoid disruption of their meetings, but the Japanese government clamped down on these payments to improve the image of the financial sector.

Sovereign wealth fund

Surging exports from East Asia and high oil prices in the Middle East have generated massive state surpluses. Some Arab and Asian countries, including Saudi Arabia, China and Singapore, have used these funds to invest in companies in developed countries in industries such as telecommunications, technology, real estate, ports, transport and, following the 2008 credit crisis, finance. Sovereign wealth funds raise two basic CORPORATE GOVERNANCE issues:

- They are secretive, neither stating their objectives nor disclosing their portfolios, being accountable only to their government paymasters.
- The sovereign nation may not be driven solely by economic motives. The investments could be used to exercise strategic, possibly political, power – for example, to promote or protect its own national champions; restrict competition; as a pawn in a diplomatic wrangle; to manipulate financial markets.

SOX

The acronym adopted in the United States for the SARBANES-OXLEY ACT, named after the two congressmen who sponsored it.

Special purpose entity

A legal entity created by a company to structure its finances. Legitimate reasons for setting up a special purpose entity (SPE) include the offsetting of risk, obtaining tax benefits and raising capital from partners. However, financial engineering through SPES has caused problems for setters of accounting standards, including the lack of DISCLOSURE, obscurity, and the distortion of financial statements by taking indebtedness off the parent company's balance sheet. ENRON had set up nearly 1,000 SPES, many in the Cayman Islands tax haven.

HOW AN SPE WORKS

Raptor was among the many hundreds of SPES set up by ENRON. It was a partnership with Enron executives. Enron lent Raptor $500m in Enron stock. Raptor then issued an IOU to Enron, which Enron guaranteed, promising to pay more stock if Raptor could not repay. Enron then treated this promissory note as an asset on its balance sheet. In other words, Enron had used its own equity shares on one side of its balance sheet to create an asset on the other. Raptor then borrowed funds secured on its Enron stock-holding and invested in Avici, a computer-network manufacturer. As Raptor's investments increased in value, Enron took a $500m profit, though no profit had actually been realised. Then the shares in Avici fell. Raptor moved into loss, could not repay the IOU and began to draw on the Enron guarantee. But the Enron share price was falling too, so more and more stock was needed. Eventually the whole house of cards collapsed.

Special purpose vehicle

A term frequently used in the UK for a SPECIAL PURPOSE ENTITY. (See also ENRON.)

Specialist

One of the roles a director can play (see PERFORMANCE ROLES).

Spinning

Bankers launching an INITIAL PUBLIC OFFERING of shares might "spin" an allotment to friends at beneficial prices, then, once the price had risen, "flip" the shares to less fortunate buyers. Spinning was investigated by American securities REGULATORS following the market collapse of 2000–02. (See GAMES DIRECTORS PLAY for an alternative meaning.)

Sponsorship

See GAMES DIRECTORS PLAY.

Staggered board

A board, sometimes called a classified board, whose members' terms of appointment are staggered, so that where, for example, directors' term of office is three years one-third retire each year. Staggered appointments bring greater stability to a board, allowing directors more freedom to exercise longer-term focus on strategic issues. Critics of staggered boards complain that hostile bidders cannot remove an entire board at a single election. Staggered boards, therefore, become a takeover defence, entrenching under-performing directors. Annual election allows a change of control through a single successful proxy contest. In the United States, resolutions opposing staggered boards and calling for declassification have topped shareholder activists' calls for change.

Stakeholders

Groups of those whose interests are affected by a company's activities. The primary stakeholder group recognised by law is the SHAREHOLDERS. Other stakeholders include company employees, whose rights are protected by employment law, creditors and those with non-equity financial stakes in the company, who are protected by contract law, and those in the company's ADDED-VALUE CHAIN such as suppliers, subcontractors, agents, distributors and the ultimate customers. Some add local, national and international societal interest groups to the list of stakeholders.

> *A key question currently confronting the Congress is whether something is so fundamentally wrong with the structure of corporate governance that it requires legislative remedy. In principle, corporations are run for the benefit of shareholders, within the context of laws that are designed to protect the rights of third parties. Such protections, whether for employees, the community or the environment, should not be obligations of corporate management. They are appropriately left to statute.*
>
> Alan Greenspan, Wall Street Journal

Stakeholder theory

A body of ideas pursued initially in the 1970s and early 1980s. In the *Corporate Report*, a study commissioned by British accounting bodies in 1975, it was suggested that major corporations had a duty to be accountable to all those who might be affected by their actions, including employees, suppliers, customers and communities, as well as SHAREHOLDERS. The political dimensions of the proposals resulted in considerable criticism and the shelving of the proposals.

Stakeholder thinking faded in the free-market growth ethos of the 1980s but subsequently reappeared (see TOMORROW'S COMPANY). Today, with the focus on CORPORATE SOCIAL RESPONSIBILITY, the need to recognise stakeholder interests is widely accepted.

❝❝ *Corporations capable of working in investors', stakeholders', and society's interests in a collaborative, creative and productive way would require a fundamental redesign of the concept of the corporation and the institution of the market. At this stage both prospects appear remote.*
Thomas Clarke, *International Corporate Governance: A Comparative Approach*, 2007

❝❝ *No business exists in a vacuum. We are conscious of the influence our business has on communities, throughout the UK both locally and nationally. If a community as a whole flourishes, the individual members of that community tend to flourish too.*
Sir Colin Southgate, quoted in the RSA Inquiry report, *Tomorrow's Company*

❝❝ *Stakeholders are popular normatively but shareholders are the reality.*
A director speaking to Richard Leblanc and Jim Gillies, *Inside the Boardroom*, 2005

State-owned Assets Supervision and Administration Commission

An influential Chinese state organisation overseeing China's listed enterprises, other than those in the finance sector, in which the state owns a majority holding. Eight of these are in the top 100 companies listed in the United States. The State-owned Assets Supervision and Administration Commission (SASAC) is the largest INSTITUTIONAL INVESTOR in the world. Its administration duties include being involved in the appointment of senior executives and independent NON-EXECUTIVE DIRECTORS. (See CHINESE CORPORATE GOVERNANCE.)

State-owned enterprise

A self-explanatory but perhaps misleading term. State-owned enterprises (SOEs) include nationalised businesses, entirely owned by a country. But they also include an increasingly significant number of LISTED COMPANIES in which the state retains a majority control. Chinese SOES are an example: eight are now in *Fortune's* list of 100 top companies listed in the United States. (See CHINESE CORPORATE GOVERNANCE.)

Status provider

One of the roles a director can play (see PERFORMANCE ROLES).

Stewardship theory

The original theory underpinning company law recognises that directors should be trusted to exercise a FIDUCIARY DUTY of trust towards the company, acting as stewards of the SHAREHOLDERS' interests, which they place ahead of personal ambition. Thus stewardship theory runs contrary to the ideas of AGENCY THEORY, which proposes that individual directors, given the chance, will maximise their own utility and cannot be expected to adopt a stewardship perspective if checks and balances are not put in place.

❝❝ *Saying that we work for our shareholders may sound simplistic – but we frequently see companies that have forgotten the reason they exist. They may even try to be all things to all people and serve many masters in many different ways. In any event they miss their primary calling, which is to stick to the business of creating value for their owners.*
Roberto Goizueta, former head of Coca-Cola

Stock option

See SHARE OPTION.

Strategic alliance

Strategic alliances with other companies are the preferred way for many companies to enter markets, transfer technology, procure supplies or manufacture products around the world, or share risk on an international scale. Sometimes the partners in the strategic alliance are competitors in other fields. Many alliances involve the incorporation of a joint-venture company owned by two or more partner companies. Directors of such companies are typically drawn from the senior management of the partners. Governing joint-venture companies can present special challenges. Disagreements not envisaged in the initial joint-venture agreement can arise between the partners. Directors then face conflicts of interest between their responsibilities to the joint-venture company and to the partner company that employs them. Moreover, many joint-venture companies are incorporated in foreign jurisdictions, with diverse and different company laws and regulatory regimes, and have overseas partners with different cultures.

Strategic intent

The underlying drive of a board of directors to achieve strategic success in the longer term. It might be, for example, to become the largest company in the software industry, to be the best airline in the world or to put a specific competitor out of business. Strategic intent enables a company to make the most of its CORE COMPE-TENCIES, to establish CORE VALUES throughout the organisation that unite everyone to the common goal, and to achieve better results than would have occurred had the board merely sought to fit their resources to the strategic situation.

Strategic vision

Directors need a shared perception of the future for their company, a perspective that encapsulates their aspirations for the enterprise. Some call this a strategic vision. It reflects what the board wants to achieve; the direction they want the organisation to take; where they want the enterprise to be in the future. "When you don't know where you're going, all roads lead you there." Information about the strategic context is, obviously, fundamental to this process. One of the important developments in the provision of information at board level in recent years has been the creation of customer and competitor information systems, monitoring not what is going on inside the company, as most traditional management information systems do, but what is going on outside in the strategic milieu. Sometimes a strategic vision is articulated in no more than a general statement of overall aims (see STRATEGIC INTENT); in other cases, quantified aims or goals are determined. Of course, a strategic vision remains no more than a dream unless management can turn it into reality.

“ *Directors love strategy sessions and strategy retreats because that's where they learn*
A CEO speaking to Richard Leblanc and Jim Gillies, *Inside the Boardroom*, 2005

“ *The board of a large public corporation is an inappropriate body for developing strategy, setting corporate culture and policy and initiating major decisions. Instead the board should concentrate on the critical review of proposals, with management having the primary duty to formulate and then implement proposals.*
Hilmer Report, *Strictly Boardroom*, Australia 1993

Strategy formulation

Setting the direction for a business in the context of the external competitive and customer market situation, and in the light of prevailing economic, political and technological factors. This is a crucial aspect of the board's role; it is after all why directors are so called.

Strategy formulation is typically an iterative process leading from perceptions of the strategic situation, through possible strategies, choices, projects, plans, implementation and outcomes. Strategic thinking is continuous, and strategies emerge over time rather than being created by a deliberate planning process.

The crucial discovery in formulating corporate strategy, which had been known by military strategists for thousands of years, was that it is not possible to create strategies for an organisation until the strategies being pursued (and capable of being pursued) by rival (and potential rival) organisations are understood. Company-centred planning systems often fail to adopt this perspective. HELICOPTER VISION is needed to see the business in the context of its competitors and customers, and of the political, economic, social, and technological setting.

Other strategies need to be developed, evaluated and, eventually, choices have to be made by the directors. Then the chosen strategies need supporting by appropriate POLICYMAKING, which lays down the guidelines for management. In formulating strategy and making related policy, a particular challenge to directors is to make sure that the long-term interests of the company are balanced with the short-term goals. Pressure to show strong performance in annual (even quarterly) directors' reports can adversely affect the pursuit of strategies that would fit the company for a better strategic future.

A significant trend in recent years has been away from strategies that emphasise business as a battlefield with global competitors, towards searching out strategic allies with whom mutually beneficial STRATEGIC ALLIANCES can be built.

In earlier days, when change and strategic challenge came more slowly, CORPORATE PLANNING was often an annual process, associated with budget preparation. Today, strategy formulation, in most professionally led companies, is a continuous activity for senior management and the directors. Strategies emerge as strategically significant information is digested and strategic options are discussed. Some boards of directors delegate much of the strategy formulation to the CEO and senior management. The OUTSIDE DIRECTORS act more as catalysts, probing the management's proposals, questioning their assumptions, challenging their conclusions, until a consensus is reached. Other boards are more closely involved in the details of strategic thinking. Recognising the importance of board-led strategic thinking, directors seem increasingly to be devoting specific board time and effort to strategy formulation, both during BOARD MEETINGS and by creating specific strategy sessions, often away from the boardroom.

66 *All men can see the tactics whereby I conquer: but none can see the strategy out of which victory is evolved.*
Sun Tze, *The Art of War*, 6th century BC

Suboptimisation

See GAMES DIRECTORS PLAY.

Subsidiary company

A company in a group of companies in which another company in the group holds all or a majority of its voting shares.

Supervisor

One of the roles a director can play (see CONFORMANCE ROLES).

Supervisory board

The upper board in the TWO-TIER BOARD approach to CORPOR-
ATE GOVERNANCE. In the continental European model, the supervisory board monitors and supervises the performance of the
executive board. Its power is derived from the ability to hire and
fire the CEO and other members of the executive. Common membership between the supervisory board and the executive board
is not allowed. Some protagonists argue that the supervisory
board distinguishes the PERFORMANCE ROLES and CONFORM-
ANCE ROLES that can become confused in a UNITARY BOARD.
(See also AUFSICHTSRAT, MITTAL, SIEMENS and VORSTAND.)

Sustainable development

The new orthodoxy of strategic thinking around the world. Sustainable development meets the needs of the present without
compromising the ability of future generations to meet their own
needs. Stemming from radical environmental movements of the
1970s, which offered apocalyptic visions of the earth's future, sustainable development is being embraced by boards as part of their
strategic thinking. Some companies report regularly to their shareholders on the sustainable implications of their longer term plans
(for an example see www.mtrc.com.hk). The GLOBAL REPORTING
INITIATIVE, established by the American environmental lobby
CERES and backed by the UN, aims to provide companies of all
sizes and in all markets with a template for reporting on sustainability issues, including the environment, labour practices, corrup-
tion, human rights and health and safety. (See also CORE VALUES,
CORPORATE SOCIAL RESPONSIBILITY and ETHICS.)

www.globalreporting.org, www.wbcsd.ch

66 *Corporate sustainability is a business approach that creates long-term shareholder value by embracing opportunities and managing risks deriving from economic, environmental and social development.*
Dow Jones Sustainability Indexes, www.sustainability-index.com

SWOT analysis

A CORPORATE PLANNING tool which involves taking a rigorous review of the strengths and weaknesses that a company has and the opportunities and threats that it faces. The technique is still used by many boards, although its fundamental weakness is that it is company-centred. In rapidly changing strategic situations, the strategist must consider the strategies of competitors and customers in the context of its industry (see HELICOPTER VISION and STRATEGY FORMULATION).

Tt

Titles

Not all people who carry the title of director are directors; and some who are not called director may be held liable as though they were. Titles such as director of long-range planning may add status or director of private banking may add authority, but they do not necessarily imply membership of the board. Such people would be ASSOCIATE DIRECTORS. Conversely, a SHADOW DIRECTOR, though not formally having the title of director, can influence board decisions and could be held responsible, in law, for the exercise of that power.

Tokenism

The inclusion on the board of a PUBLIC COMPANY of directors because they reflect (and can be seen to reflect) minority or other STAKEHOLDER interests, such as gender or ethnic background, consumers or the environment, rather than because of any specific contribution they might make to the board's work. Tokenism was at its height during the stakeholder debates of the 1970s, particularly among American corporations. Some NOMINATION COMMITTEES do recommend members with such backgrounds, but primarily because of their potential to contribute to the board's work, not because of their background.

Tomorrow's Company

The title of a report published in the UK in 1995 by the Royal Society of Arts. Written by a group of business people, the report argued that successful companies did not act solely for the benefit of SHAREHOLDERS but took an inclusive view of the interests of other STAKEHOLDERS (without using that word), including customers, suppliers and employees. The HAMPEL REPORT took a contrary view, arguing that although a company had to satisfy its customers, suppliers and employees, it is accountable to its shareholders.

> *Shareholder value is the imperative commanding a lot of attention, but you cannot create shareholder value by talking to your shareholders. You create it by looking at the four drivers of a successful business: how good you are at involving and motivating your staff; how close you are to your customers; how good you are at removing wastage from the supply chain and maintaining good relations with suppliers; what your reputation is in the community at large. We don't believe that the board is there purely to create shareholder value. I'm sure nobody leaps out of bed in the morning and says "I want to create shareholder value!" It's unrealistic.*
>
> Sir Stuart Hampson, chairman, John Lewis Partnership and Tomorrow's Company

Treadway Commission

The popular name for the National Commission on Fraudulent Financial Reporting (named after its first chairman, James Treadway). Since 1934 the SECURITIES AND EXCHANGE COMMISSION has been responsible for the oversight of the securities market in the United States. Subsequent developments have been influenced by a series of reports, including the 1978 Cohen Commission Report from the American Institute of Certified Public Accountants (AICPA) on AUDITORS' responsibilities; the 1987 Treadway

Report of the National Commission of Fraudulent Reporting, again from the AICPA; and the 1992 COSO Report, which provided an integrated framework for internal control. (COSO is the Committee of Sponsoring Organizations of the Treadway Commission of the American Institute of Certified Public Accountants.)

Triple bottom line

See CORPORATE SOCIAL RESPONSIBILITY.

Trust

The underpinning concept of the JOINT STOCK LIMITED LIABILITY COMPANY: the SHAREHOLDERS trust the directors to be stewards of their funds. Essentially, trust involves the agreement between parties with asymmetrical access to information. In companies, of course, the directors know far more about the enterprise than the shareholders, who must trust them. The AGENCY THEORY of CORPORATE GOVERNANCE, however, takes a less sanguine view of directors' behaviour.

Turnbull Report

A UK report on CORPORATE GOVERNANCE which explored some issues raised by the HAMPEL REPORT in more depth, particularly the board's responsibility for RISK MANAGEMENT. The COMBINED CODE incorporated the findings of the Turnbull Report.

www.dti.gov.uk/cii, www.icaew.co.uk/internalcontrol, www.iia.org.uk, www.globalcommunity.com

Two-hat dilemma

The potential problem facing all executive directors: in the board-room are they wearing the hat of a director responsible for the governance of the company as a whole, or are they wearing their executive hat representing the interests and defending the performance of their part of the organisation?

❝ *I make it clear to all my executive directors that when they are in my boardroom they take off their executive hat and accept responsibility with me for the direction of the company as a whole.*
Lord Caldecote, when chairman of Delta Group

Two-tier board

A governance structure found in some continental European countries, including Germany and the Netherlands, in which the executive board comprising the senior executive team is entirely separate from the upper SUPERVISORY BOARD. (See also AUFSICHTSRAT and VORSTAND.)

❝ *The same reason which induced the Romans to have two consuls makes it desirable for there to be two chambers of parliament; that neither of them may be exposed to the corrupting influence of undivided power.*
John Stewart Mill

TYCO

Dennis Kozlowski became CEO of Tyco in 1992. Treating the company as a private fiefdom, he siphoned off hundreds of millions of pounds in private expenditure, including an infamous gold and burgundy shower curtain, allegedly costing £6,000. His compliant board gave Kozlowski a contract saying that he would not be dismissed if convicted of a felony, unless it directly damaged the company. Subsequently, it transpired that he had also authorised the funding of $4m to support a chair in CORPORATE GOVERNANCE at Cambridge University. He claimed that this was jointly funded by the company and himself. Some irate Tyco shareholders, hoping to retrieve some of their squandered funds, tried to recover these university funds. But the powers behind the chair of corporate governance insisted that they would hang on to the cash. No matter how tainted by corporate excess it might be, they could put it to good use. However, they did have some difficulty in finding a suitable professor.

Uu

Unitary board

In many jurisdictions company law requires a company to have a single or unitary board of directors. This could consist entirely of EXECUTIVE DIRECTORS (as in some FAMILY COMPANIES), entirely of OUTSIDE DIRECTORS (as in some companies established for charitable purposes) or a mix of executive and NON-EXECUTIVE DIRECTORS. In the United States major LISTED COMPANIES usually have a majority of independent, outside directors. In the UK executive directors used to form a majority on the board, but the trend is towards board structures with a majority of non-executive directors. By contrast, a company incorporated in some continental European jurisdictions has a TWO-TIER BOARD. (See BOARD STRUCTURES and MITTAL.)

UNIVERSITY OF OXFORD

Oxford is a collegiate university, each college with its own constitution, finances and governance, operating under the umbrella of the university, which confers degrees and provides facilities such as laboratories, libraries and museums. Unsurprisingly, change comes slowly to an ancient institution. It took many years in the late 19th century for the study of science to be accepted, alongside the long-standing study of philosophy and theology, and nearly as long for management studies to be recognised in the late 20th century. Some of the colleges are affluent; others are less so. Each college has its own governing body. Governance of the university is in the hands of around 4,000 members of Congregation

– self-rule by the dons – which elects a Council composed almost entirely of dons to oversee the running of the university's finances and administration.

Aware that its traditional governance processes had become inappropriate in the 21st century, the university had been reviewing its governance since the early 2000s. Facing a financial shortfall, calls for a change in governance increased in 2006, with questions being asked in the media and Parliament about the Oxford admissions process. The vice-chancellor, John Hood (the first vice-chancellor to be appointed from outside Oxford), proposed a major shift towards a more modern corporate style of governance, introducing a new governing body composed of half dons and half independent OUTSIDE DIRECTORS, who would approve budgets and oversee the university's affairs. Only thus, he argued, could Oxford retain its international pre-eminence. His proposals had the backing of the government's Higher Education Funding Council and the university's chancellor, Lord Patten. However, Congregation had other ideas. Opponents of the proposals argued that reducing the number of directly elected university members would involve a loss of sovereignty and could affect the personal interests of dons and the academic well-being of students. Congregation met in the 17th-century Wren-built Sheldonian Theatre and voted convincingly against the proposals.

W

Vice-chairman

A title used by some boards to spread the work of the CHAIRMAN; by others to mark the chairman-elect; and by a few to confer prestige without necessarily giving additional responsibilities or powers.

> ❝ *Chairman, Vice-chairman, President – the titles do not always mean quite what they seem. Analysing the hierarchies at the top of American public companies can be a little like working out where real power lies in the Kremlin. The man at the top of the pecking order may, indeed, be the big potato, but it is just as likely that he counts for nothing at all.*
> Robert Lacey, *Detroit's Destiny*

Viénot Report

A report on CORPORATE GOVERNANCE in France, published in 1995. It recommended:

Every board should set up an accounts or audit committee to ensure that the accounting methods used in preparing the accounts are pertinent and consistent, and should inform the AGM of its existence and the number of times it had met during the year.

VODAFONE/MANNESMANN

The first hostile takeover by a foreign firm in German corporate history occurred in 2000 when Vodafone, then a British company, made a successful bid for Mannesmann, a German company, creating a European mobile telephone group. Mannesmann used the classic German two-tier CORPORATE GOVERNANCE structure with a wholly executive board appointed and overseen by a SUPERVISORY BOARD, which had both SHAREHOLDER and employee representatives.

Following the acquisition, an acrimonious meeting of the Mannesmann shareholders claimed that severance bonuses of around £50m paid as part of the bid negotiations to Klaus Esser, head of Mannesmann, and other senior executives were immoral, had reduced the company's value and had been designed to influence the bid. Members of both the executive and supervisory boards were called "crooks" and "looters". Klaus Zwickel, a member of the supervisory board and head of IG Metall, the metalworkers' union, protested that the bonuses were "indecently high", until it was pointed out that he had voted in favour of them at the supervisory board meeting. Initially, Vodafone said it knew nothing of the bonuses, but later conceded that the idea had come from Hong Kong-based Hutchinson Whampoa, one of Mannesmann's major shareholders, and that Vodafone had agreed to permit any such payments provided that they were made legally.

In Anglo-American corporate governance an open market for control, which assists takeover activity, is seen as essential to a healthy capital market. But in Germany hostile takeovers were viewed with suspicion by both management and unions. The Mannesmann case reinforced this opinion. The European Union had been trying to develop Europe-wide laws to facilitate hostile bids. But the German government actively sabotaged these proposals, following pressure from companies and unions.

Some years later, another governance issue arose. The CHAIRMAN, Lord MacLaurin, appeared to be at loggerheads with the CEO, Arun Sarin. But further investigation questioned the independence of the deputy chairman, Paul Hazen, who was the board's senior INDEPENDENT DIRECTOR responsible for liaising with investors. Hazen was shown to have worked with Sarin for many years at Airtouch, an American mobile business, which had also been acquired by Vodafone. INSTITUTIONAL INVESTORS demanded changes to the board. One institutional investor said:

"Hazen is more like Sarin's mentor than an independent." Another commented that some of the other so-called independent directors had in fact joined the board as part of takeover agreements with companies that had been acquired by Vodafone. "The board is being run as a Sarin fiefdom," he said. Subsequently, the company added new independent directors. Sarin retired as chief executive in 2008.

Voluntary organisations' governance

See NON-PROFIT DIRECTORS.

Vorstand

The executive committee or board in the German TWO-TIER BOARD system (see GERMAN CORPORATE GOVERNANCE).

Voting rights

A company's ARTICLES OF ASSOCIATION typically include the procedures for members' voting in general meetings. If a meeting votes by a show of hands, those present have one vote each and the size of individual shareholdings will not count; if a poll is called for, the usual clause in the articles provides for one vote for each share. (See also PROXY VOTES and DUAL VOTING RIGHTS.)

Voting with their feet

Some INSTITUTIONAL INVESTORS who prefer not to become involved in the governance issues of companies in which they have invested reserve the right to sell their shares rather than voting them and becoming involved in governance issues. (See also RELATIONSHIP INVESTING.)

Ww

WALLENBERG

CORPORATE GOVERNANCE in Sweden has some distinctive characteristics: mandatory CO-DETERMINATION, high private share ownership, dual-class shares and directors nominated by a SHAREHOLDERS' NOMINATION COMMITTEE. But arguably the most interesting characteristic is the influence of the Wallenberg family, which owns some 40% of the value of the Swedish stock exchange, and through dual-class shares exercises even greater VOTING RIGHTS. This massive empire is now in its fifth generation of family control and planning for the sixth. The Wallenbergs own some 19% of Saab, a car and aeroplane maker, and control 38% of the voting rights. They also own 5% of Ericsson, a leading telecommunications company, 11% of Electrolux, a white goods manufacturer, and 10% of Scania, a truck manufacturer, and in each of these three companies they control at least double those percentages in voting rights. The family has major interests in Atlas Copco, a compressor manufacturer, ABB, a global engineering group, SEB, one of Scandinavia's largest banks, and many other companies, together with 4% of AstraZeneca, a pharmaceuticals company listed in London where dual-class shares are not permitted.

Wallenberg ownership is exercised through the Wallenberg foundations (assets $6 billion), which exercise control through Investor, a PUBLIC COMPANY chaired by Jacob Wallenberg, with over 100,000 other investors. Companies dominated by Investor are run by professional managers with their own boards of directors. The family justify their special multiple-voting rights because they founded and continue to contribute strategically to these Swedish companies through strong and involved ownership.

WALT DISNEY COMPANY

In 2003 the governance and nomination committee of the board of the famous Disney company lowered the mandatory retirement age for directors to 72. Roy Disney, Walt Disney's nephew, the last remaining member of the Disney family on the board, was 73. He was told that the board intended to make no exceptions. Roy Disney, who was VICE-CHAIRMAN of the board and the executive chairman of the Animated Features Division, was not surprised by this news. For years, relations between him and Michael Eisner, the CHAIRMAN and CEO of Disney, had been poor. Together with some of the OUTSIDE DIRECTORS, Disney had criticised poor performance, falling profits and dropping share price, complaining that the company had lost its creative energy. But other directors on the board of 18 supported Eisner. Disney decided to resign, making public his concerns for the future of the company. Other outside directors resigned. One of them, Stanley Gold, commented that "this is yet another attempt by this board to squelch dissent by hiding behind the veil of 'good governance'". INSTITUTIONAL INVESTORS also complained about the company's performance and the lack of succession planning for Eisner. Disney and Gold launched a campaign to unseat Eisner. Their website claimed:

Shareholder democracy, while lauded as the centerpiece of democratic capitalism, has in fact become an oxymoron, with the vast majority of corporations firmly in the grip of their chief executives and acquiescent boards.

At the next AGM 43% voted against the renewal of Eisner's contract. Subsequently, the board created a new role of chairman of the board separate from that of CEO. Eisner then announced that he would stand down when his contract expired in two years' time. The board thanked him for his 20 years' service and looked forward to his continuing leadership throughout his remaining tenure. Disney and Gold called it window-dressing (see GAMES DIRECTORS PLAY). In the event Eisner went a year later.

War room

A few boards have their boardroom fitted out with display screens and information retrieval facilities to provide information pertinent to decisions under discussion. The analogy with the military operations room in a battle situation is, however, suspect since military operations involve real-time tactical responses as situations evolve, whereas the time horizon of board-level decisions ought to be long-term and strategic.

WASTE MANAGEMENT

In 1992, ARTHUR ANDERSEN, the AUDITOR of Waste Management, a refuse collection company in the United States, identified some improper accounting practices, which had resulted in an overstatement of reported profits. These misstatements totalled $93.5m, which was less than 10% of reported profit. Furthermore, one-off gains of over $100m, which should have been shown separately in the accounts, had been netted against other expenses. A "clean" AUDIT certificate was signed.

In 1993, Andersen identified further misstatements of $128m, which represented 12% of reported profit. Again it decided that these misstatements were not sufficiently material for the audit report to be qualified. But it did decide to allow the company to write off prior misstatements over a number of years, instead of making immediate DISCLOSURE, as required by GENERALLY ACCEPTED ACCOUNTING PRINCIPLES. In 1994, the company continued its practice of netting expenses against one-off gains.

Waste Management was an important and lucrative client for Andersen. Between 1991 and 1997, audit fees totalled $7.5m, and other fees, such as consulting services, contributed $11.8m. In Andersen's words, Waste Management was a "crown jewel" among its clients. Moreover, Waste Management's senior finance executives had all previously been Andersen auditors.

In June 2001, the SECURITIES AND EXCHANGE COMMISSION (SEC) found that Arthur Andersen and four of its partners had failed in their responsibilities in connection with the audits of the annual financial statements of Waste Management for the years 1992–96. These financial statements, on which Andersen issued unqualified or "clean" opinions, overstated Waste Management's pre-tax income by more than $1 billion.

The SEC found that:

[Andersen] knowingly or recklessly issued false and misleading audit reports ... [which] falsely stated that the financial statements were presented fairly, in all material respects, in conformity with generally accepted accounting principles.

Without admitting or denying the allegations or findings, Andersen agreed to pay a civil penalty of $7m, the largest ever SEC enforcement action against a then big five accounting firm.

This case raises the vexed issue of auditor independence. Andersen had a close relationship with a valuable client, which led to creeping year-on-year acceptance of less than acceptable auditing standards. The SEC's director of enforcement commented:

Arthur Andersen and its partners failed to stand up to company management and thereby betrayed their ultimate allegiance to Waste Management's shareholders and the investing public.

Watchdog

One of the roles a director can play (see CONFORMANCE ROLES).

Whistle-blowing

The reporting by an employee, often anonymously, of illegal practices or breaches in a company's CORPORATE GOVERNANCE code or ethical guidelines. In the past, whistle-blowing carried connotations of "snitching" or betrayal, and it still does in some countries. But many companies now recognise the need for an anonymous internal communication channel to guarantee good corporate governance. Boards need to establish whistle-blowing policies, which should lay down the procedures to be followed and protect the whistle-blower. The SARBANES OXLEY ACT in the United States requires companies to create channels for whistle-blowers and to protect them from retaliation. (See Public Concern at Work at www.pcaw.co.uk.)

White knight

In a hostile takeover bid, the attacked company may look for another more-acceptable company – a white knight – to protect it with a counter offer.

Window dressing

See GAMES DIRECTORS PLAY.

Window-on-the-world

One of the roles a director can play (see PERFORMANCE ROLES).

Wise man

One of the roles a director can play (see PERFORMANCE ROLES).

Woman director

More and more women are becoming directors of major British and American organisations, although the numbers are still small and almost all of them are NON-EXECUTIVE DIRECTORS.

❝ *Women directors used to be in politics or good works: today they are younger, with relevant business experience.*
Viki Holton, *Corporate Governance: An International Review*, Vol. 3, No. 2, 1995

Worker director

Proponents of industrial democracy argue that governing a major company involves an informal partnership between labour and capital, and that consequently labour should be represented in the CORPORATE GOVERNANCE processes. In a German SUPERVISORY BOARD, for example, half of its members are chosen under the CO-DETERMINATION laws through the employees' trade union processes. In the 1970s, the draft Fifth Directive of the European Community (now the European Union) proposed supervisory boards with employee representation for all large companies. The BULLOCK REPORT was the British response. Since then the company law harmonisation process in the EU has been over-taken by social legislation, including recent requirements that all major firms should have a WORKS COUNCIL through which employees can participate in significant strategic developments and policy changes.

Works council

The draft Fifth Directive of the European Community proposed that companies incorporated in the EC should have WORKER DIRECTORS on their boards. However, the Social Chapter of the Maastricht treaty superseded this proposal. Large companies in the EU must now have a works council and inform and consult with employees on strategic issues and plans that might affect employment. Since 2008 any firm in the EU with 50 or more employees must inform and consult with its workers about business and employment prospects.

❝ *I think compulsory works councils are a waste of time and money because most large companies have consulting mechanisms, so it's an attempt to reinvent the wheel.*
Richard Wilson, Institute of Directors, 2000

WORLDCOM

"WorldCom systematically flouted the rules of accounting and lied outright to investors", according to the Justice Department investigating the collapse of this huge American company. The company was founded by Bernie Ebbers, a charismatic entrepreneur, whose first job was delivering milk in Canada as a boy; this was followed by a basketball scholarship at Mississippi College and work as a basketball coach, nightclub bouncer and motel owner. In 1983, he saw the opportunity to create a long-distance telecommunications carrier by buying capacity from the newly deregulated AT&T. It is said that he scrawled his vision on a restaurant table napkin.

The build-up

Long Distance Discount Services (LDDS) was formed and Ebbers spent the next 18 years building a global telecoms powerhouse, mainly through acquisitions. These included TCL Telecom, a major player in Ireland, SkyTel's paging business and UUNET Technologies, an internet service provider that carried half of America's internet traffic. Then in 1997 Ebbers gazumped BT to acquire the long-distance phone business of MCI, a company three times its size, for $37 billion. By 2000, WorldCom had more than 20m customers in over 200 countries.

The acquisitions were nearly always paid for in WorldCom shares, which Ebbers believed would continue to surge in value in the new information age. An exception was the purchase of BT's share in MCI, which BT insisted was bought for cash – a wise decision that made BT over £2 billion instead of the massive loss had it taken WorldCom shares.

Ebbers's personal wealth grew with the massive growth of WorldCom's share price, at its peak reaching over $60 a share. Moreover, he gambled on it increasing further, taking from the company a personal loan of $343m to meet a call on WorldCom shares he had bought.

In April 2002 he resigned. The compliant board agreed a generous severance package: $22m GOLDEN HANDSHAKE, $1.5m a year for life, the continuation of his low-interest loan now standing at $408m and unlimited use of the company's jet. Later, as the debacle unfolded, the board reviewed these terms. John Sidgmore, who had previously run UUNET Technologies (acquired by World-Com in 1996), became chief executive following Ebbers's resignation. He was a hard-driven man, who claimed he needed only three hours' sleep a night.

Unwelcome revelations

The revelation that over the past five quarters $3.8 billion of expenditure, which should have been charged against annual profits, had been capitalised came in June 2002. The accounts, which should have disclosed a significant loss, showed a profit of $1.4 billion. The extent of the fraud was increased to $9 billion after a SECURITIES AND EXCHANGE COMMISSION investigation revealed inflation of profits since 1999.

ARTHUR ANDERSEN, WorldCom's AUDITOR, had been dismissed, following the adverse publicity of the firm's handling of the ENRON AUDIT. When WorldCom's internal auditors discovered the accounting irregularities, Cynthia Cooper, vice-president of internal audit, alerted KPMG, the new external auditor.

Three members of the accounting staff were indicted for fraud by a federal grand jury: Scott Sullivan, the chief financial officer; Burford Yates, the former director of general accounting; and David Myers, the former controller who was dismissed in June 2002. Sullivan stepped down and exercised his constitutional right not to testify to a Congressional inquiry. Ebbers also invoked the Fifth Amendment, but told Congress he had done nothing wrong, and the investigations did not link him directly with the fraud.

Bankruptcy protection under Chapter 11 was sought in July 2002. This was the largest filing in corporate history, surpassing even ENRON. The share price, which had peaked at over $60, collapsed; 17,000 jobs were lost worldwide.

Most of WorldCom's $422 billion debt was in corporate bonds, mainly held by INSTITUTIONAL INVESTORS around the world. They were appalled. Many pension funds, concerned at the fall in the equity market, had switched to the supposedly less erratic bond market. CALPERS admitted a $330m unrealised loss on WorldCom bonds. Yet many INVESTMENT ANALYSTS had been promoting WorldCom shares to the very end.

Bert Roberts Jr, WorldCom's CHAIRMAN, who had deflected calls from investors and creditors for his resignation, stood down in November 2002, opening the way for a wholesale clearout of the boardroom.

What went wrong?

Unlike Enron's, WorldCom's failure was basically caused by a classic accounting fraud: its accounts did not conform to GENERALLY ACCEPTED ACCOUNTING PRINCIPLES. In governance terms this was a company that seemed to meet many of the guidelines on good CORPORATE GOVERNANCE. The roles of chairman and CEO were split between different people, unlike most American companies, and a majority of the board members were OUTSIDE DIRECTORS.

But look more closely: of the 12 directors, five were WorldCom executives but two more worked for companies acquired by WorldCom. Max Bobbitt, chairman of the AUDIT COMMITTEE, had benefited from selling WorldCom shares and, at the time of the collapse, held nearly 500,000 shares. This was a board with a DOMINANT DIRECTOR/founder lacking truly independent and tough-minded outside members. Directors were beholden and sycophantic towards Ebbers, who some now suggested was an overbearing buccaneer who took pride in his lack of technical knowledge of the telecoms industry.

A corporate culture of fiddling the figures also emerged. Sales staff had increased the reported revenues by registering a single sale many times over, paying the salesman commission on each occasion, in a practice known as "rolling the revenues".

❝ *I continued to be positive about WorldCom because it fits my thesis of what a strong, valuable company should be.*
Jack Grubman, an investment analyst accused of bias in favour of WorldCom

❝ *The only experience Bernie Ebbers had operating a long-distance carrier is that he used the phone.*
A friend commenting on the founder of WorldCom

Yakusa

Japanese underworld organisations often run in a business-like, corporate manner. The *yakusa* sometimes threaten disruption of companies' AGMs if they are not suitably rewarded. Consequently, many companies hold their AGMs on the same day.

YUKOS

Following the dissolution of the Soviet Union, Boris Yeltsin became president of Russia in 1991 with a mission to turn a communist centrally-planned economy into a capitalist-market economy. The reforms proved turbulent. In 1998, Russia's economy collapsed, bringing economic chaos, humiliation and suffering. The state was unable to pay its workers, millions of Russians were plunged into poverty and the value of the currency fell by 70%. However, a few people, the *novi Russki* or oligarchs, benefited from the privatisation of Russia's state assets, becoming super-rich. Mikhail B. Khodorkovsky was one of them. He built a vast energy empire from the privatisation of state enterprises, creating Yukos Oil Company.

In 1999, Vladimir Putin, a former secret service chief, was elected president. He proved a great success, ending the chaos of the Yeltsin years, bringing millions of people out of poverty and repaying the country's international loans. Russians' confidence grew and in 2004 Putin was re-elected with a huge majority. But he saw Khodorkovsky, who was said then to be Russia's richest man, as a potential threat. Yukos had agreed to combine with

Sibneft, Russia's fifth largest oil company, 73% owned by GAZPROM, a Russian state company. Sibneft was led by Roman Abramovich, governor of Russia's remote Chuotka region and owner of London's Chelsea football club, who is said now to be Russia's richest man.

In 2004, Khodorkovsky was charged with fraud, embezzlement, forgery and tax evasion. He was found guilty and jailed. He described his imprisonment as a political strike against him by Putin because he had shown a political interest in the presidency. Yukos was seized by the state and charged with tax evasion. The company claimed its use of tax havens had been legal, and that it faced "an unprecedented campaign of illegal, discriminatory and disproportionate tax claims escalating into raids and confiscation, culminating in intimidation and arrests". Yukos's assets were confiscated by the revenue authorities and sold to state-owned Gazprom and Rosneft. Rosneft's shares are listed in London. Khodorkovsky is still in jail in Siberia.

Appendices

1 Directors and the global financial crisis

It began innocuously enough in 2007. After more than a decade of substantial growth, house prices in the United States began to fall, leaving some owners in negative equity, their mortgage loans greater than the value of their homes. Worse, it emerged that many of these loans had been made to people who were not good credit risks, the so-called sub-prime market. Foreclosures escalated, driving house prices down further.

But the real problem had been growing for a decade. Lax monetary policies, cheap money and massive liquidity produced a lending and asset bubble in the western world. Companies used low-interest loans to leverage their financial strategies. World trade boomed, with some countries facing vast trade imbalances. Personal borrowing soared, some secured on inflating house prices, some on extended credit-card debt.

The catalyst for the subsequent chaos was financial engineering in which banks had bundled their loan assets into securities, which they then sold on to other financial institutions. This securitisation of debt spread the risk around the world's financial system, but because these instruments were complex and sophisticated, there were problems matching exposure to security.

Rumours of banks overexposed to sub-prime debt circulated. Confidence began to wane. But confidence is the foundation stone of every financial system: confidence that credit will be available when needed and trust that debts will be repaid when due. Facing uncertainty, banks began to tighten their lending polices. Funds became scarce. Central banks had to make special arrangements to provide money to meet some institutions' liabilities.

In 2007, the first run on a UK bank for over a century occurred at Northern Rock, which was bailed out and then taken over by the British government. In the United States, Bear Stearns, a financial institution, was also bailed out. Then, dramatically, the two huge American mortgage organisations, Fannie Mae and Freddie Mac, which account for a large part of all mortgages to homeowners in the United States, were given government guarantees of up to $5 trillion. Next AIG (American International Group), the world's biggest insurer and provider of hedging cover to the banking system, imploded. The American government, believing that it could not countenance the adverse economic effects of an AIG failure, provided a loan facility of $85 billion to protect the interests of its taxpayers, secured on assets of AIG, taking an 80% equity stake in the company. Lehman Brothers was not so fortunate; the Federal Reserve refused support, and after 158 years in business the firm went bankrupt. In retrospect this was a questionable decision because it drove down market confidence still further.

Some hedge funds were accused of exacerbating the crisis by short selling bank shares. They responded that this was normal practice when markets were expected to fall. Short-term curbs were introduced, which exposed the massive extent of the shorting of stocks.

In September 2008 in the United States, the Fed and the Treasury tried to restore confidence. They proposed a bail-out in which the American government would take on banks' bad debts, including the sub-prime loans, with the underlying collateral security. Some complained that this would allow the financial executives, whose reckless investments had caused the crisis in the first place, to unload their risky assets and then walk away with their bonuses and golden parachutes intact.

Other countries also experienced liquidity problems. In September 2008 there was a run on the Bank of East Asia in Hong Kong, which was quickly met by reassurances from Hong Kong's financial authorities. In October 2008 all the banks and the stock exchange in Iceland were closed when depositors' demands for cash could not be met. Iceland, a country of around 300,000 people, which had previously relied on fishing and tourism, had been encouraged by a handful of financial entrepreneurs to hit way above its economic power.

When the full story of the global financial crisis that started in 2007 is written Monday October 13th 2008 will stand out. To prevent the collapse of the world's financial system, governments in Australia, Austria, Finland, France, Germany, Indonesia, India, Italy, Japan, New Zealand, South Korea, Spain, Sweden, the UK and the United States all went to extraordinary lengths to bail out their banks, guarantee savers' funds and provide state investment to recapitalise their banks to the tune of an estimated US$1.8 trillion. Subsequently, it was thought to cost more.

In retrospect, the global financial crisis has raised some fundamental corporate governance issues:

- Where were the directors of the failed financial institutions, particularly the independent outside directors who were supposed to provide a check on overenthusiastic executive directors? Did they really understand the strategic business models and sophisticated securitised instruments involved? In other words, did they appreciate the risk inherent in their companies' strategic profile?

- Where were the banking regulators? Although the extent of the crisis was unprecedented, the regulators seem to have been beguiled into complacency, perhaps taken over by the industry they were there to regulate. New rules seem inevitable.

- Where were the auditors? In approving the accounts of client financial institutions, did they fully appreciate and ensure the reporting of exposure to risk? Expect some major legal actions as client companies fail.

- Did the credit agencies contribute to the problem by

awarding high credit ratings to companies exposed to significant risk?

■ Government bail-outs also raised the question of so-called moral hazard: by protecting bankers from their past reckless decisions, would others be encouraged to take excessive risks in the future?

■ Will the experts who designed the sophisticated loan securitisation vehicles and other financial engineering systems be held to account? Are their ideas and enthusiasms now under control?

■ Were any of the financial institutions' activities illegal? Compare the situation with Enron, where some senior executives continued to believe that nothing they had done was illegal, even after they were in jail.

■ Lastly, did excessive bonuses and share options encourage short-term and unrealistic risk-taking with shareholders' funds? In the future, controls are likely on performance-related remuneration and on the practice of guaranteed bonuses. The news that some bankers had lost their fortunes as share prices collapsed was cold comfort to mortgagees who lost their homes, shareholders who lost their savings and employees who lost their livelihoods.

In any market those involved must both trust those they are dealing with and have confidence in the market overall. Such confidence and trust in the financial markets were sorely weakened in this crisis and the fallout from it is of direct concern to all directors and likely to be significant and long lasting. It will include curbs on lending and an increased cost of capital; tighter credit; a dearth of insurance cover including hedging and directors and officers (D&O) insurance; a greater emphasis on every board's responsibility for strategic risk assessment and management; stronger and co-ordinated regulation of finance markets; and a greater emphasis on director remuneration, with rewards for true long-term strategic success, rather than the achievement of short-term and potentially manipulated performance measures.

The global economic impact of the financial crisis – falling production, slowing economies, increasing unemployment, failing companies, volatile stock and currency markets, falling tax revenues, rising taxes, recession, even depression in some countries – all, ultimately, reflect failures of corporate governance.

66 *A banker is a fellow who lends you an umbrella when the sun is shining but wants it back the minute it begins to rain.*
Mark Twain

2 The UK Combined Code on Corporate Governance

The UK Combined Code sets out standards of good practice in relation to issues such as board composition and development, remuneration, accountability and audit and relations with shareholders. All companies incorporated in the UK and listed on the main market of the London Stock Exchange are required under the listing rules to report on how they have applied the Combined Code in their annual report and accounts. Overseas companies listed on the main market are required to disclose the significant ways in which their corporate governance practices differ from those set out in the code. The Combined Code contains broad principles and more specific provisions. Listed companies are required to report on how they have applied the main principles of the code, and either to confirm that they have complied with the code's provisions or – where they have not – to provide an explanation.

The UK Combined Code was first issued in 1998 and has been updated at regular intervals since then. The edition which follows applies from July 2008.

Financial Reporting Council
June 2008

SECTION 1   COMPANIES

A Directors

A1 The board

Main principle

Every company should be headed by an effective board, which is collectively responsible for the success of the company.

Supporting principles

The board's role is to provide entrepreneurial leadership of the company within a framework of prudent and effective controls which enables risk to be assessed and managed. The board should set the company's strategic aims, ensure that the necessary financial and human resources are in place for the company to meet its objectives and review management performance. The board should set the company's values and standards and ensure that its obligations to its shareholders and others are understood and met. All directors must take decisions objectively in the interests of the company. As part of their role as members of a unitary board, non-executive directors should constructively challenge and help develop proposals on strategy. Non-executive directors should scrutinise the performance of management in meeting agreed goals and objectives and monitor the reporting of performance. They should satisfy themselves on the integrity of financial information and that financial controls and systems of risk management are robust and defensible. They are responsible for determining appropriate levels of remuneration of executive directors and have a prime role in appointing, and where necessary removing, executive directors and in succession planning.

Code provisions

A1.1 The board should meet sufficiently regularly to discharge its duties effectively. There should be a formal schedule of matters specifically reserved for its decision. The annual report should include a statement of how the board operates, including a high level statement of which types of decisions are to be taken by the board and which are to be delegated to management.

A1.2 The annual report should identify the chairman, the deputy chairman (where there is one), the chief executive, the senior independent director and the chairmen and members of the nomination, audit and remuneration committees. It should also set out the number of meetings of the board and those committees and individual attendance by directors.

A1.3 The chairman should hold meetings with the non-executive directors without the executives present. Led by the senior independent director, the non-executive directors should meet without the chairman present at least annually to appraise the chairman's performance (as described in A6.1) and on such other occasions as are deemed appropriate.

A1.4 Where directors have concerns which cannot be resolved about the running of the company or a proposed action, they should ensure that their concerns are recorded in the board minutes. On resignation, a non-executive director should provide a written statement to the chairman, for circulation to the board, if they have any such concerns.

A1.5 The company should arrange appropriate insurance cover in respect of legal action against its directors.

A2 Chairman and chief executive
Main principle
There should be a clear division of responsibilities at the head of the company between the running of the board and the executive responsibility for the running of the company's business. No one individual should have unfettered powers of decision.

Supporting principle
The chairman is responsible for leadership of the board, ensuring its effectiveness on all aspects of its role and setting its agenda. The chairman is also responsible for ensuring that the directors receive accurate, timely and clear information. The chairman should ensure effective communication with shareholders. The chairman should also facilitate the effective contribution of non-executive directors in particular and ensure constructive relations between executive and non-executive directors.

Code provisions

A2.1 The roles of chairman and chief executive should not be exercised by the same individual. The division of responsibilities between the chairman and chief executive should be clearly established, set out in writing and agreed by the board.

A2.2 The chairman should on appointment meet the independence criteria set out in A3.1 below. A chief executive should not go on to be chairman of the same company. If exceptionally a board decides that a chief executive should become chairman, the board should consult major shareholders in advance and should set out its reasons to shareholders at the time of the appointment and in the next annual report.

A3 Board balance and independence
Main principle

The board should include a balance of executive and non-executive directors (and in particular independent non-executive directors) such that no individual or small group of individuals can dominate the board's decision taking.

Supporting principles

The board should not be so large as to be unwieldy. The board should be of sufficient size that the balance of skills and experience is appropriate for the requirements of the business and that changes to the board's composition can be managed without undue disruption. To ensure that power and information are not concentrated in one or two individuals, there should be a strong presence on the board of both executive and non-executive directors. The value of ensuring that committee membership is refreshed and that undue reliance is not placed on particular individuals should be taken into account in deciding chairmanship and membership of committees. No one other than the committee chairman and members is entitled to be present at a meeting of the nomination, audit or remuneration committee, but others may attend at the invitation of the committee.

Code provisions

A3.1 The board should identify in the annual report each non-executive director it considers to be independent. The board should determine whether the director is independent in character and judgment and whether there are relationships or circumstances which are likely to affect, or could appear to affect, the director's judgment. The board should state its reasons if it determines that a director is independent notwithstanding the existence of relationships or circumstances which may appear relevant to its determination, including if the director has been an employee of the company or group within the last five years; has, or has had within the last three years, a material business relationship with the company either directly, or as a partner, shareholder, director or senior employee of a body that has such a relationship with the company; has received or receives additional remuneration from the company apart from a director's fee, participates in the company's share option or a performance-related pay scheme, or is a member of the company's pension scheme; has close family ties with any of the company's advisers, directors or senior employees; holds cross-directorships or has significant links with other directors through involvement in other companies or bodies; represents a significant shareholder; or has served on the board for more than nine years from the date of their first election.

A3.2 Except for smaller companies, at least half the board, excluding the chairman, should comprise non-executive directors determined by the board to be independent. A smaller company should have at least two independent non-executive directors.

A3.3 The board should appoint one of the independent non-executive directors to be the senior independent director. The senior independent director should be available to shareholders if they have concerns which contact through the normal channels of chairman, chief executive or finance director has failed to resolve or for which such contact is inappropriate.

A4 Appointments to the board
Main principle
There should be a formal, rigorous and transparent procedure for the appointment of new directors to the board.

Supporting principles
Appointments to the board should be made on merit and against objective criteria. Care should be taken to ensure that appointees have enough time available to devote to the job. This is particularly important in the case of chairmanships. The board should satisfy itself that plans are in place for orderly succession for appointments to the board and to senior management, so as to maintain an appropriate balance of skills and experience within the company and on the board.

Code provisions
A4.1 There should be a nomination committee which should lead the process for board appointments and make recommendations to the board. A majority of members of the nomination committee should be independent non-executive directors. The chairman or an independent non-executive director should chair the committee, but the chairman should not chair the nomination committee when

it is dealing with the appointment of a successor to the chairmanship. The nomination committee should make available its terms of reference, explaining its role and the authority delegated to it by the board.

A4.2 The nomination committee should evaluate the balance of skills, knowledge and experience on the board and, in the light of this evaluation, prepare a description of the role and capabilities required for a particular appointment.

A4.3 For the appointment of a chairman, the nomination committee should prepare a job specification, including an assessment of the time commitment expected, recognising the need for availability in the event of crises. A chairman's other significant commitments should be disclosed to the board before appointment and included in the annual report. Changes to such commitments should be reported to the board as they arise, and included in the next annual report. No individual should be appointed to a second chairmanship of a FTSE 100 company.

A4.4 The terms and conditions of appointment of non-executive directors should be made available for inspection. The letter of appointment should set out the expected time commitment. Non-executive directors should undertake that they will have sufficient time to meet what is expected of them. Their other significant commitments should be disclosed to the board before appointment, with a broad indication of the time involved, and the board should be informed of subsequent changes.

A4.5 The board should not agree to a full-time executive director taking on more than one non-executive directorship in a FTSE 100 company or the chairmanship of such a company.

A4.6 A separate section of the annual report should describe the work of the nomination committee, including the process it has used in relation to board appointments. An explanation should be given if neither an external search consultancy nor open advertising has been used in the appointment of a chairman or a non-executive director.

A5 Information and professional development

Main principle

The board should be supplied in a timely manner with information in a form and of a quality appropriate to enable it to discharge its duties. All directors should receive induction on joining the board and should regularly update and refresh their skills and knowledge.

Supporting principles

The chairman is responsible for ensuring that the directors receive accurate, timely and clear information. Management has an obligation to provide such information but directors should seek clarification or amplification where necessary. The chairman should ensure that the directors continually update their skills and the knowledge and familiarity with the company required to fulfil their role both on the board and on board committees. The company should provide the necessary resources for developing and updating its directors' knowledge and capabilities. Under the direction of the chairman, the company secretary's responsibilities include ensuring good information flows within the board and its committees and between senior management and non-executive directors, as well as facilitating induction and assisting with professional development as required. The company secretary should be responsible for advising the board through the chairman on all governance matters.

Code provisions

A5.1 The chairman should ensure that new directors receive a full, formal and tailored induction on joining the board. As part of this, the company should offer to major shareholders the opportunity to meet a new non-executive director.

A5.2 The board should ensure that directors, especially non-executive directors, have access to independent professional advice at the company's expense where they judge it necessary to discharge their responsibilities as directors. Committees should be provided with sufficient resources to undertake their duties.

A5.3 All directors should have access to the advice and services of the company secretary, who is responsible to the board for ensuring that board procedures are complied with. Both the appointment and removal of the company secretary should be a matter for the board as a whole.

A6 Performance evaluation
Main principle
The board should undertake a formal and rigorous annual evaluation of its own performance and that of its committees and individual directors.

Supporting principle
Individual evaluation should aim to show whether each director continues to contribute effectively and to demonstrate commitment to the role (including commitment of time for board and committee meetings and any other duties). The chairman should act on the results of the performance evaluation by recognising the strengths and addressing the weaknesses of the board and, where appropriate, proposing new members be appointed to the board or seeking the resignation of directors.

Code provision
A6.1 The board should state in the annual report how performance evaluation of the board, its committees and its

individual directors has been conducted. The non-executive directors, led by the senior independent director, should be responsible for performance evaluation of the chairman, taking into account the views of executive directors.

A7 Re-election
Main principle
All directors should be submitted for re-election at regular intervals, subject to continued satisfactory performance. The board should ensure planned and progressive refreshing of the board.

Code provisions

A7.1 All directors should be subject to election by shareholders at the first annual general meeting after their appointment, and to re-election thereafter at intervals of no more than three years. The names of directors submitted for election or re-election should be accompanied by sufficient biographical details and any other relevant information to enable shareholders to take an informed decision on their election.

A7.2 Non-executive directors should be appointed for specified terms subject to re-election and to Companies Acts provisions relating to the removal of a director. The board should set out to shareholders in the papers accompanying a resolution to elect a non-executive director why they believe an individual should be elected. The chairman should confirm to shareholders when proposing re-election that, following formal performance evaluation, the individual's performance continues to be effective and to demonstrate commitment to the role. Any term beyond six years (e.g. two three-year terms) for a non-executive director should be subject to particularly rigorous review, and should take into account the need for progressive refreshing of the board. Non-executive directors may serve longer than nine years (e.g. three three-year terms), subject to annual re-election. Serving more than nine years could be relevant to the determination of a non-executive director's independence (as set out in provision A3.1).

B Remuneration

B1 The level and make-up of remuneration

Main principles
Levels of remuneration should be sufficient to attract, retain and motivate directors of the quality required to run the company successfully, but a company should avoid paying more than is necessary for this purpose. A significant proportion of executive directors' remuneration should be structured so as to link rewards to corporate and individual performance.

Supporting principle
The remuneration committee should judge where to position their company relative to other companies. But they should use such comparisons with caution, in view of the risk of an upward ratchet of remuneration levels with no corresponding improvement in performance. They should also be sensitive to pay and employment conditions elsewhere in the group, especially when determining annual salary increases.

Code provisions
Remuneration policy
B1.1 The performance-related elements of remuneration should form a significant proportion of the total remuneration package of executive directors and should be designed to align their interests with those of shareholders and to give these directors keen incentives to perform at the highest levels. In designing schemes of performance-related

remuneration, the remuneration committee should follow the provisions in Schedule A to this code.

B1.2 Executive share options should not be offered at a discount save as permitted by the relevant provisions of the listing rules.

B1.3 Levels of remuneration for non-executive directors should reflect the time commitment and responsibilities of the role. Remuneration for non-executive directors should not include share options. If, exceptionally, options are granted, shareholder approval should be sought in advance and any shares acquired by exercise of the options should be held until at least one year after the non-executive director leaves the board. Holding of share options could be relevant to the determination of a non-executive director's independence (as set out in provision A3.1).

B1.4 Where a company releases an executive director to serve as a non-executive director elsewhere, the remuneration report should include a statement as to whether or not the director will retain such earnings and, if so, what the remuneration is.

Service contracts and compensation

B1.5 The remuneration committee should carefully consider what compensation commitments (including pension contributions and all other elements) their directors' terms of appointment would entail in the event of early termination. The aim should be to avoid rewarding poor performance. They should take a robust line on reducing compensation to reflect departing directors' obligations to mitigate loss.

B1.6 Notice or contract periods should be set at one year or less. If it is necessary to offer longer notice or contract periods to new directors recruited from outside, such periods should reduce to one year or less after the initial period.

B2 Procedure
Main principle
There should be a formal and transparent procedure for developing policy on executive remuneration and for fixing the remuneration packages of individual directors. No director should be involved in deciding his or her own remuneration.

Supporting principles
The remuneration committee should consult the chairman and/or chief executive about their proposals relating to the remuneration of other executive directors. The remuneration committee should also be responsible for appointing any consultants in respect of executive director remuneration. Where executive directors or senior management are involved in advising or supporting the remuneration committee, care should be taken to recognise and avoid conflicts of interest. The chairman of the board should ensure that the company maintains contact as required with its principal shareholders about remuneration in the same way as for other matters.

Code provisions
B2.1 The board should establish a remuneration committee of at least three, or in the case of smaller companies two, independent non-executive directors. In addition the company chairman may also be a member of, but not chair, the committee if he or she was considered independent on appointment as chairman. The remuneration committee should make available its terms of reference, explaining its role and the authority delegated to it by the board. Where remuneration consultants are appointed, a statement should be made available of whether they have any other connection with the company.

B2.2 The remuneration committee should have delegated responsibility for setting remuneration for all executive directors and the chairman, including pension rights and any compensation payments. The committee should also recommend and monitor the level and structure of remuneration for senior management. The definition of "senior management" for this purpose should be determined by the board but should normally include the first layer of management below board level.

B2.3 The board itself or, where required by the articles of association, the shareholders should determine the remuneration of the non-executive directors within the limits set in the articles of association. Where permitted by the articles, the board may however delegate this responsibility to a committee, which might include the chief executive.

B2.4 Shareholders should be invited specifically to approve all new long-term incentive schemes (as defined in the listing rules) and significant changes to existing schemes, save in the circumstances permitted by the listing rules.

C Accountability and audit

C.1 Financial reporting
Main principle
The board should present a balanced and understandable assessment of the company's position and prospects.

Supporting principle
The board's responsibility to present a balanced and understandable assessment extends to interim and other price-sensitive public reports and reports to regulators as well as to information required to be presented by statutory requirements.

Code provisions

C1.1 The directors should explain in the annual report their responsibility for preparing the accounts and there should be a statement by the auditors about their reporting responsibilities.

C1.2 The directors should report that the business is a going concern, with supporting assumptions or qualifications as necessary.

C2 Internal control
Main principle
The board should maintain a sound system of internal control to safeguard shareholders' investment and the company's assets.

Code provision

C2.1 The board should, at least annually, conduct a review of the effectiveness of the group's system of internal controls and should report to shareholders that they have done so. The review should cover all material controls, including financial, operational and compliance controls and risk management systems.

C3 Audit committee and auditors
Main principle
The board should establish formal and transparent arrangements for considering how they should apply the financial reporting and internal control principles and for maintaining an appropriate relationship with the company's auditors.

Code provisions

C3.1 The board should establish an audit committee of at least three, or in the case of smaller companies two, members who should all be independent non-executive directors. The board should satisfy itself that at least one member of the audit committee has recent and relevant financial experience.

C3.2 The main role and responsibilities of the audit committee should be set out in written terms of reference and should include: to monitor the integrity of the financial statements of the company, and any formal announcements relating to the company's financial performance, reviewing significant financial reporting judgments contained in them; to review the company's internal financial controls and, unless expressly addressed by a separate board risk committee composed of independent directors, or by the board itself, to review the company's internal control and risk management systems; to monitor and review the effectiveness of the company's internal audit function; to make recommendations to the board, for it to put to the shareholders for their approval in general meeting, in relation to the appointment, reappointment and removal of the external auditor and to approve the remuneration and terms of engagement of the external auditor; to review and monitor the external auditor's independence and objectivity and the effectiveness of the audit process, taking into consideration relevant UK professional and regulatory requirements; to develop and implement policy on the engagement of the external auditor to supply non-audit services, taking into account relevant ethical guidance regarding the provision of non-audit services by the external audit firm; and to report to the board, identifying any matters in respect of which it considers that action or improvement is needed and making recommendations as to the steps to be taken.

C3.3 The terms of reference of the audit committee, including its role and the authority delegated to it by the board, should be made available. A separate section of the annual report should describe the work of the committee in discharging those responsibilities.

C3.4 The audit committee should review arrangements by which staff of the company may, in confidence, raise concerns about possible improprieties in matters of financial reporting or other matters. The audit committee's objective should be to ensure that arrangements are in place for the proportionate and independent investigation of such matters and for appropriate follow-up action.

C3.5 The audit committee should monitor and review the effectiveness of the internal audit activities. Where there is no internal audit function, the audit committee should consider annually whether there is a need for an internal audit function and make a recommendation to the board, and the reasons for the absence of such a function should be explained in the relevant section of the annual report.

C3.6 The audit committee should have primary responsibility for making a recommendation on the appointment, reappointment and removal of the external auditors. If the board does not accept the audit committee's recommendation, it should include in the annual report, and in any papers recommending appointment or reappointment, a statement from the audit committee explaining the recommendation and should set out reasons why the board has taken a different position.

C3.7 The annual report should explain to shareholders how, if the auditor provides non-audit services, auditor objectivity and independence are safeguarded.

D Relations with shareholders

D1 Dialogue with institutional shareholders

Main principle

There should be a dialogue with shareholders based on the mutual understanding of objectives. The board as a whole has responsibility for ensuring that a satisfactory dialogue with shareholders takes place.

Supporting principles

While recognising that most shareholder contact is with the chief executive and finance director, the chairman (and the senior independent director and other directors as appropriate) should maintain sufficient contact with major shareholders to understand their issues and concerns. The board should keep in touch with shareholder opinion in whatever ways are most practical and efficient.

Code provisions

D1.1 The chairman should ensure that the views of shareholders are communicated to the board as a whole. The chairman should discuss governance and strategy with major shareholders. Non-executive directors should be offered the opportunity to attend meetings with major shareholders and should expect to attend them if requested by major shareholders. The senior independent director should attend sufficient meetings with a range of major shareholders to listen to their views in order to help develop a balanced understanding of the issues and concerns of major shareholders.

D1.2 The board should state in the annual report the steps they have taken to ensure that the members of the board, and in particular the non-executive directors, develop an understanding of the views of major shareholders about their company, for example through direct face-to-face contact, analysts' or brokers' briefings and surveys of shareholder opinion.

D2 Constructive use of the AGM
Main principle
The board should use the AGM to communicate with investors and to encourage their participation.

Code provisions

D2.1 At any general meeting, the company should propose a separate resolution on each substantially separate issue, and should in particular propose a resolution at the AGM relating to the report and accounts. For each resolution, proxy appointment forms should provide shareholders with the option to direct their proxy to vote either for or against the resolution or to withhold their vote. The proxy form and any announcement of the results of a vote should make it clear that a "vote withheld" is not a vote in law and will not be counted in the calculation of the proportion of the votes for and against the resolution.

D2.2 The company should ensure that all valid proxy appointments received for general meetings are properly recorded and counted. For each resolution, after a vote has been taken, except where taken on a poll, the company should ensure that the following information is given at the meeting and made available as soon as reasonably practicable on a website which is maintained by or on behalf of the company: the number of shares in respect of which proxy appointments have been validly made; the number of votes for the resolution; the number of votes against the resolution; and the number of shares in respect of which the vote was directed to be withheld.

D2.3 The chairman should arrange for the chairmen of the audit, remuneration and nomination committees to be available to answer questions at the AGM and for all directors to attend.

D2.4 The company should arrange for the Notice of the AGM and related papers to be sent to shareholders at least 20 working days before the meeting.

SECTION 2 INSTITUTIONAL SHAREHOLDERS
E Institutional shareholders

E1 Dialogue with companies
Main principle
Institutional shareholders should enter into a dialogue with companies based on the mutual understanding of objectives.

Supporting principles
Institutional shareholders should apply the principles set out in the Institutional Shareholders' Committee's "The Responsibilities of Institutional Shareholders and Agents – Statement of Principles", which should be reflected in fund manager contracts.

E2 Evaluation of governance disclosures
Main principle
When evaluating companies' governance arrangements, particularly those relating to board structure and composition, institutional shareholders should give due weight to all relevant factors drawn to their attention.

Supporting principle
Institutional shareholders should consider carefully explanations given for departure from this code and make reasoned judgments

in each case. They should give an explanation to the company, in writing where appropriate, and be prepared to enter a dialogue if they do not accept the company's position. They should avoid a box-ticking approach to assessing a company's corporate governance. They should bear in mind in particular the size and complexity of the company and the nature of the risks and challenges it faces.

E3 Shareholder voting
Main principle
Institutional shareholders have a responsibility to make considered use of their votes.

Supporting principles
Institutional shareholders should take steps to ensure their voting intentions are being translated into practice. Institutional shareholders should, on request, make available to their clients information on the proportion of resolutions on which votes were cast and non-discretionary proxies lodged. Major shareholders should attend AGMs where appropriate and practicable. Companies and registrars should facilitate this.

See www.frc.org.uk/corporate/combinedcode.cfm for:

- Schedule A: Provisions on the design of performance related remuneration
- Schedule B: Guidance on liability of non-executive directors: care, skill and diligence
- Schedule C: Disclosure of corporate governance arrangements

3 The OECD Principles of Corporate Governance

1 Ensuring the basis for an effective corporate governance framework

The corporate governance framework should promote transparent and efficient markets, be consistent with the rule of law and clearly articulate the division of responsibilities among different supervisory, regulatory and enforcement authorities.

A The corporate governance framework should be developed with a view to its impact on overall economic performance, market integrity and the incentives it creates for market participants and the promotion of transparent and efficient markets.

B The legal and regulatory requirements that affect corporate governance practices in a jurisdiction should be consistent with the rule of law, transparent and enforceable.

C The division of responsibilities among different authorities in a jurisdiction should be clearly articulated and ensure that the public interest is served.

D Supervisory, regulatory and enforcement authorities should have the authority, integrity and resources to fulfil their duties in a professional and objective manner. Moreover, their rulings should be timely, transparent and fully explained.

2 The rights of shareholders and key ownership functions

The corporate governance framework should protect and facilitate the exercise of shareholders' rights.

A Basic shareholder rights should include the right to:
1   secure methods of ownership registration;
2   convey or transfer shares;
3   obtain relevant and material information on the corporation on a timely and regular basis;
4   participate and vote in general shareholder meetings;
5   elect and remove members of the board; and
6   share in the profits of the corporation.

B Shareholders should have the right to participate in, and to be sufficiently informed on, decisions concerning fundamental corporate changes such as:
1   amendments to the statutes, or articles of incorporation or similar governing documents of the company;
2   the authorisation of additional shares; and
3   extraordinary transactions, including the transfer of all or substantially all assets that in effect result in the sale of the company.

C Shareholders should have the opportunity to participate effectively and vote in general shareholder meetings and should be informed of the rules, including voting procedures that govern general shareholder meetings.
1   Shareholders should be furnished with sufficient and timely information concerning the date, location and agenda of general meetings, as well as full and timely information regarding the issues to be decided at the meeting.
2   Shareholders should have the opportunity to ask questions of the board, including questions relating to the

annual external audit, to place items on the agenda of general meetings, and to propose resolutions, subject to reasonable limitations.

3 Effective shareholder participation in key corporate governance decisions, such as the nomination and election of board members, should be facilitated. Shareholders should be able to make their views known on the remuneration policy for board members and key executives. The equity component of compensation schemes for board members and employees should be subject to shareholder approval.

4 Shareholders should be able to vote in person or *in absentia*, and equal effect should be given to votes whether cast in person or *in absentia*.

D Capital structures and arrangements that enable certain shareholders to obtain a degree of control disproportionate to their equity ownership should be disclosed.

E Markets for corporate control should be allowed to function in an efficient and transparent manner.

1 The rules and procedures governing the acquisition of corporate control in the capital markets, and extraordinary transactions such as mergers, and sales of substantial portions of corporate assets, should be clearly articulated and disclosed so that investors understand their rights and recourse. Transactions should occur at transparent prices and under fair conditions that protect the rights of all shareholders according to their class.

2 Anti-takeover devices should not be used to shield management and the board from accountability.

F The exercise of ownership rights by all shareholders, including institutional investors, should be facilitated.

1 Institutional investors acting in a fiduciary capacity should disclose their overall corporate governance and voting

policies with respect to their investments, including the procedures that they have in place for deciding on the use of their voting rights.

2 Institutional investors acting in a fiduciary capacity should disclose how they manage material conflicts of interest that may affect the exercise of key ownership rights regarding their investments.

G Shareholders, including institutional shareholders, should be allowed to consult with each other on issues concerning their basic shareholder rights as defined in the principles, subject to exceptions to prevent abuse.

3 The equitable treatment of shareholders

The corporate governance framework should ensure the equitable treatment of all shareholders, including minority and foreign shareholders. All shareholders should have the opportunity to obtain effective redress for violation of their rights.

A All shareholders of the same series of a class should be treated equally.

1 Within any series of a class, all shares should carry the same rights. All investors should be able to obtain information about the rights attached to all series and classes of shares before they purchase. Any changes in voting rights should be subject to approval by those classes of shares which are negatively affected.

2 Minority shareholders should be protected from abusive actions by, or in the interest of, controlling shareholders acting either directly or indirectly, and should have effective means of redress.

3 Votes should be cast by custodians or nominees in a manner agreed upon with the beneficial owner of the shares.

4 Impediments to cross-border voting should be eliminated.

5 Processes and procedures for general shareholder meetings should allow for equitable treatment of all shareholders. Company procedures should not make it unduly difficult or expensive to cast votes.

B Insider trading and abusive self-dealing should be prohibited.

C Members of the board and key executives should be required to disclose to the board whether they, directly, indirectly or on behalf of third parties, have a material interest in any transaction or matter directly affecting the corporation.

4 The role of stakeholders in corporate governance

The corporate governance framework should recognise the rights of stakeholders established by law or through mutual agreements and encourage active co-operation between corporations and stakeholders in creating wealth, jobs and the sustainability of financially sound enterprises.

A The rights of stakeholders that are established by law or through mutual agreements are to be respected.

B Where stakeholder interests are protected by law, stakeholders should have the opportunity to obtain effective redress for violation of their rights.

C Performance-enhancing mechanisms for employee participation should be permitted to develop.

D Where stakeholders participate in the corporate governance process, they should have access to relevant, sufficient and reliable information on a timely and regular basis.

E Stakeholders, including individual employees and their representative bodies, should be able to freely communicate their concerns about illegal or unethical practices to the board and their rights should not be compromised for doing this.

F The corporate governance framework should be complemented by an effective, efficient insolvency framework and by effective enforcement of creditor rights.

5 Disclosure and transparency

The corporate governance framework should ensure that timely and accurate disclosure is made on all material matters regarding the corporation, including the financial situation, performance, ownership and governance of the company.

A Disclosure should include, but not be limited to, material information on:
   1   the financial and operating results of the company;
   2   company objectives;
   3   major share ownership and voting rights;
   4   remuneration policy for members of the board and key executives, and information about board members, including their qualifications, the selection process, other company directorships and whether they are regarded as independent by the board;
   5   related party transactions;
   6   foreseeable risk factors;
   7   issues regarding employees and other stakeholders;
   8   governance structures and policies, in particular, the content of any corporate governance code or policy and the process by which it is implemented.

B Information should be prepared and disclosed in accordance with high-quality standards of accounting and financial and non-financial disclosure.

C An annual audit should be conducted by an independent, competent and qualified auditor in order to provide an external and objective assurance to the board and shareholders that the financial statements fairly represent the financial position and performance of the company in all material respects.

D External auditors should be accountable to the shareholders and owe a duty to the company to exercise due professional care in the conduct of the audit.

E Channels for disseminating information should provide for equal, timely and cost-efficient access to relevant information by users.

F The corporate governance framework should be complemented by an effective approach that addresses and promotes the provision of analysis or advice by analysts, brokers, rating agencies and others, that is relevant to decisions by investors, free from material conflicts of interest that might compromise the integrity of their analysis or advice.

6 The responsibilities of the board

The corporate governance framework should ensure the strategic guidance of the company, the effective monitoring of management by the board, and the board's accountability to the company and the shareholders.

A Board members should act on a fully informed basis, in good faith, with due diligence and care, and in the best interest of the company and the shareholders.

B Where board decisions may affect different shareholder groups differently, the board should treat all shareholders fairly.

C The board should apply high ethical standards. It should take into account the interests of stakeholders.

D The board should fulfil certain key functions, including:

1 Reviewing and guiding corporate strategy, major plans of action, risk policy, annual budgets and business plans; setting performance objectives; monitoring implementation and corporate performance; and overseeing major capital expenditures, acquisitions and divestitures.

2 Monitoring the effectiveness of the company's governance practices and making changes as needed.

3 Selecting, compensating, monitoring and, when necessary, replacing key executives and overseeing succession planning.

4 Aligning key executive and board remuneration with the longer-term interests of the company and its shareholders.

5 Ensuring a formal and transparent board nomination and election process.

6 Monitoring and managing potential conflicts of interest of management, board members and shareholders, including misuse of corporate assets and abuse in related party transactions.

7 Ensuring the integrity of the corporation's accounting and financial reporting systems, including the independent audit, and that appropriate systems of control are in place, in particular, systems for risk management, financial and operational control, and compliance with the law and relevant standards.

8 Overseeing the process of disclosure and communications.

E The board should be able to exercise objective independent judgment on corporate affairs.

1 Boards should consider assigning a sufficient number of non-executive board members capable of exercising independent judgment to tasks where there is a potential for conflict of interest. Examples of such key

responsibilities are ensuring the integrity of financial and non-financial reporting, the review of related party transactions, nomination of board members and key executives, and board remuneration.

2   When committees of the board are established, their mandate, composition and working procedures should be well defined and disclosed by the board.

3   Board members should be able to commit themselves effectively to their responsibilities.

F   In order to fulfil their responsibilities, board members should have access to accurate, relevant and timely information.

Source: www.oecd.org/dataoecd/32/18/31557724.pdf

4 The core competencies of company directors

What competencies should people have if they are to perform effectively as company directors? This beguilingly straightforward question lacks a straightforward answer.

The legal duties, rights and liabilities of directors are well documented in major jurisdictions. Legal commentaries on directors' roles and responsibilities usually emphasise the fiduciary duty to act honestly in good faith for the benefit of all shareholders and, consequently, comment on the importance of independence and personal integrity. Similarly, the requirement to exercise reasonable care, diligence and skill is rehearsed, focusing on the need for appropriate knowledge, experience and skill. But companies are now so disparate in size, complexity and ownership structure that such guidance is, at best, at a high level of abstraction. Neither the legal literature nor the common law provides an answer to the question of what core competencies are necessary for effective company direction.

The descriptive and anecdotal literature of corporate governance lays great store on board procedures, emphasising the importance of interpersonal skills if directors are to interact effectively, and of the need for directors to have the moral fibre to take tough-minded decisions with the necessary authority, supplemented by an appropriate amount of business knowledge and experience. Of the theoretical bodies of knowledge, stewardship theory adopts a socio-legal perspective, assuming that directors are capable of fulfilling their fiduciary duties; agency theory assumes that they are not, with each director maximising his or her own personal advantage; and stakeholder theories take a socio-philosophical view of corporations in society. But none addresses the question of what competencies are needed to be an effective company director. Little serious research has been done on defining, measuring and refining such core competencies.

The Institute of Directors study

In 1993–94 the UK's Institute of Directors (IOD) sponsored Henley Management College to research directors' perceptions of good board level practice. The results were claimed to represent:

A comprehensive view of good practice drawn from a very broad cross section of commercial companies in diverse settings ... covering a greatly varied spectrum of corporate size and type, encompassing small firms, private and public companies, and subsidiaries of both UK and foreign-owned companies.

Subsequently, the IOD developed a set of standards for good board practice, based on research and grouped under three headings: organising and running the board; the tasks of the board and indicators of good practice; and building an effective board. The primary focus was on the activities of the board as a whole. However, the following suggestions are made for the personal qualities required by directors:

- Strategic perception and decision-making – perspective, organisational awareness, vision, imagination, judgment and change-oriented.
- Analytical understanding – information collection, detail consciousness, numerical interpretation, problem analysis, critical faculty.
- Communication – oral communication, listening, openness and written communication.
- Interacting with others – co-ordinating, assertiveness, impact, persuasiveness, motivating others, sensitivity and flexibility.
- Board management – planning, delegating, appraising and developing directors.
- Achieving results – energy, achievement and motivation,

determination, independence, risk-taking, business sense, resilience and integrity.

(Institute of Directors, 1995)

Inevitably these suggestions are descriptions of generalised personal qualities that every director needs, rather than core competencies that are necessary to be a successful director on a specific board. They reflect personality attributes, such as independence, determination and the ability to take risks; they do not claim to be core competencies that can be learned, either through formal training or from experience. Others involve moral characteristics, such as integrity and resilience, which underpin core competencies. However, core competencies are more likely to be contingent on the culture of a specific company and its board, on the industry context, and perhaps on the national culture and company law jurisdiction.

The MTRC project on executive directors' competencies

The Hong Kong Mass Transit Railway Company (MTRC) established a project to determine the core competencies of its executive directors. These were defined as the competencies critical to success as an executive director of that company and aimed to identify the high-level discriminators for success. They were derived from in-depth job analysis. Then the organisation used these criteria to assess potential executive directors.

The core competencies identified by the MTRC were as follows.

Strategic vision and planning
The ability to:

- think independently, originally and proactively;
- take a broad cross-functional corporate view;

- have vision for the future;
- take into account and foresee the implications of important economic, social and political developments;
- identify strategic direction for the corporation and develop broad comprehensive strategies for introducing change or preventing recurrences of problems which are clearly capable of being translated into management action.

Strategic reasoning skills
- To be capable of synthesising and integrating information from a number of sources and establish hypotheses, theories or a more complete body of related information.
- To possess strong powers of analysis and be capable of quickly reading and accurately interpreting large volumes of often technically complex information and data.
- To be able to apply principles of logic to solve both conceptual and practical problems.
- To have highly developed critical faculties and be capable of objectively discriminating between the relative priorities of strategic issues.

Decision-making
The ability to:

- exercise judgment, bringing to bear all relevant information to arrive at decisions often involving the allocation of fiscal resources;
- decide action through consensus with others and take tough commercially necessary decisions as well as difficult decisions affecting the welfare of others;
- objectively and pragmatically evaluate information and draw sound logical conclusions even when under pressure and on occasion extreme time constraints.

Team membership and directing skills
The ability to:

- work effectively and flexibly as a member of a peer group team, taking charge of the team in crisis where his or her technical expertise is required, while at the same time being capable of deferring to other team members as more appropriate leaders in other situations and giving them full support;
- provide strategic direction for others and delegate and empower management to implement appropriate action;
- act as an objective overseer of management performance and decisions.

Communication skills
The ability to:

- express ideas clearly and persuasively to both internal and external bodies;
- listen carefully and act as a sounding board for the chairman and other directors;
- be culturally sensitive and capable of creating empathy with a wide range of diverse people;
- be a strong negotiator able to remain calm and controlled in often emotional situations and under aggressive questioning.
- To have good formal presentation skills.

Personal strength and motivation
- To have high personal integrity and strong motivation for achievement.
- To be prepared to stand his or her ground.
- To have the courage of his or her convictions and yet at the same time be prepared to reach reasonable compromise.
- Not to be unreasonably stubborn but persistent.
- Not give in to difficulties and to be dedicated to completing tasks whatever the time or effort required.

■ To be loyal to the corporation and prepared to put the organisation ahead of personal preferences.

Political awareness and networking skills
The ability to:

■ initiate and maintain a wide range of contacts in government and political circles;
■ keep up professional contact;
■ command respect in the international community.
■ To be diplomatic and demonstrate good social skills.
■ To be politically astute, skilful at lobbying support internally and externally and capable of persuading and influencing individuals of equal or greater status and power.

Professional corporate and commercial understanding
■ To keep up-to-date with and be able to command professional respect within own field of expertise.
■ To have a good understanding of the workings of the corporation as well as a sound grasp of developments in the transport industry worldwide.
■ To be customer oriented as well as concerned with getting a good deal for the corporation, alert to commercial opportunities, and sensitive to market movements.
■ To have a good understanding of financial management and the operations of international money markets.

Source: Mass Transit Railway Corporation, Internal Assessment Centre, 1995

5 Induction checklist for new directors

Outside directors never know enough about the business to be useful and inside directors always know too much to be independent. So runs a criticism of traditional board practice. Working through the items on this checklist will improve the quality of directors' contributions and reduce the time it takes for them to contribute fully and effectively. Induction exercises for directors ensure that all board members are fully informed about the company, the business and its financials, the three fundamental areas in which directors need to be conversant and competent. Obviously, directors vary in the extent of their knowledge of the company and its business, but the checklist will provide an *aide-memoire* for both outside and inside directors.

1 Knowledge of the company

The first broad focus of the induction programme is on the company and its governance. The chairman, other long-serving directors and the company secretary can often be helpful in this regard. If in any doubt, it is always wise to seek legal opinion.

Ownership power
In a joint stock limited liability company ownership is the ultimate basis of governance power. What is the balance of the equity shareholding and voting power? Has the balance changed in the past and how have the votes been used? How might it change and the voting strength be used in the future? For example, consider in a family company what might happen as shares are transferred on succession; or in a widely held public company the potential for a merger or hostile bid. What anti-takeover provisions, if any, are in place? How effective might they be?

In a company limited by guarantee, or any other corporate entity governed by its members, how active is the membership in governance matters? Could this situation change in the future? Explore the way that the board communicates with the members and whether there have been any attempts by members to influence corporate affairs. Not-for-profit organisations often seem to generate controversial, even adversarial, member activity.

Governance rules, regulations and company law

Study the articles of association and memorandum or corporate rule book. These are the formal documents created on incorporation and updated subject to the approval of the members. Within the constraints of the company law and the listing rules (for a quoted public company), they determine the way the company can be governed. The memorandum, for example, could limit the size of the board, lay down rules for the selection of the board chairman, or define conditions for the meeting and voting of the members. All too often directors are not familiar the contents of the company's memorandum and are surprised to find themselves constrained in some way, for example in the percentage of members' votes needed to change the capital structure or sell off part of the enterprise.

In a listed public company, be familiar with the listing rules of the stock exchanges on which the company's shares are quoted. Some directors feel that this is a matter that can reasonably be left to the company secretary, share registrar or corporate legal counsel. It is difficult to ask appropriate questions that ensure compliance if you are not familiar with the basic requirements. There is an important distinction between delegation and abdication of responsibility.

Be familiar with the broad scope of the company law of the jurisdiction in which the company is incorporated and has its major bases. Obviously, the detailed requirements of company law vary between Delaware and California, Australia and Canada, or the UK and France, but there can also be fundamental differences, particularly in the handling of private companies. Companies incorporated in the British Virgin Islands, for example, are not required to have an audit, there is virtually no public filing of documents and the rights of members can be severely limited if they are not also directors.

It is not necessary for a director to be a lawyer or accountant to fulfil such responsibilities, but company law around the world typically expects directors to show the degree of knowledge and skill that a reasonable person would associate with company directorship. In the old days this might not have amounted to very much; today expectations are running high.

Board structure, membership and processes
What is the structure of the board? In other words, what is the balance between executive and non-executive directors? In your opinion is this appropriate? Are the outside, non-executive directors independent, or do they have some connection with the company? For example, are they nominees for a major shareholder or lender, are they members of the family of the chairman or CEO, or have they held an executive directorship in the past? Such matters could affect your assessment of the position they take on board issues.

Is the board chairmanship separated from the role of chief executive? If not, is there a danger that a single individual will dominate the board, and are you able to operate in such a climate? Who are the other board members? Do you know them? If not, some effort to learn about their background, experience and reputation could reinforce your early contributions to board discussions. Meeting individual directors to discuss corporate matters before you accept the appointment might help you to discover whether the chemistry of the board is likely to be appropriate for you. Is there a succession plan for key directors and senior management? Is there a strategy for development at board level to ensure that the business does not outgrow the board?

How often does the board meet? Typically, how long do the meetings last? What role does the chairman play in board matters? Ask for the agenda and minutes of recent board meetings. Talk to the company secretary about the way the board meetings are run. Does the board operate with committees, an executive committee, audit, remuneration or nomination committees, for example? Find out what you can about the membership, chairmanship and style of these committees. Again study their minutes and discuss with their chairman or the company secretary how they operate.

What information do the directors routinely receive? Ask for all the documentation provided for recent meetings; study the reports and consider the scope of the routine performance data provided. Is it adequate? Does the board have briefings and presentations from non-board senior executives or other experts from time to time? Do the directors meet with the auditors periodically?

2 Knowledge of the business

The second focus of this induction checklist is on the business itself. Do you know enough about the business to make an effective contribution? Obviously, this is a reasonable question to ask an outside director who has little or no experience in this particular industry. Interestingly, though, it is also a pertinent question to put to many executive directors. Expertise and success in a particular function (finance and accounting, perhaps), or high managerial performance in running a division or group company, do not necessarily provide a view of the business as a whole. Indeed, they might have created a narrow window of experience through which the entire corporate business is viewed. This part of the checklist is relevant to all directors.

The basic business processes

Can you outline the fundamental steps in the added-value chain or network of the firm? What are the crucial risks facing the business? Where is the business most exposed to risk? These questions are just as pertinent for directors of a bank, a telecommunications company or an airline as they are to those of a manufacturing business (although the basic processes are often more difficult to identify). Are you familiar with the major sources of the business inputs – where they come from and who provides them? Within the business processes, which add the value and provide competitive advantage; which drive the costs? What are the core competencies or capabilities of the business? What is the range of products and services provided by the business? Find out all you can from catalogues, trade literature, customer promotions, trade shows and similar sources of information. Who are the customers? What sectors and markets are served? Pareto's law often applies to products and customers – 80% of the value comes from 20% of the list. Which products and customers form this 20%?

Corporate strategies

Does the firm have a written mission statement or statement of core values? Is there a shared view of the business direction, clearly articulated in strategies, plans and projects? Obtain copies, discuss them with the chairman or CEO. If not, what is the broad direction of the business; what strategies are emergent from recent actions, such as strategies of growth through investment in new product development or through acquisition and divestment? Are there any written policies or management manuals? Again study and discuss them. For example, as far as customers are concerned, are there specific pricing policies and credit policies?

Who are the principal competitors? What competitive advantages and disadvantages do they have, and what strategies are they pursuing? Are there potential new entrants into the market or new technological developments, products or services that might provide alternative competition? Is the business involved in strategic alliances; for example, joint ventures to develop new strategic areas, to supply goods or services, or provide access to distribution channels?

How is strategic change initiated in the firm? Does the board respond to ideas put up by the CEO and senior management, or is the board intimately involved in strategy formulation?

Organisation, management and people
What is the formal organisation structure? Discuss with the CEO and other members of senior management how the organisation works in practice. Form a view of the management culture and style throughout the business: it may differ around the world.

What management control systems are used, for example for budgetary planning and control, profit centres and performance centres? Is there a formal enterprise risk management system? What management performance measures are used? Are they linked to managerial incentives? Are there employee or senior management share option schemes?

How many employees are there in the various parts of the business? What are the characteristics of the workforce? Are trade unions important and is there a policy towards them? What are the remuneration and other employment policies?

Overall, how would you assess the current position of the business? What needs to be done to maintain and enhance future performance?

3 Knowledge of the financials

The financial aspects of the organisation inevitably feature strongly in typical board discussions.

Study the annual accounts and directors' reports for the past few years. What have been the trends? Consider the trends of key financial ratios, for example: overall performance ratios, such as return on equity and return on investment, and working capital management ratios, such as inventory turnover rates, liquidity ratios and debt collection rates. What criteria do the board use to measure and assess corporate performance?

Trends are likely to convey more information than the ratios for the business itself, but the financial ratios at a point in time can be useful for cross-industry comparisons. What are the future projections for these financial criteria? How does the financial position of the company compare with that of its main competitors?

Review the financial performance of parts of the business, such as product or geographical divisions or subsidiary companies. Review the criteria used in investment project appraisals.

How is the company financed? What is the financial structure? What implications might the debt/equity ratio have for the future? For example, what might be the effect of a significant change in interest rates given this gearing or leverage?

Who are the auditors? Ask to see the any management letter written after the last audit discussing any issues that arose during the audit.

4 Expectations on appointment

All directors should discuss with the chairman what is expected of their directorship before accepting nomination. Consequently, a crucial part of any induction briefing should review the expectations of the chairman and the other directors.

Is a specific role expected of you? Was there a special reason, perhaps, for your nomination to the board? For example, did it reflect your particular knowledge in some area, or special skills or experience you could bring to board discussions, or a special channel of communication and information you could provide? Or was the nomination made because of your overall experience and potential contribution to all aspects of the board's work? Are you capable of fulfilling these expectations? If not, what other information, knowledge, or skills will you need to obtain?

How much time are you expected to give to the board, its committees and other aspects of the company's affairs? This should cover not only attendance at regular meetings, but also the time needed for briefings and discussions, visits within the company and preparation. Outside directors will have to ensure that this is compatible with other demands on their time. Inside executive directors will need to harmonise these expectations and their director responsibilities with the duties required under their contract of employment with the company.

Although all directors have the right to be informed on all board matters, confirm that you will have appropriate access to the information you require. This should cover not only formal board papers, but also the right to seek additional information if necessary. Are you able to talk to members of the management team, and if so, under what circumstances?

Last, but not least, review the details of the contractual relationship between you and the company. What are the terms of appointment as a director? Is there a written contract or a formal letter of appointment from the chairman? What is the length of the appointment? What are the terms and likelihood of reappointment; the basis of the remuneration package and manner of review; the details of director and officers indemnity insurance (particularly important in the increasingly litigious climate facing directors in many parts of the world)?

All directors face a challenge as they join a new board. Effective board membership involves a learning experience. It should start well before the director attends the first board meeting and should continue during all the rest. The successful director is the one who can say, "Aha! I hadn't realised that, now I understand", not once but continuously, throughout his or her service to the board.

6 Effectiveness checklist for boards

There is no board of directors or governing body in the world which, if the members think about it, cannot improve its effectiveness. That is the belief behind this checklist of opportunities. All too readily board members grow old together. Often the business outgrows the board. Few boards take a rigorous look at themselves. A review of board effectiveness can be a salutary experience, but it can lead to important changes. Many codes of corporate governance now require a regular appraisal of the performance of the board and board committees.

Essentially, a board review involves a comprehensive and tough-minded look at the board and its activities. The aim is to explore the board's structure, style and processes in the light of changing company needs to highlight potential problems for the future and provide the basis for improving effectiveness today.

A board review needs the enthusiastic support and co-operation of all members if it is to succeed. It can be led by the board chairman, one of the outside directors, an ad hoc board committee or someone with suitable experience from outside the board. Some professional directors' organisations and corporate governance consultancies now provide appraisal services. Obviously, it is a highly confidential activity.

The review process involves marshalling a lot of information about the underlying governance power-base in the company, the board structure and its members, and the way the board and its committees work, including the information they receive and the way they allocate their time. Various ideas, issues and opinions will then emerge. Alternatives can be developed and evaluated. In due course the options can be discussed by the directors, leading eventually to a strategy for the development of the board and the way it works. The process needs to be taken step by step.

1 Set the board review in the context of the company's business strategy

As companies grow in complexity, diversity and size, it seems obvious that their boards ought also to evolve to reflect such changes. Unfortunately, this is not always the case. If, for example, the company's strategy involves new technologies, markets or international locations, if it is developing new strategic alliance or acquisition strategies, or if its plans call for alternative global financing strategies such as the use of derivatives, it is essential that among the board members are those able to understand the issues and, in due course, monitor executive management's performance (see NORTHERN ROCK). Thus the first step towards creating a strategy for board development is to consider the implications at board level of the corporate business strategy as a whole. The board review must be in line with, preferably part of, the company's overall business strategy.

2 Review the overall governance situation

This can be particularly important, yet easily overlooked. The key question is: who has ultimate power over the company and might this change over the strategic time horizon of the board review? If so, what would be the implications for governance and the board? For example, in a public listed company, what are the prospects of a change of ownership through a friendly or hostile bid? Or in a company with a dominant shareholder, what might happen to the board if this shareholding changed hands? In a family firm, how might the balance of power change on succession? It is important not only to know precisely the current ownership of the voting equity but also to consider possible future scenarios. Detailed knowledge of the company's articles of association is important as well. There may be unexpected clauses about percentages of shareholder votes needed to approve various strategic changes, such as introducing new capital or divesting part of the business.

3 Consider relevant external factors

This means looking at the context in which the governance of the company must operate over the time horizon of the review. Are there any legal, political or societal factors that could affect the governance of the company? Examples include possible changes to company legislation in any of the countries in which the company operates, new regulations from the European Union about worker representation in strategic decision-making, the imposition of new disclosure requirements in the stock exchange listing rules, or the possible effects of a change of government. Any plans for developing the board must take account of the changing governance environment.

4 Review board structure

Consider the size of the board. Is it appropriate for the task that needs to be done? There may be a case for additional members, or the board may have grown too big. Consider the structure of the board. Is the balance between executive and non-executive members appropriate? This issue will have to be reviewed along with the identification of board style and the way the members work together. Are enough of the non-executive directors genuinely independent? This means ensuring that the independent outside directors have no relationships with the company that could affect the exercise of genuinely objective judgment. Are the posts of chairman of the board and chief executive separate? Is the present arrangement the most satisfactory for the future?

5 Identify board style

Consider how the board's work has evolved in recent years. Reflect on the effects of changes in chairman and other members. Review the way the directors work together. Is this a genuinely professional board style or are there elements of rubber-stamp, representative or country-club boards? What changes might be necessary to meet different circumstances in the future? How might the board style change should there be a change of board leadership?

6 Review board membership and the roles directors play, formulate succession plans

Consider the detailed membership of the board. Summarise the résumé of each director. Does the board have the balance of knowledge, skills and experience that will be needed for the planned future of the company? Look at the age profile of members. Are any directors likely to retire over the review's time horizon? What is the probability of any directors resigning? Develop succession plans for both executive and non-executive directors. Boards should always have a portfolio of potential non-executive directors who could be considered for board appointment, and the management development plans for senior executive staff should also include their potential as directors. (See also Appendix 4.)

7 Consider director development and training

As much attention should be given to director development and training as is given to management development and training, but it seldom is. Directors all too readily assume that, having reached the board, they must have the experience to perform as directors. But governance, the work of the board, is not the same as management. It calls for additional knowledge and different skills.

Consider the director development needs of each director. This could involve a carefully developed induction or updating programme on the company and its work; or experiential development, such as chairing a board task force or one of the board committees; or it might be achieved through participation in the growing number of director-level courses and programmes around the world.

8 Achieving greater efficiency: review directors' time and information

How does the board spend its time? Is this the most effective use of one of the company's most valuable resources? Does the board delegate some of its work to board committees? Are these as effective as they could be? This information can be extracted from an analysis of the agenda and minutes of meetings of the board and its committees, and by discussing the issue with each director. Similarly, review the nature, extent and adequacy of the information available to directors. How could the routine board papers be improved? Can directors readily obtain the additional information they want? Do the outside directors have access to management information? Is there a case for board-level briefings to keep directors up-to-date and provide the context for board-level discussions? What ideas does each director have for improvement in the information process?

9 Achieving greater effectiveness: better strategy formulation and policymaking

Review the board's contribution to the performance roles of strategy formulation and policymaking. Is adequate time devoted to this part of the board's responsibilities? Are all board members adequately informed about strategic matters? Is there a shared vision and understanding of the company's core values and competencies among all the directors? Are there any differences of view as to the strategic direction of the firm? Are the policy guidelines laid down by the board adequate for management decision-making, balancing control and freedom appropriately? Are the risk management processes and policies adequate? What ideas do directors have for improvement?

10 Achieving greater effectiveness: better executive supervision and accountability

Turning to the conformance roles of the board, do the directors adequately monitor and supervise executive management? Is the feedback of information relevant and timely? How might the process be improved? Seek the opinions of all directors and senior managers as well as the auditors and others in a position to take a view on board activities. Is the accountability of the board appropriate to all those with a legitimate claim to be informed? Does this include a commitment to employees, customers, suppliers? Or does the board accept a responsibility only to be accountable to the shareholders? Is this responsibility adequately fulfilled? Consider the published report, websites and other communications and meetings with the members, analysts and the media. What ideas are there for improvement?

11 Develop and agree the strategy for board development

From the mass of hard data, opinion and ideas for improvement that have been gathered, marshal the facts, identify alternatives and articulate their implications. Develop a report for discussion by the board. Such a review might well take place as part of a strategy seminar, rather than in a formal board meeting, to encourage open discussion and creativity. Move towards developing a strategy for developing the board. This could include planned changes to board size, structure or membership, a new committee structure, new sources and ways of providing information, other uses of directors' time, programmes for director and board training and development, different formats for board meetings, or calling on some directors to commit different amounts of time to their board duties. Agree the strategy, ensuring that it is consistent with, indeed part of, the overall business strategy.

12 Determine action plans and projects

Lastly, develop the procedures, plans and projects that will turn the strategy into realised change. Ensure commitment from all those involved. Get feedback periodically to confirm that the changes are taking place as planned and that the results are as expected. Continue the strategic review and change programme as part of the board's constant learning and relearning process.

7 Sources of information

www.acga-asia.org
Asian Corporate Governance Association

www.blackwellpublishing.com/corg
Corporate Governance: An International Review – the first
academic corporate governance journal

www.businesslink.gov.uk
Business information with recommendations on business risk
analysis

www.cgfrc.nus.edu.sg
National University of Singapore, Corporate Governance and
Financial Reporting Centre – updates on current topics in
corporate governance

www.charity-commission.gov.uk; www.ncvo-vol.org.uk
Information on governance in voluntary and community
organisations

www.charteredsecretary.net; www.icsa.org.uk
Institute of Chartered Secretaries and Administrators (UK) – best
practice guides and other publications

www.companieshouse.gov.uk
Registrar of Companies

www.conference-board.org/knowledge/govern
The Conference Board (US), Corporate Governance Center

www.corpgov.net
A valuable site, full of corporate governance information by company, country and topic; reviews, updates, library and links to other relevant corporate governance sites

www.csr.gov.uk
UK government gateway to corporate social responsibility

www.ecgi.org
European Corporate Governance Institute – a forum for dialogue among academics, legislators and practitioners

www.ecgi.org/codes/all_codes.php
Index of corporate governance codes around the world with access to texts

www.encycogov.com/WhatIsGorpGov.asp
Web encyclopedia of corporate governance

news.findlaw.com/hdocs/docs/gwbush/sarbanesoxley072302.pdf
The Sarbanes-Oxley Act

www.frc.org.uk
UK Financial Reporting Council for latest on UK codes

www.fsa.gov.uk
Financial Services Authority – search on "corporate governance"

www.gcgf.org
Global Corporate Governance Forum of the World Bank

www.icgn.org
International Corporate Governance Network – exchanging corporate governance information internationally and raising standards

www.iod.com
Institute of Directors (UK)

www.ifc.org/corporategovernance
International Finance Corporation (IFC) a member of the World
Bank

www.ifc.org/ifcext/corporategovernance.nsf/Content/CG_Tools
Corporate governance tools for family and founder-owned
unlisted companies, listed companies, financial institutions,
privatised transition economy companies and state-owned
enterprises

www.mapnp.org/library/boards/boards.htm
Management Library guidelines for not-for-profit organisations

www.nacdonline.org
National Association of Corporate Directors (US)

www.oecd.org
Organisation for Economic Co-operation and Development –
corporate governance principles and discussion of corporate
governance topics (follow links by topic or country to corporate
governance)

www.opsi.gov.uk/acts/acts2006/ukpga_20060046_en.pdf
UK Companies Act 2006

www.riskassessment101.com
Guide to risk management

www.sec.gov
US Securities and Exchange Commission – its role, latest
regulations

www.sustainability-reports.com
Portal for sustainability reports of multinational companies all
over the world

www.swd.gov.hk/doc/ngo/corp-gov-eng.pdf
Leading your NGO board (Canada)

www.thecorporatelibrary.com
An independent research firm providing corporate governance
data, analysis, board effectiveness rating, risk assessment tools,
regular corporate governance reading and reviews

www.wcfcg.net
World Council for Corporate Governance – an international
network to galvanise good governance practices worldwide

8 Recommended reading

Cadbury, A., *Corporate Governance and Chairmanship: A Personal View*, Oxford University Press, 2002.

Carter, C.B. and Lorsch, J.W., *Back to the Drawing Board*, Harvard Business School Press, 2004.

Carver, J., *Corporate Boards that Create Value*, Jossey-Bass, 2002.

Clarke, T., *International Corporate Governance: A Comparative Approach*, Routledge, 2007.

Cornforth, C., *The Governance of Public and Non-Profit Organizations: What Do Boards Do?*, Routledge, 2003.

Hancock, J., *Investing in Corporate Social Responsibility: A Guide to Best Practice, Business Planning and the UK's Leading Companies*, Kogan Page, 2004.

Kakabadse, A. and Kakabadse, N., *Leading the Board: The Six Disciplines of World Class Chairmen*, Palgrave Macmillan, 2007.

Kotler, P. and Lee, N., *Corporate Social Responsibility: Doing the Most Good for Your Company and Your Cause*, John Wiley & Sons, 2004.

LeBlanc, R. and Gillies, J., *Inside the Boardroom*, Wiley, 2005.

Lipton, M., *Some Thoughts for Boards of Directors*, Watchell, Lipton, Rosen & Katz, 2007.

Mallin, C.A., *Corporate Governance*, 2nd edition, Oxford University Press, 2007.

Monks, R.A.G. and Minow, N., *Corporate Governance*, 4th edition, Wiley, 2007.

Monks, R.A.G., *Corpocracy: How CEOs and the Business Roundtable Hijacked the World's Greatest Wealth Machine*, Wiley, 2008.

Solomon, J., *Corporate Governance and Accountability*, 2nd edition, Wiley, 2007.

Tricker, R.I., *Corporate Governance: Principles, Policies and Practices*, Oxford University Press, 2008.

UK Stationery Office, *How to Use the CSR Competency Framework: A Resource Pack for Using the CSR Competency Framework*, www.tso.co.uk